KNOW THE COUNTRYSIDE SERIES

ADVANCED TAXIDERMY

OTHER BOOKS AVAILABLE

The Sporting Shotgun
Robin Marshall-Ball

The Sportsman's Companion
Edited by Eric Begbie

Wildlife Conservation and the Modern Zoo
Gordon Woodroffe

Parrots, Lories, and Cockatoos
David Alderton

Hummingbirds
A. J. Mobbs

Pheasants of the World
Dr J. Delacour

ADVANCED TAXIDERMY

by

P. A. O'Connor

Taxidermist and Naturalist

DISTRIBUTOR: SAIGA PUBLISHING CO. LTD.,
1 Royal Parade, Hindhead, Surrey, GU26 6TD,
England
Produced by Triplegate Ltd.

ISBN 086230 062 2

Typeset and Printed by
Broglia Press, Bournemouth

SAIGA PUBLISHING CO. LTD.,
1 Royal Parade, Hindhead, Surrey, GU26 6TD,
England

CONTENTS

MONOCHROME ILLUSTRATIONS

COLOUR PLATES

PREFACE

I have written this book for the person who has read a beginner's book, and has tried a few specimens himself, and wishes to know more. The photographs were taken by David 'Cyclops' Nye, the wildlife photographer, and are of specimens set up by myself. My daughters, Elaine and Dawn O'Connor, spent many hours helping to prepare and make this book possible. Not all the ideas are my own, but they are techniques I practise because I think they are sound and give excellent results.

It is impossible to write such a book without the support background of master craftsmen, both from the past and present, and their willingness to share their knowledge. America has many great taxidermists alive today, so it would be unfair to name some of them, and omit others. In my earlier days the written works that impressed me and shaped my future were those of Montagu Browne, John Rowley, and John Moyer. Two great taxidermists in the British Isles today are Eric Hare and Roy Hale. There must be others I have not met personally. To me they are special; like Vermeer and Van Gogh. Not that one is crazy; they both are, when it comes to taxidermy.

The taxidermist plays an important role in today's awakening awareness of Natural History. If he sets up a creature well, it becomes an ambassador for its species over the next century, long after today's people are dead. If there is a magic formula to this art, I would say it is that effort, patience, and observation, equals skill.

To all taxidermists, amateur and professional, past and present, my friendship. To the beginner and the unborn, welcome to wonderland.

March 1983 P. A. O'Connor

Frontispiece Hooded crow, in classical style

CHAPTER 1

BIRDS

SELECTING A BIRD SPECIMEN

For the beginner it is very important that one selects the correct specimen. Birds he should avoid for his first few encounters are seabirds, because they are far too oily, and birds that live around houses and gardens, as they have too much fat from such an easy living, which makes their skin very thin around their bellies. Waders can cause great confusion, with their long awkward legs and stances. They also go bad very quickly, due to their crab and seashore diets. Small birds such as warblers, tits, and pipits, are too small to be done easily. Large birds like swans and geese are too large to begin with, and as their heads are too big to be tackled via the normal technique, they have to be done separately. This also applies to ducks, woodpeckers and most of the crow family.

Birds like martins and swallows have such delicate plumage that it becomes an expert's job. Fat is also a problem with caged and pet birds. Birds with naked areas of skin, such as turkeys, poultry, peafowl, and vultures, are best left until some experience is gained. Rare birds should not be attempted by the beginner, because of their rarity. These should be set off to their best advantage, and this normally takes a professional or a very skilled amateur. **Never touch a bird which looks as if it has been ill for some time before death;** it could put you in the same condition.

The ideal specimen

What is required is a fresh, small to medium sized, tough skinned bird with mannerisms known to all of us in our everyday living. A number of birds fit the bill; the starling, (which is a member of the crow family without the head problem), most seedeaters, like the sparrow, and finches, are ideal. So too are the larks, gulls, blackbirds, thrushes, hawks, and small game birds. Where to obtain such specimens can be a problem. Suggestions are the R.S.P.C.A., P.D.S.A., museums, gamekeepers, zoos, lighthouse keepers, pest and rodent officers, farmers, shooting clubs, and ornithology societies, as all will come in contact with specimens from time to time.

When one receives a specimen, it is worth recording the colour of its eyes, beak, legs, and bare skin areas; a paint colour chart may help with the colours. Other useful data includes district, date of death, weather, and cause of death, if known. This is important if from farmers or rodent officers, as the specimen may have been poisoned. Another useful tip is that if a bird has bars or lines, below, or behind the eye, or crests of any description, then it is advisable to do a rough instructive drawing to help make sure the finished specimen has them in the correct places.

Freezing

Push cotton wool in the throat, nostrils and vent of your specimen to prevent any seepage from the crop and bowels. Now the specimen is ready for the freezer, where it can be stored for months, or until required. It is not necessary to freeze a bird, but this process does kill all vermin living among the feathers. It also destroys the bluebottle eggs and larva, if left for a period of not less than a fortnight.

SKINNING A BIRD

There is an array of equipment for skinning, but it can be said that these items are important but not essential. I have skinned many hundreds of specimens using no more than a pair of domestic scissors, a penknife, a small screwdriver, and a razor-blade. Equipment used by the taxidermist is mainly for his own ease of working and speed.

Stages

The bird is laid on its back, with its head on the left hand side, the tail to the right, provided one is right-handed; reverse for left-handers. The feathers on the breast of the bird are moved to either side, and this will expose a feather-free area from the breastbone to the vent. Make a cut along this length, but do not press too hard after the blade leaves the breastbone or you will cut through two skin layers; one of them belonging to the walls of the intestines, and this will make things messier.

Starting at the skin on the further side to you, at the breastbone, pick up the cut skin with blunt-nosed forceps, or tweezers, and gently lift it up, while releasing the underside with a scalpel. Release down to the end of the breastbone, and then reverse the scalpel and slide the handle between the skin layer holding the feathers and the skin layer, or wall of the intestines. At this stage it will be necessary to use the scalpel blade to release points here and there, especially in the pelvic region, where a single rib-like bone becomes attached to the skin.

Breast

Put aside the tools and return to the breast, using your fingers to release the skin around the 'knee', until it is completely clear; now cut through the knee joint, making sure you do not catch the skin. Then do the same to the other leg. Loosen the skin further down the back towards the 'parsons-nose'. When the skin is completely free around the bird's body at the tail end, cut through the parsons-nose, making sure you do not cut through the base of the tail feathers. It is better to leave a little flesh on the skin and trim later.

Back and wings

The skin is carefully freed up the back until the wing bones are cleared at the junction of the scapula (shoulder bone), and the humerous (arm bone) joint; cut through this joint on both wings. The skin is only held now by the crop, neck and head. The skin can now be turned inside out and the problem of protecting feathers becomes much easier.

Crop

The crop can be freed by fingers, and great care must be taken not to squeeze this bag, otherwise the contents will be forced into the windpipe and perhaps out of the beak. Throughout the whole of this skinning process, the use of borax powder may be of assistance, to prevent feathers becoming soiled, and in preserving the skin. Cotton wool tucked into the sides that are not being worked can sometimes be of great value, especially when one is dealing with a greasy or white breasted bird.

Head

The skin can now be turned inside out over the head as it is worked down the neck. The base of the skull soon becomes visible, and now care must be taken because of the ear coverts. In small birds these can be prised out from the concave by the fine pointed forceps; in larger birds they have to be cut out.

Work in a circular movement around the head, so the skin is released evenly from the throat, cheeks, and crown; even greater care must be taken as one approaches the eyes, because it is very easy to nick the thin skin. Cut as close to the eyeball as safety allows, as nicking the eye can release a surprising amount of fluid; then trim the surplus skin around the eye later. Release the eyes and free the skin to the base of the beak. Now cut the body and neck from the skin; but leave the tongue with the skin if you wish to do a singing specimen, as this is simply preserved with borax powder.

Final touches

The bones still adhering to the skin are cleaned up by cutting the surplus flesh from them, dusting well with borax, and plumbers hemp or tow bound around to take the place of the flesh removed. A cut is placed in the sole of the bird's foot and the tendons removed from the scaly part of the leg. Later the leg wires will run down the channels left by these tendons.

The brains need to be removed from the skull via the hole in its base. This hole is enlarged and the soft tissue withdrawn, and the interior dusted with borax. It is well to keep this hole small, to allow the false neck to lie in its correct position. The eyes and flesh are removed from the rest of the head, dusted, and modelling clay inserted into the eye sockets and glass eyes lightly pressed into place.

When all surplus fat has been removed from the skin, and cotton tied to each wing bone, the skin can be turned feather side out. If however the skin has become dry, it will be necessary to dampen it first with water, using only minute quantities ; wet fingers might be enough. Never work with a dried out skin.

FALSE BODIES OR MANIKINS FOR BIRDS

My own method makes the whole wire frame carry the strain, and not the packing. I start with a wine cork (half a cork for blackbird size) then I pass one wire through one end to make the neck, passing it out through the far end. I bend this into a hook and pull it back into the cork so it is firmly anchored. At the other end, I pass two wires through the cork for the tail. These I also hook over and pull back, until they are firmly embedded; the two wires allow one to have

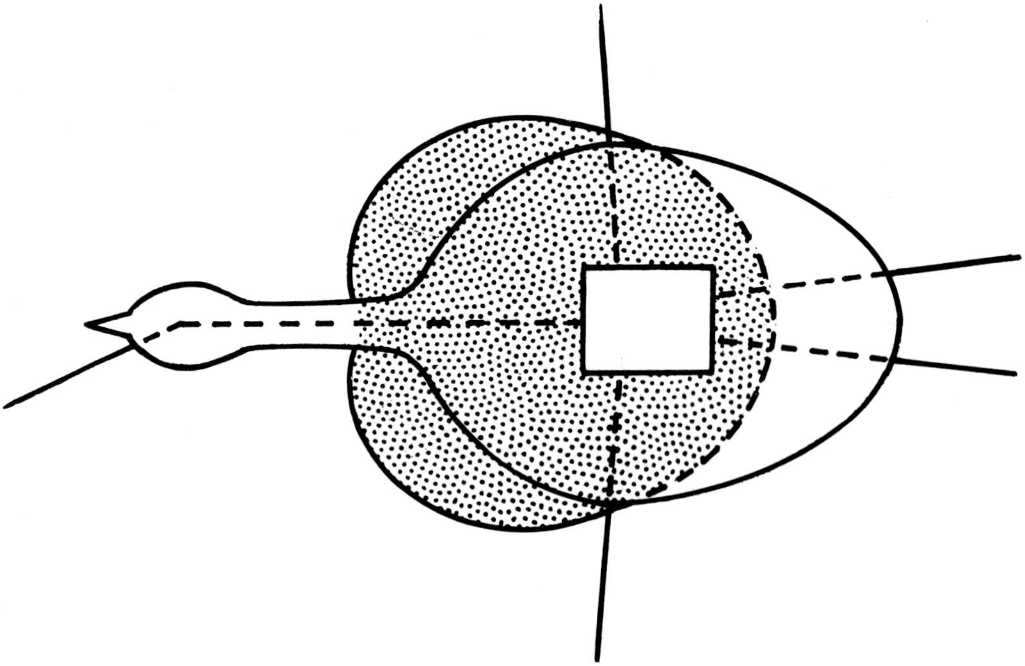

Figure 1.1 Positioning of leg and tail wires

the tail spread if required (see figures 1.1 and 1.2). Next I pass two wires through opposite sides of the cork and anchor them like the earlier wires; this pair of wires is for the legs.

Tow or plumbers hemp is then wound around the body in a figure of eight and bound with cotton until the shape is roughly achieved. Then the neck is built up, and I always give my specimens a 'windpipe' of tow and bind it into position, as this prevents a round neck appearance. Finally a soft breast is added, again made of tow; this allows the neck to lie further back on the body (see figures 1.1 and 1.3). Most beginners would find it an advantage to make the manikin smaller than the true body, as they will have less trouble with it when it comes to sewing on the birdskin.

The neck and leg wires are filed to a very sharp point. The leg wires are passed through the leg from the inside, and down the tendon cavity and out through the bottom of the foot. It will be easier to pass these wires through the legs if the wires are bent towards the bird's back during assembling, as this will take up the strain from the birdskin. Once the specimen is sewn up and placed on a stand, the wires can be tightened to hold the bird into its stance. The wires then carry the weight of the specimen.

Mounting the bird

The last stage is to unite the manikin and the birdskin. If the skin has become dry, dampen and redust with borax, and lay it in front of you with the head to the left and tail to the right. Remove any cotton filling, and tie the wing bones together, leaving the same space between them as they had in the real body. Pack a little loose tow between them and the skin; this

Plate 1 Fox, mounted in classical method

Plate 2 Yellow wagtail, freeze-dried

Plate 3 Tawny owl in classical style; note house mouse

Plate 4 Green woodpecker, male, set up using classical methods, but finished by the skin being freeze-dried

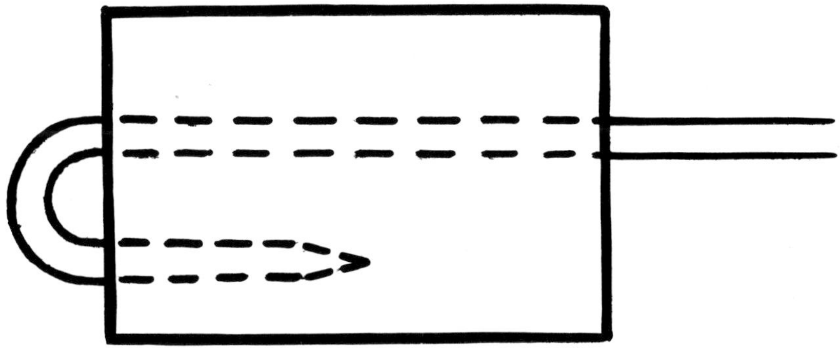

Figure 1.2 Anchoring the wire in the cork

prevents a sunken back appearance, as in the real body these wing bones are embedded within the body. Pick up the manikin and guide the neck wire through the hole in the base of the skull and force the wire through the skull and birdskin, near the bird's forehead or crest. If the wire's location is at the nostril, it will be difficult to trim, and if too far back, then the head is apt to wobble, and full control of the specimen is lost. It is also a weaker specimen.

First leg

Ease the wire through, and the manikin's neck up to the base of the skull. This brings the leg wires near their positions. Work first with the leg furthest from you. Push the wire down the tow and on into the back of the scaly part of the leg, where the tendons have been removed, and out through the sole of the claw. Make sure you have not nipped any skin with the wire while doing so.

Second leg

Now the second leg. You will find it easier to do if you bend the leg towards the back while doing so. When this is completely finished, the skin will be around the manikin. Adjust the plumage, and stitch up using a loose zig-zag stitch. Grasp the cotton and pull firmly, and all the feathers will be drawn into place; it should now look like a dead bird, bedraggled, lying on its back.

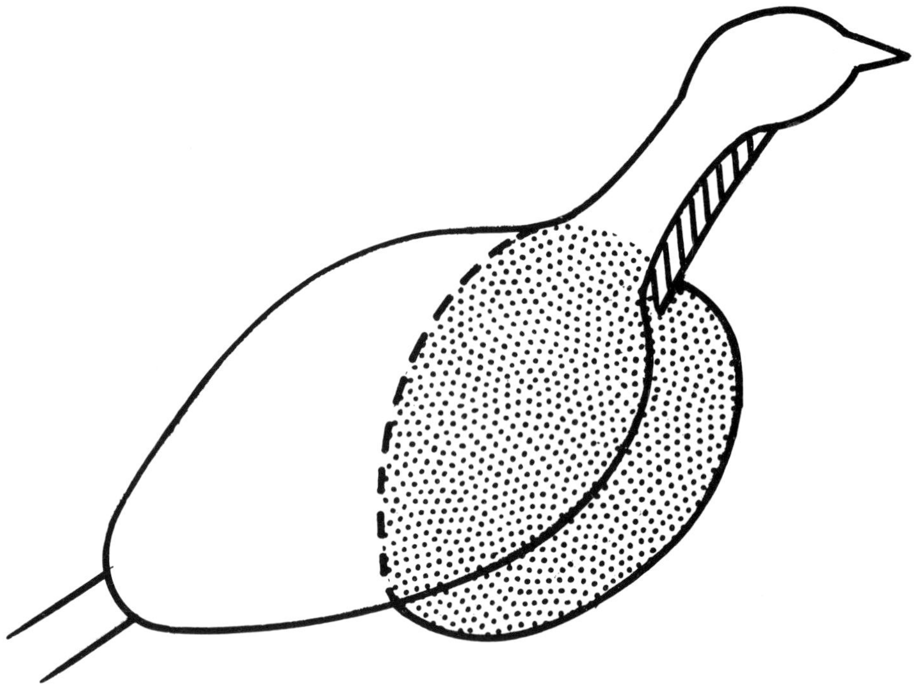

Figure 1.3 Building up the neck and breast

Neck

Bend the neck, to give it an 'S' bend, and pull the leg wires tight to make sure the leg bones are fully in position, but do not overdo this or the specimen will have short stubby legs and an unreal stance. Then mount the specimen on stiff cardboard and bend the wires over to secure them in a temporary manner.

Plumage

The specimen needs adjustment to its plumage. A sharp wire is driven into each wing, to hold it in position, the end of the wire protruding out from the body by an inch or more. Cotton can be anchored to this, in a figure of eight around the body, to give a final support, and hold many of the feathers flat. This starts at one wing wire, then across the back, under the tail, and across the second wing to the other wire.

Tail

Now the tail wire can be opened, slightly for a normal tail position, or wide for a full bird display, and the feathers spread between them. Make sure they are lying correctly, uppermost to the centre, lower to the outer edge. Cardboard is placed above and below the feathers and wires, which are sandwiched in the middle, and held in place with paperclips.

Legs and claws

The position of the legs and claws are all important. Too many beginners are apt to place the legs too far back. The bird must look balanced, and to achieve this, at least one claw should be so far forward as to be level with the bird's breast. A photograph or good picture can help at this stage. The legs should be slightly bent to give a more natural appearance. In life, they act as shock-absorbers and not pogo sticks. The claws can be held in position by household pins until dry.

Head, throat, and mantle

There now remains the head, throat, and mantle to correct. If the throat looks too thin, then push a little cotton wool down the throat via the beak. Birds such as starlings often bristle the throat feathers, and to achieve this effect, it needs to be well packed. Finish by passing a needle and cotton through the nostrils and tie both bills together.

Make sure the ears are in place, and the lines, markings, or bars on the head are correct, and adjust the eyes for the final time. There is a choice of methods here. The simplest is with a hair-dryer, and we will describe this first. Place the eyelids in a natural position, and use the hot air from the hair-dryer to blow on them for a few minutes; this dries them onto the lid, preventing distortion.

The second and most popular method is to allow natural drying to take place. With this technique it is necessary to pull the eyelid slightly lower than its natural position, because as it dries naturally over the next ten days or so, the eyelid will shrink and lift. Failure to do this gives the bird a mad, staring look.

The mantle is the feathers between the bird's neck and its wings or 'shoulders'. If they look out of place, they can be lightly moved into position with forceps, by stroking the thin skin underneath. The strokes should be made from the side of the neck, at the base, to the centre of the back, both sides being treated separately.

Some taxidermists then cover the whole specimen in cotton wool, and bind it lightly with cotton; this keeps the feathers in tightly against the bird while drying. The cotton 'figure of eight' already mentioned also does for most specimens. If the bird is completely bound in cotton wool, then it must be checked in a few days to see that the feathers are lying correctly. While the bird is drying out, it must be placed in an airy, dry, fly-proof cupboard until completely dry.

When dry, the surplus wire can either be cut off, or bent into a hook and pressed into the body, and hidden by the feathers above. Cotton and tail wires should be cut off, eyes cleaned, and oil-paint applied to the legs and beak, if required. When the paint has dried, then artist's picture varnish can be applied to the bill and legs. This type of varnish is used because it can be removed with petrol, whereas normal varnish will resist such efforts.

BLOODIED BIRD SPECIMENS

From time to time, specimens obtained are covered in blood, mud, and dirt. These specimens have to be washed. First skin down the bird, and clean the skull and bones. Then mix a little detergent, Daz or Ariel, the latter being better, with hot water, to allow the particles to dissolve; then add cooler water to make the liquid tepid. If the blood has dried on the specimen then it is advisable to soak the skin in cold clean water, and if soaked overnight, then a few drops of Carbolic Acid may be added, to prevent bacteriological action.

The skin is passed into tepid, soapy water, and quickly washed. All blood clots have to be removed in the process, then it is rinsed several times in clean water to remove all trace of the detergent. If any remains then it may well prevent the feathers returning to a fluffy state. Allow the bird to drain for a time, then use a towel and absorbent paper to remove as much surplus water as possible, before using the hair-dryer. There will be far more water retained among the wing feathers than those of the head, so for the beginner it is advisable to start at the head, so he can see the success of this technique as soon as possible.

First put some cotton wool into the eye-sockets via the neck, to keep the moisture of the skull away from the eyelid and feathers, then apply the hair-dryer, taking care not to expose the delicate eyelids to too much heat.

Soon the feathers will begin to lift and then fluff up. Move the dryer around so the heat is applied over an area, rather than just one spot; a finger or a hand slipped into the skin will also assist with the control of the feather areas being dried. Continue until all feathers are dry, then proceed to mount the eyes and treat as a normal skin.

Hints for cleaning

With a very bloodied specimen which has dried, or perhaps for a bird with a large white area, then the skin can be left overnight in a cold solution of Ariel and water, and in a cool place, and the process continued next day. I have tried this method on a terribly mutilated little owl which had been run over by a number of cars, and had dried itself onto the roadway. I thought at the time I could not have chosen a much worse skin to work on, but for a bet and out of sheer curiosity, I did. The finished specimen was beautiful, and could not be picked out as the damaged broken creature it had been. However it is a method I would only recommend to the more advanced student. The danger of using ammonia to remove blood stains is that it can also cause fading in the skin as a whole. Finally, rinse with cold water, before draining and drying. If a few drops of Carbolic Acid are added to the warm water, it helps prevent any bacteriological action while drying. I also use this method overnight for skins with a great deal of dried blood.

ANCHORING OF FINISHED SPECIMENS

The method of anchoring specimens to a stand or twig is quite simple, but seems to cause confusion. Drill two holes through the wooden stand, false rock or bark, or twig, and pass the bird leg wires through, pull tight and bend over. Then, using pliers, bend the end of the wires at right angles and press sharpened ends firmly into the stand, rock or twig, until flush with it. With the false rock or stand, a groove can be made to sink the wire in, and covered with polyfiller, thus hiding it completely. With the twigs, a thin layer of dyed moss can hide the wire. If the wires are trimmed to shorten them, make sure that a new point is filed on, otherwise it will be difficult to press the wires in (see figure 1.4). Heavy wires, such as those used for swans and geese can be treated in the same way, but may need staples to secure them along their length.

Birds to be mounted on twigs and branches should be done immediately, and then allowed to dry; this makes sure the stance is correct. This also allows one to curl the claws around the

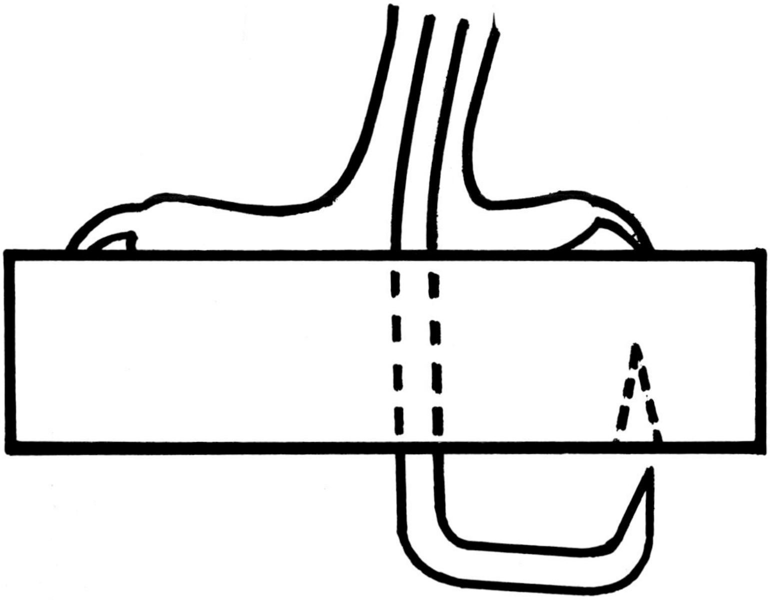

Figure 1.4 Anchoring the specimen

branch, and pin or bind them down until they harden, otherwise they will spring up, especially the hind claw.

Mounting medium to large birds

An extra wire added to the manikin of many birds allows far more control of the finished specimens, until they are fully dried out. A bird like a goose, with neck forward, as in a feeding position, is very unbalanced on two wires only. Once the webbing of the foot has fully dried out, the specimen becomes very rigid on its temporary stand. The extra wire is added to the rear of the manikin, and extends out with the tail wires while the false body is made up, as in figure 1.5.

It is also a useful wire to add when birds are standing on one foot, flying, or alighting. Once the goose is fully dried out, the wire is cut off close to the bird's body. With flying birds, it may be retained, and the leg wires removed, giving a true flying stance (see figures 1.6 and 1.7).

Single legged stance

Birds which have a single legged stance need a manikin built in the normal way, but the leg wires will differ. One leg wire will carry the full weight of the finished specimen, while the other only has to carry the weight of the leg.

Figure 1.5 Mounting a medium to large bird

Positioning of leg wires

The position of the leg wiring will depend on whether the bird is standing or running, because with each of these positions, the leg holds a different position in relation to the body (see figure 1.8).

MOUNTING BIRDS USING THE SKELETON

With some larger birds, one can use a method incorporating the whole or part of the skeleton. With a long necked bird, such as a heron, there is a distinct advantage in incorporating the neck from the skeleton. The angle and position of the neck, using this method, are true to life. The head wire is placed through the hollow of the vertebrae and out through the bird's forehead. The flesh is removed as far as possible before incorporating it with the manikin, and the remaining flesh can either be rubbed with alum or painted with Formaldehyde (40%). The missing muscles and windpipe are replaced with tow which is bound into position with cotton.

With really large specimens, such as the ostrich, the bones may have to be cooked, and then reassembled. However, if one does this, then it is necessary to place pads between each vertebra, to take the place of the natural disc, to retain true neck length. These pads can be made of cardboard, polystyrene, carpet underlay, or a similar material.

Using the whole skeleton, the bird is skinned in the normal way. The skin, however, is removed completely from the legs and the skull, leaving the skeleton complete, except wing bones, which stay with the skin. The flesh and organs are removed. Heavy bones, such as the

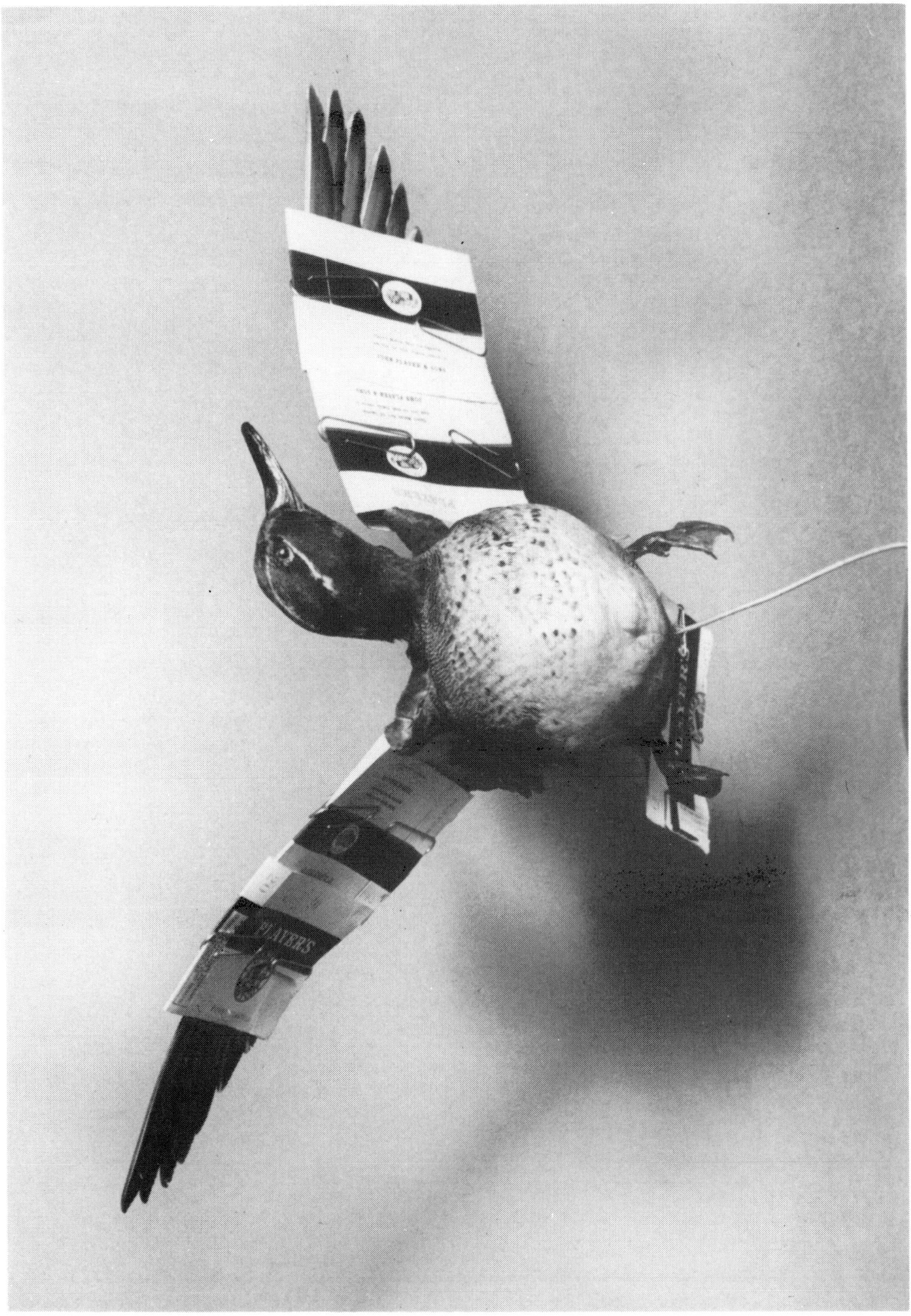

Figure 1.6 Male teal in 'springing' flight, showing how feathers are pinned

Figure 1.7 Male teal with the cardboard removed

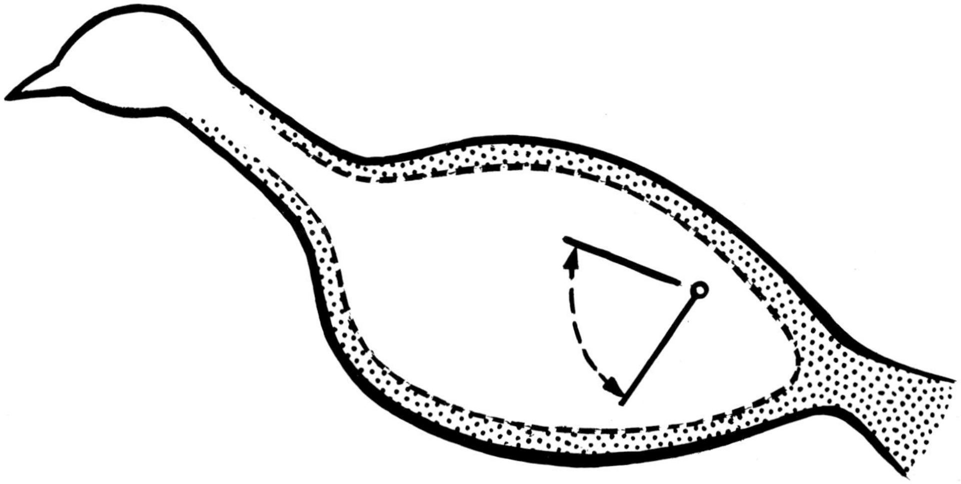

Figure 1.8 Positioning of leg wires

femur, may have to be drilled, and the bone marrow either removed or preserved. It could become a problem years after the specimen has been mounted. The skeleton is washed to clean it. Clean water will do, a solution containing alum or borax is even better.

A wooden block is placed in the body cavity. This block carries the wires for the legs, head, and tail. Once in place the cavity is shaped with tow, and the missing flesh replaced with the same material (see figure 1.9). The manikin is now mounted onto a suitable base and the skeleton painted with Formaldehyde (40%), and allowed to dry. This will cause the skeletal parts to harden and stiffen. Tow is the suggested medium to replace muscles, but papier mâché, balsa wood, or many other materials can be used for this job. The final decision depends on the materials available and the choice made by individual taxidermists.

The skin is preserved and mounted in the normal way, the only difference being that the skin joining the base of the beak, and the skin joining the legs, is secured with an adhesive, the choice of which ranges from No. 1 Clear Bostik to the modern instant impact ones.

RELAXING BIRD SKINS

Relaxing skins is a delicate job, and cabinet skins a job for an expert. The problem is that it is possible to relax some parts of the skin easier than other parts. The wing area around the 'thumb' takes so much time to relax that feathers from the rest of the body fall out. Even professional taxidermists, when mounting a bird from a cabinet skin, normally have a notice attached stating so, in case that particular specimen is taken as his normal standard of mounting. Even then, they are not placed in a wing-raised position. Small birds relax more readily than larger ones.

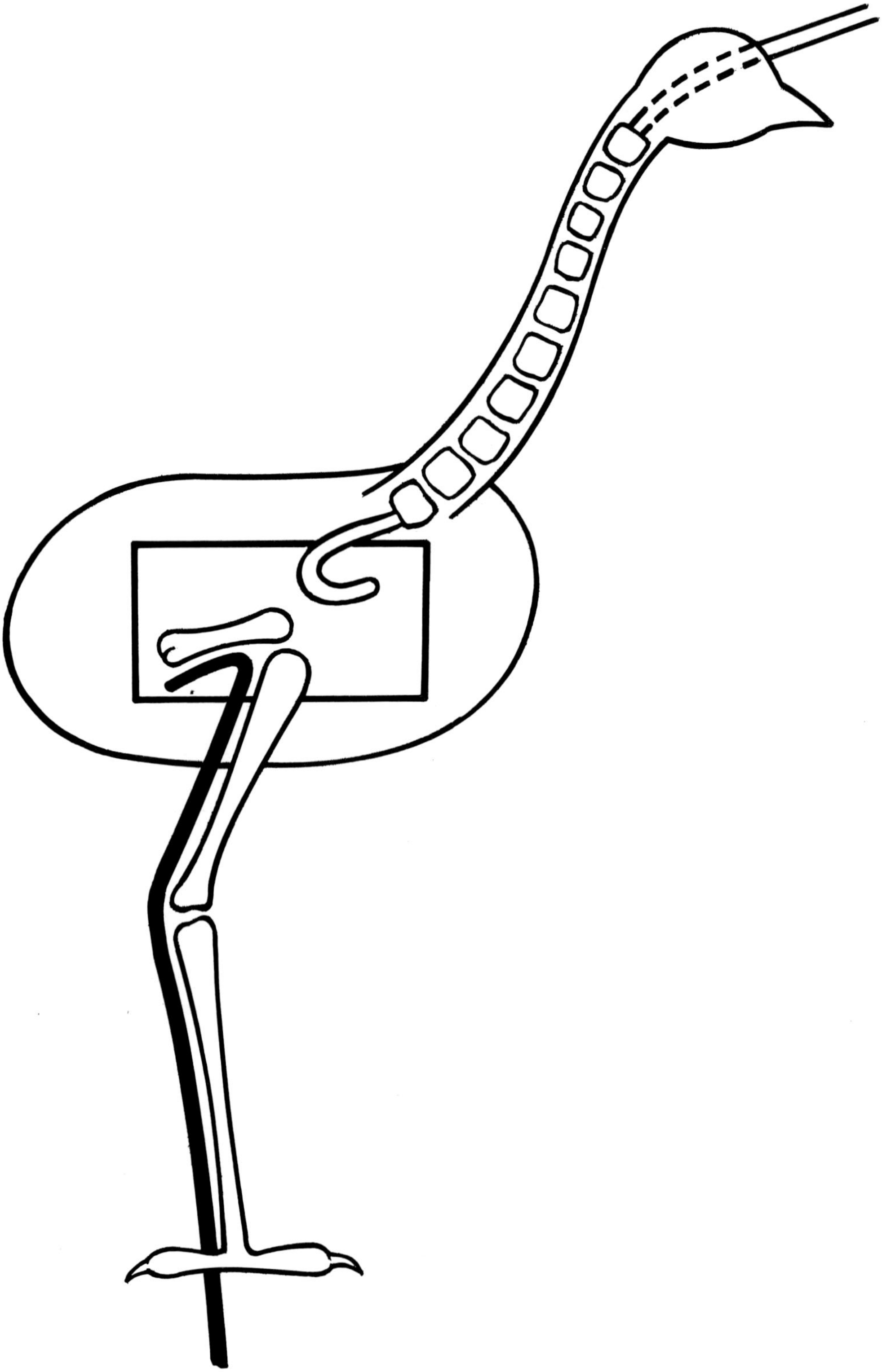

Figure 1.9 Mounting a bird using the skeleton

Method

Remove the belly stitches as far as possible. Dampen interior with cold water, and place in an air-tight box or plastic bag. It is an advantage to dampen the tougher areas a day before, with damp cotton wool pads. Small birds relax in 24 to 48 hours, but need regular supervision. An unsightly eye can be corrected with a damp cotton wool pad placed in position for a few hours.

PRESERVING GREASY BIRD SKINS

Firstly skin out, then clear off blood stains, and rub in salt well and fold back into position. It is important to note that if salt is applied to bloodstained feathers or fur, it will cause a permanent stain. The specimen so treated can be stored for a few days in a damp place.

Relax by soaking in water, and washing all traces of salt from the skin, by numerous water changes, or running water. When fat is removed, submerge in **Hubers Solution** for a full day. Repeat if necessary. Dry by draining, using paper absorbent towels, and hair-dryer, in that order.

MAGGOTS AND FLY EGGS

Even fresh specimens can have eggs laid on them. It is almost impossible to clear every single egg or maggot by hand. The answer is to deep freeze the specimen, by the following method.

If the specimen is a day or so old, remove the body. This allows the minimum of time for thawing out when one wishes to work on the specimen. Then fast freeze the specimen. Maggots are quickly killed off in deep freeze temperatures. With eggs, it is difficult to tell whether they are killed as easily as maggots, so to be safe I allow a time of fourteen days for the eggs and 48 hours for maggots. These times are probably far longer than is necessary, but they have become a routine safety factor with me. I find this a far superior way to treat a skin, to avoid using yet another chemical, as it does not damage the skin. If no freezer is available use Hubers Solution and immerse specimen completely.

Hubers Solution

2 gallons Petrol (Colourless)
1 pint Alcohol (Industrial Methylated Spirit)
4 ozs Spirit of Turpentine

WATTLES AND COMBS

There are a number of ways of dealing with these. The easiest produce the poorer results, and rely more on the patience and ability of the taxidermist. The simplest is to paint the wattles and comb with Formaldehyde (40%), and allow to dry completely. Then, using coloured beeswax, build up the now shrunken parts and add fine detail while the wax is soft, with hot needles and other heated tools. Another method is to cut them off and take a plaster cast of them, then build new ones completely from wax, as described in the section for leaves and grasses. The finest classic method is described in the next section.

CASTING NAKED BIRD HEADS

The extremes in this case include turkeys, vultures, and the like. Remove the head and neck at the base of the feathers. Run a strong wire up the spinal cord of the vertebrae and into the brain cavity. Anchor the other end of the wire to a wooden base. Clean the head of blood, and pose it to the required stance, fluffing any hair, or bristles, out to their original positions. Grind marble dust to a fine powder and sieve through a fine cloth, to obtain only the powder. This is then mixed dry with Plaster of Paris, one part marble to two parts Plaster, by volume. From this mixture, plus water, a mould is made in two parts.

Detail

In order to obtain the finest detail, a thin solution is painted onto the wet head by means of a soft paint brush, allowing the bristles to stiffen and stand out. Apply in layers to a thickness of up to half an inch. Do not allow any oil or grease to come into contact with the skin from the mould dividing line.

Now place the cast and head in a warm place to allow decomposition to start and the mould to dry hard. After a few days, open the mould. The feathers and bristles will stay with the two halves. Remove any adhering skin. The beak with some bone is removed, cleaned, dried, and replaced into the mould, and the two halves clamped together. The mould is placed in hot water for a quarter of an hour before use. Equal quantities of beeswax and paraffin wax are blended together by heating, and coloured. A quantity of this is poured into the mould and shaken around to allow a good coating on the inside. A wire and tow neck, smaller in diameter than the original one, is made. The wire has to be long enough to fit to the intended manikin. The neck is then inserted into the mould, and the rest of the hot wax poured in. Allow to cool.

Submerge neck, cast and all into a solution of Muriatic Acid 20% and water 80% for a number of hours. The plaster will dissolve and crumble off with care. It will be necessary to replenish the solution until the mould has dissolved, leaving the rest intact.

Finally, rinse in clean water. Make eye sockets, and fit eyes. Final contrasting shades of colour can be added for finer detail. The manikin can now be made incorporating the head and neck and the skin is finally secured in this region, by gluing and pinning.

BIRDS WITH LARGE HEADS

Some birds present a special problem with the size of their head in relation to their neck, such as the goose, duck, woodpecker, and some marginal cases in the crow family. These are skinned in the normal way until one comes to the neck, or as far as one can, before it is cut off and the body removed. A useful tip is to pack a quantity of cotton wool down the windpipe, past where one intends to cut. This way all blood is retained in the body.

Cleaning

To clean the head, a second, smaller cut is made in the skin. Some taxidermists do it at the back of the head. This can affect a crest display, and leaves a longer 'scar' on the skin. If, however the bird is cut under the throat, and the head cleaned from there, the 'scar' is far

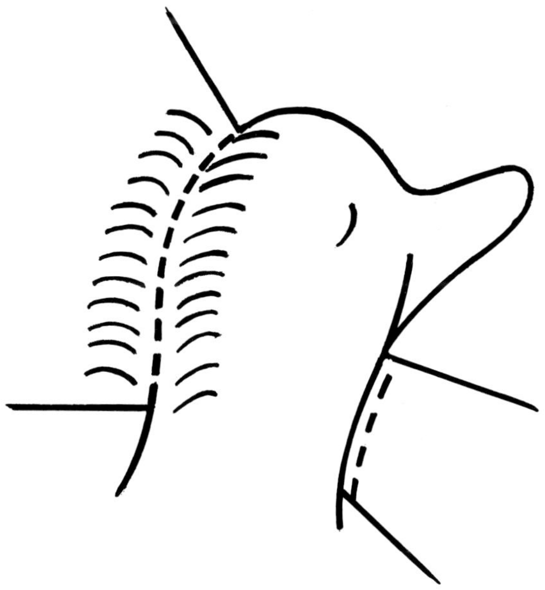

Figure 1.10 Concealing the scar when the head is cleaned

smaller when restitched, and is tucked from sight (see figure 1.10). The head is cleaned in the normal manner.

On mounting the skin, the neck of the manikin is put into position before the head cut is restitched. This way, it allows an observation point, which is useful for long necked birds. With short necked birds, restitch after completing head, as this helps prevent bedraggled feathers.

OWL EYES

Owls have a different type of eye to other birds, the eyeball being a tough sac. This is retained with the specimen. The lens is cut from the front of this sac, and the soft eye fluid removed. The interior is then powdered with borax, and packed hard with cotton wool, the glass eye fitting in front (see figure 1.11).

FLYING BIRDS

A specimen in a flying or wings raised position is a more impressive and eye-catching object, and is well worth the extra patience needed to produce it. The hidden problem in mounting such a specimen is the extra weight of cardboard strips, pins, and paperclips, combined with the bird being clear of the actual base. Excessively heavy wires to support the specimen are ugly, and detract from the desired finish of a light buoyant bird.

Figure 1.11 Mounting owl eyes

Method of support

Once it is fully dried, and the supporting material removed, the flying bird can be supported by a modest, less eye-catching wire. The length of the supporting wire, between the base board and the specimen, will determine how much weight it can carry.

In figure 1.12, the surplus wire is wrapped around the base block. Note the distance between the base and the bird in A & B. 'B' can support a far greater weight. Another way to support a drying specimen is seen in figure 1.13. This way extra wire support rods, marked B, can be used on the wings and tail to steady it. The cardboard strips are needed to hold the large primary feathers, secondaries, and coverts in position until they are dry and self supporting.

Mounting a flying bird

Proceed as if one is to do a normal bird, but do not tie the wing bones together. The position of the bird in flight will determine where the supporting wire is to be placed. It can protrude from the back, if a frontal view is envisaged, or alternatively from the tail. Yet again it could be placed on the opposite side of the body to the viewing angle.

Wings

The bird, when the manikin has been introduced and stitched up, is set roughly into position. A sharpened wire is driven down the inside of the bird's wing, from the outside, starting near the bird's thumb, protruding above the thumb. If the wing is now spread above the thumb, it

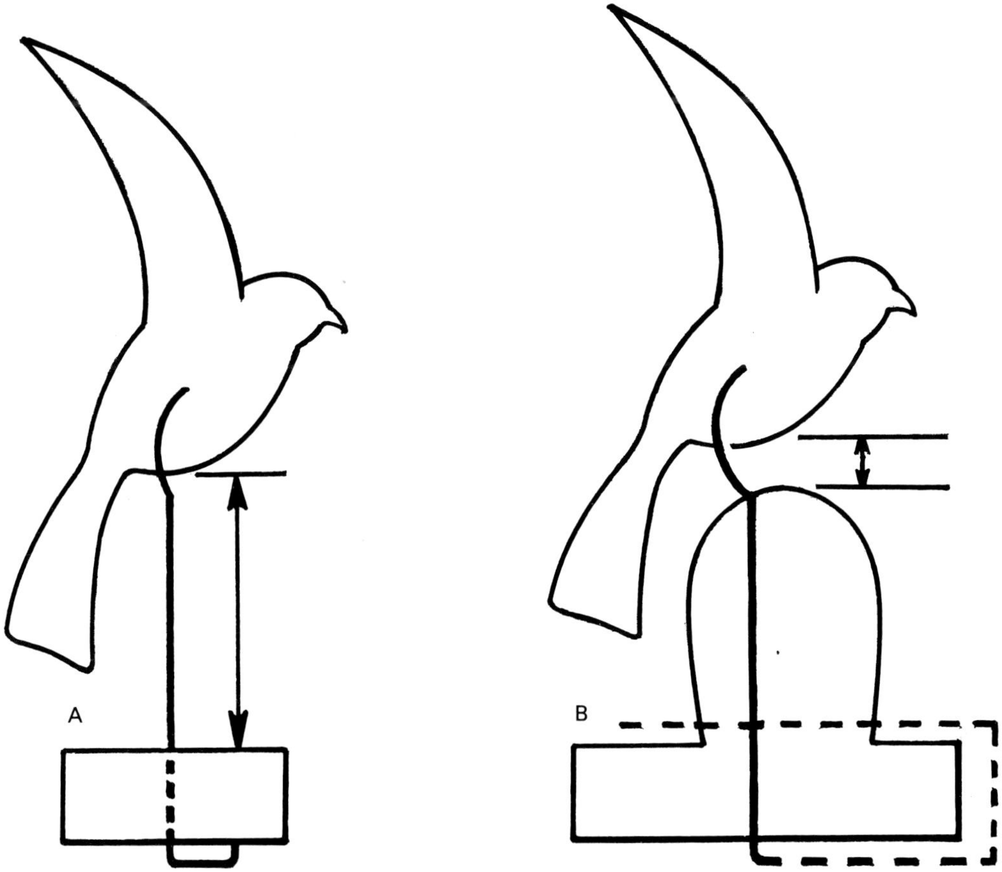

Figure 1.12 Method of supporting a flying specimen

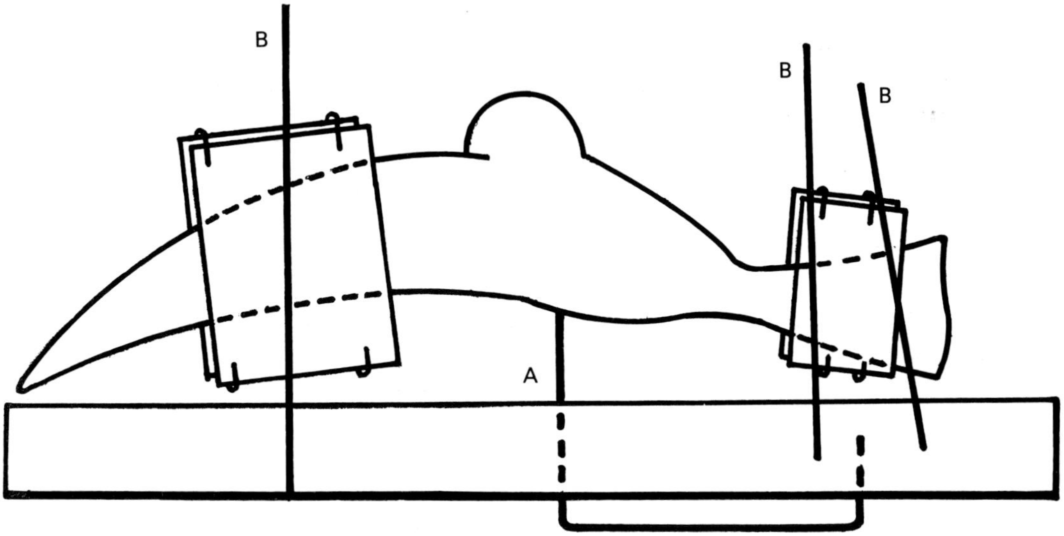

Figure 1.13 Method of support when drying

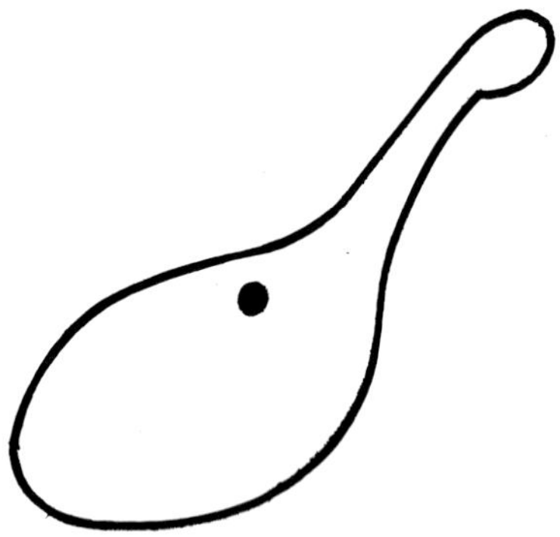

Figure 1.14 Entry point of main wire wing support

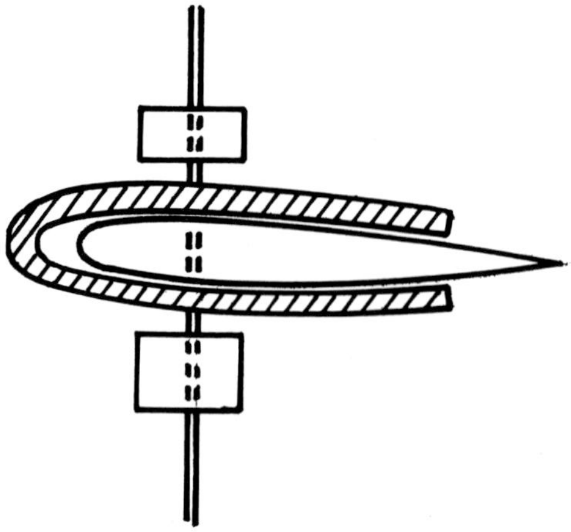

Figure 1.15 Method of clamping the wing

will readily be seen that if the thumb area is clamped with cardboard, the wing will remain spread. A cigarette pack and large paperclips will hold the position, while long strips are positioned to hold the feathers down. To prevent the paperclips sliding off, a pin may be driven through the clip and packet.

Figure 1.14 shows where the main wire wing support should enter the manikin, and figure 1.17 shows the main wire as "A" and another wire support "B", which stops the wing twisting while drying. Later it can be removed. Figure 1.16 shows two different patterns of cardboard to pin the wing feathers, one pattern on each wing. Figure 1.15 shows a pin driven through cork, cardboard, wing, cardboard and cork. This, sandwiched together, acts as a clamp for sections in the middle of the bird's wing, where the paperclips cannot reach. As many as required may be used. Figure 1.18 shows another use of clamps. Cotton or twine can be used between the wings to prevent any later movement, but should not be used to carry excess weight.

Once the stance is satisfactory, the head, tail and final adjustments to feathers and leg positions are made. Figure 1.13 shows another way a flying bird can be supported while drying. "A" wire is the main support wire. The numerous "B" wires are temporary drying supports only (see also figures 1.19 and 1.20). Frequent checks should be made during the drying period to see that no feathers are moving out of position. If so, an extra securing strip should be added to the affected area.

BIRDS LANDING OR TAKING OFF

These present an easier task than the flying birds as three base wires can be used. On completion, one or two of these wires can be removed. In figure 1.5 one can see three wires,

Plate 5 Grey squirrel, using combined methods

Plate 6 Pine marten, using combined methods

Plate 7 Coypu, using combined taxidermy

Plate 8 Deer, as trophy head

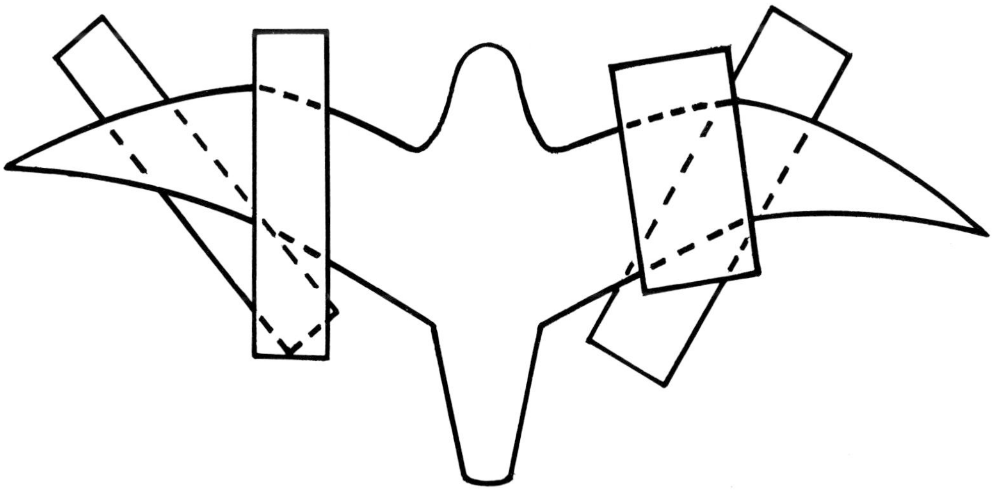

Figure 1.16 Alternative patterns of cardboard to pin the wing feathers

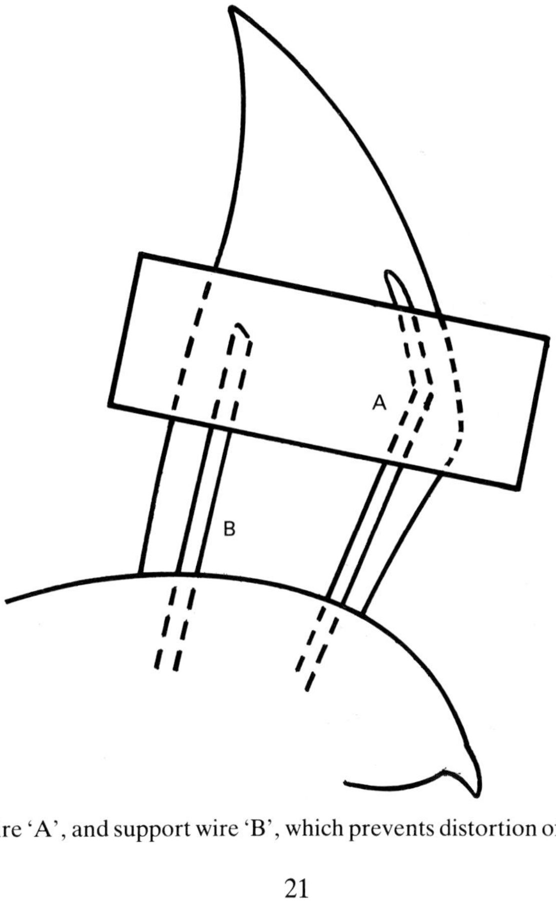

Figure 1.17 The main wire 'A', and support wire 'B', which prevents distortion of the wing during drying

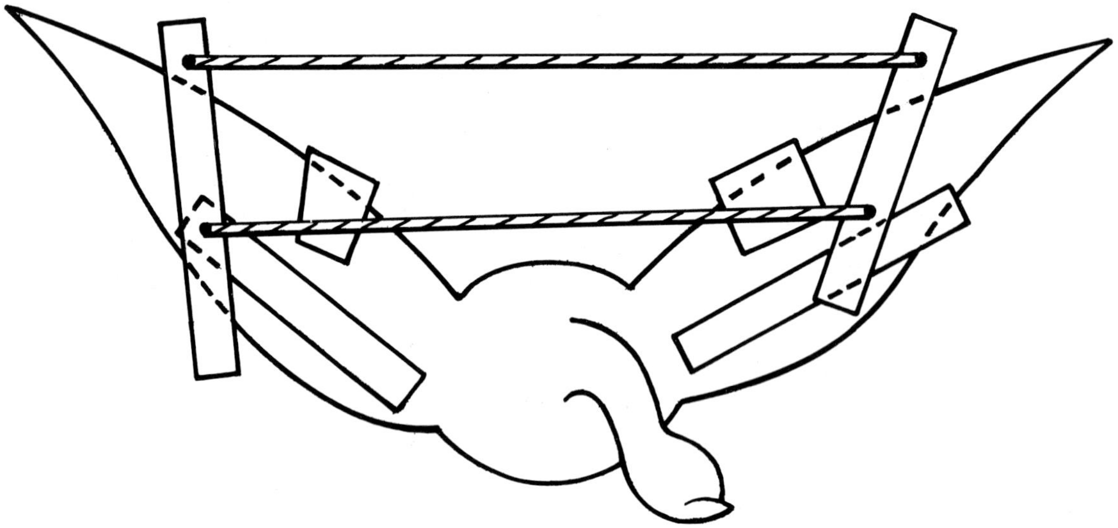

Figure 1.18 Another use of clamps; cotton or twine may be used between the wings to prevent movement, but must not be used to carry excess weight

A, B, and C. If "B" wire is to be the only retained wire to give an almost invisible wire support; i.e. launching itself from a branch, it must be strong enough to carry the whole bird. It could be lighter gauge if A and B were to be retained.

Figure 1.21 shows a talon, with a cork pushed up the wire to keep the claws open, and the pins anchoring them into the required position. When dried the cork can be cut away and the wire trimmed off. Figure 1.22 shows another method with a webbed foot. The wire is looped and modelling clay is packed into the hollow. The shape of the foot is retained by three pins.

SUSPENDED FLYING BIRDS

Birds, like the kestrel hovering, can be suspended on a fisherman's nylon line, which can have a realistic effect. The centre of balance of such a specimen can present a problem, which can easily be overcome by studying figure 1.23. A wire loop is extended an inch or two from the hovering bird. The wire can be bent to dive or climb.

Such hanging birds can be affected by convection currents, especially in large halls, which can cause the bird to turn slowly. A second nylon line attached to the wire loop will prevent this happening. See figure 1.23 "B" attachment.

BIRD TONGUES

These can be cut out by the roots and pinned into a suitable position on a cork. Dip in borax solution for an hour and allow to dry. They can then be inserted back into the birds' open

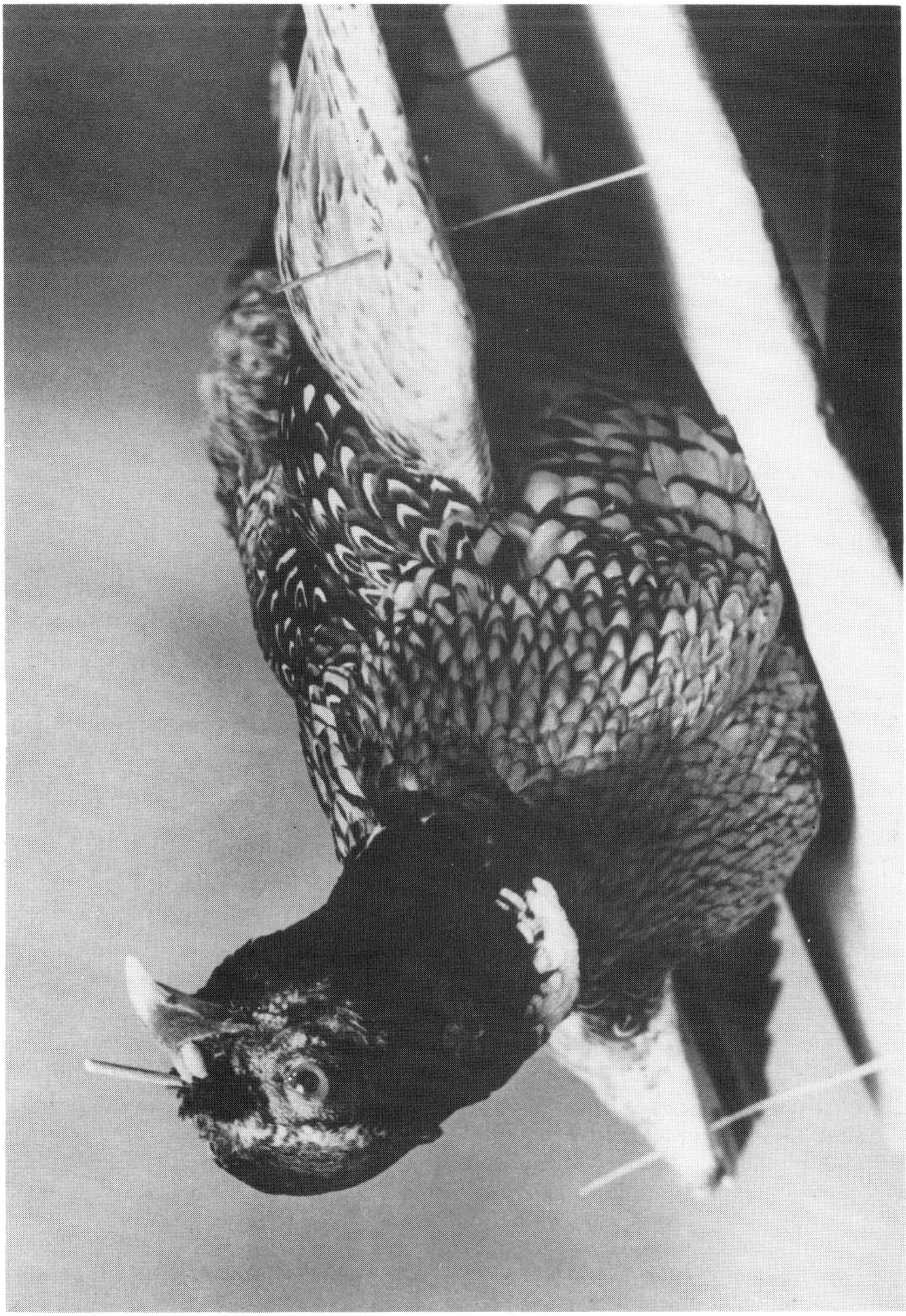

Figure 1.19 Male pheasant showing wire pins through wings

Figure 1.20 Male pheasant showing cardboard pinning areas

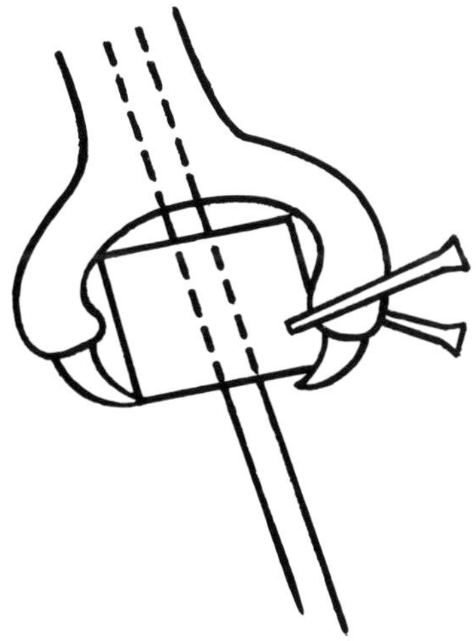

Figure 1.21 Talon with claws pinned into the required position

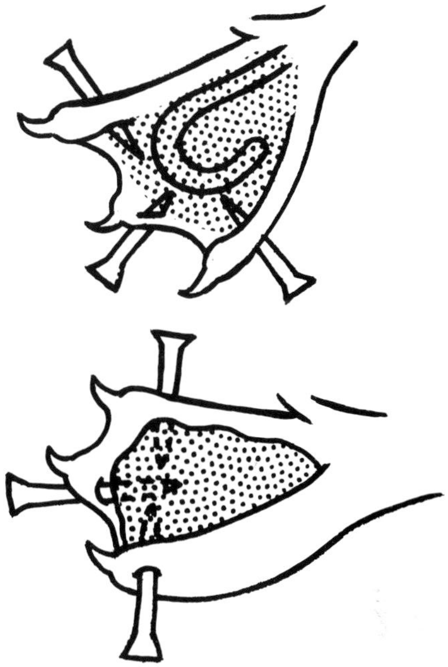

Figure 1.22 Webbed foot fixed into position

beaks, and imbedded into the throat by soft beeswax, and finally the colour restored by tinting with oil paints.

SWIMMING WATER BIRDS

Skin down in the normal manner, degrease, etc, as with a normal bird. The build up of the manikin differs from the tow body as the material to be used will be either balsa wood or a polystyrene block. The reason for this is one needs the glass sheet, or "water". There are two methods of approaching the problem. Both are simple and have their merits.

Method one

Cut a block of balsa wood to the shape of the duck's body. No neck is required, this being added by making one on a long wire, from tow. This wire is pushed through the body and anchored at the manikin's rear, and the tow neck adjusted (see figure 1.25).

The position of the waterline is decided and marked. An easy way to do this is to gently lower the manikin into a bowl of water and mark the required waterline with pins. Later mark the line and cut into two halves. The upper half is mounted into the skin, remembering to place the usual tow pad between the wing bones to prevent a hollow backed appearance. Once the skin is in position, the lower empty half can be cut away from the inside.

The upper half can be completed with a zig-zag stitch, glue, and pins (to retain the skin in position while the glue is drying). See figure 1.24. The lower half of the skin and manikin are brought together. The upper half of this is held by a zig-zag stitch, and the half turned over

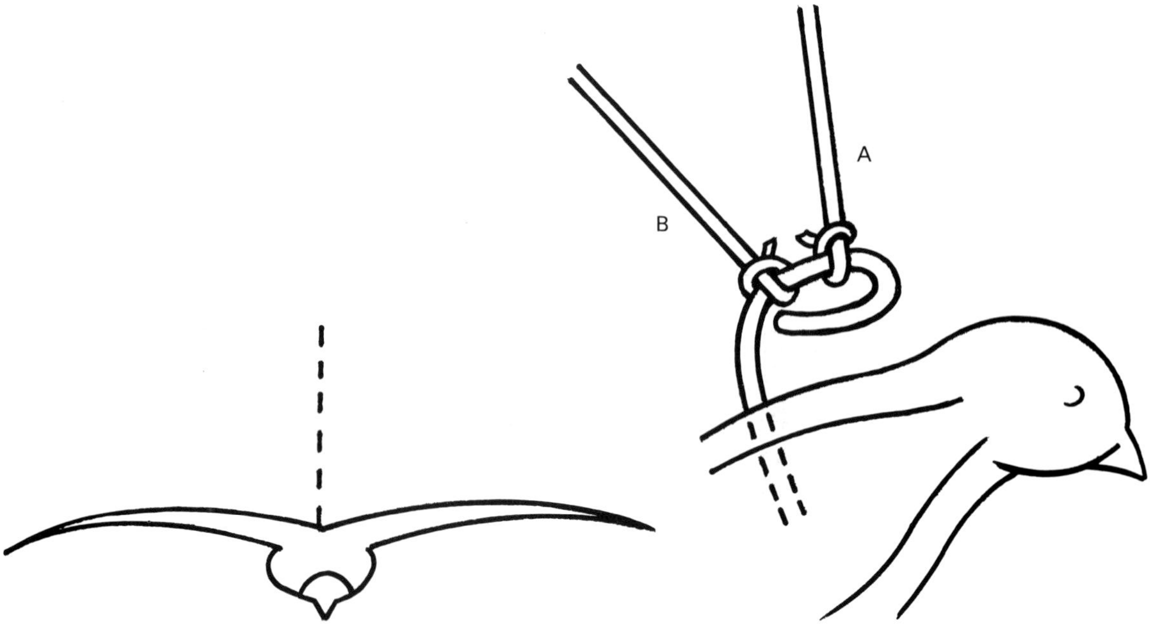

Figure 1.23 Finding the centre of balance of the specimen; if wires 'A' and 'B' are fixed from the loop, this should prevent the bird from rotating

and treated as a normal specimen. The only difference is that sharpened leg wires are driven into the leg from the outside, via the foot, and up into the manikin (see figure 1.26).

The belly opening is stitched up, and the lower half adjusted. It is now placed upside down on glass in the required position and glued or bonded. Once it has set hard, the glass can be reversed, and the upper half of the duck placed above the lower half, and glued into position, and treated as a normal specimen.

Method two

This method is perhaps more useful, when dealing with ducks in awkward underwater positions, as in figure 1.24. The manikin is made, water-marked and cut as in method one. It is then pinned together with wire prongs, and/or bound with cotton to hold it as one unit. The leg wires can be added, as seen in figure 1.27, and anchored as if in cork.

Mounting the skin is the same as for a normal bird, but before stitching up, insert two or three short guide wires from the outside to show where the manikin is joined, because later it has to be cut in two halves, from the outside. The bird can now be adjusted. As there is no stand, a strong wire carefully driven through the bird will allow it to rest on an open box, rather like an ox on a spit. It is allowed to harden and dry. Once ready for finishing the duck is cut from the outside, along the line of the two manikin halves, and levered apart. The joining wire spikes are removed, and the method continues as in method one.

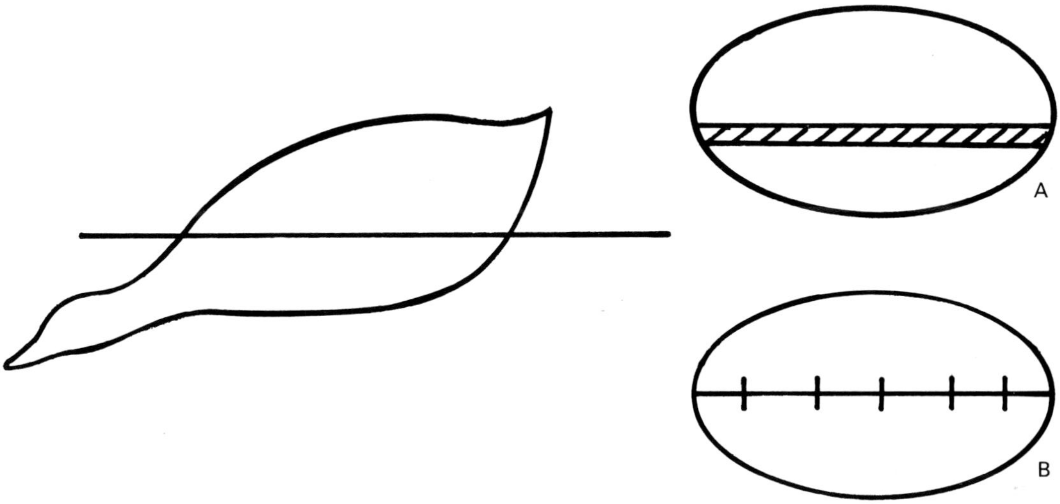

Figure 1.24 Waterline for swimming water birds

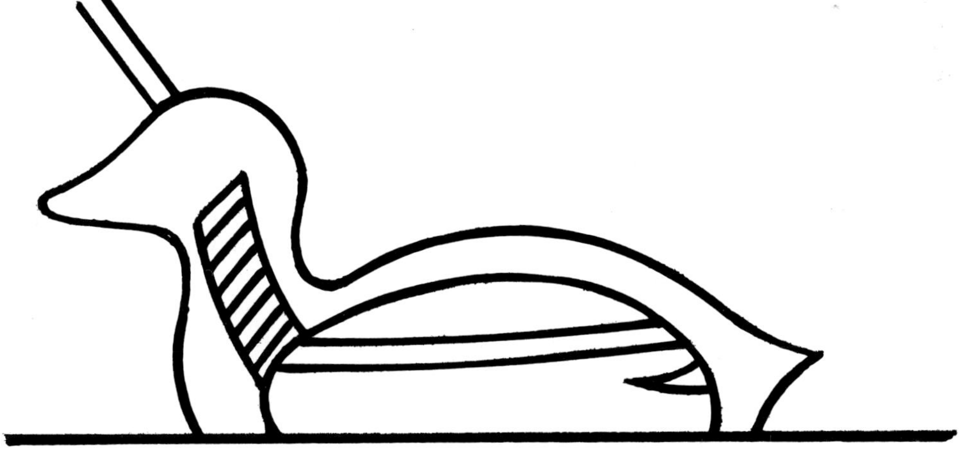

Figure 1.25 Method of supporting the body and neck of a swimming bird

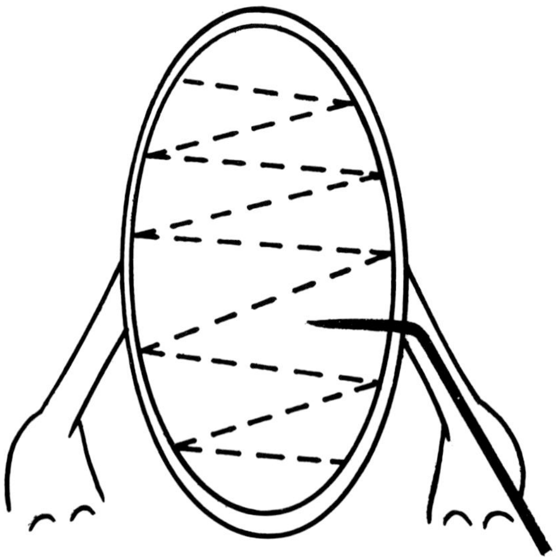

Figure 1.26 Wire driven into the manikin through the foot of an underwater specimen

Tips for water scene

If the underside and inside of the glass case is varnished, a dimmer, more blurred effect is reached. Acrylic, or plastic, water disturbance around the duck and water plants add to the interest. It can also be used as water droplets from the beak and feathers. Water Lilies and grasses stuck on the surface are more interesting, with stems stuck on the underside, to give continuity. Blanket weed can be made from teased out dyed cotton wool. Water beetles and snails can make it realistic. Tree roots can also enhance an underwater scene; examine ponds for ideas, at different times of the year.

WIRE FOR MOUNTING

The wire used for specimens, regardless of size, must have the following qualities. It must be strong, resistant to corrosion to a high degree, reasonably priced, and not inclined to 'spring'. By that, I mean that once the wire or rod has been bent into the required position, it will not try to 'creep' or attempt to return to its original position.

Copper wire, and non-corrosive wires are usually too soft and weak. Galvanised wire is excellent and stands up to corrosion in specimens very well. Mild steel and iron rods are normally chosen for larger specimens. The following is a guide to wire size:

Small birds up to blackbird size	1 to 1.25mm wire
Magpie, jackdaw	1.50 to 1.60mm wire
Carrion crow, pheasant	2mm wire
Goose, fox, badger	2.5mm wire

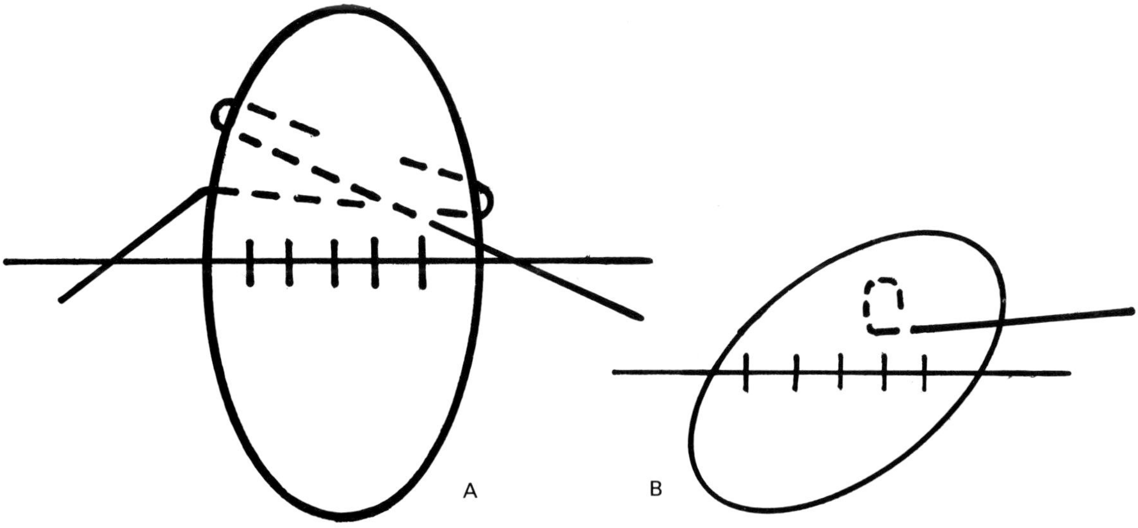

Figure 1.27 Method of mounting a duck in an awkward underwater position

DEEP FREEZERS

Although specimens can be set up without even coming into contact with a deep freezer, it is one of the main pieces of heavy equipment used by a taxidermist. Besides allowing storage of a number of unworked specimens, it also allows for many items to be tackled during a week, and left at suitable stages of the work. For instance, a fox head, once skinned and trimmed, may be returned to the freezer, while the skull is cooked and cleaned, and the manikin prepared. To do this in one day, satisfactorily, is impossible.

Sometimes I skin down birds, and refreeze the skin. This allows me to come back fresh on the assembly work, rather than to slog on, and so become careless. If such a bird is returned, and the head has been cleaned, the eye should not have modelling clay put into the eye socket, as it will become very soft on thawing. Use cotton wool pads instead. Birds prepared this way are quickly thawed and ready for mounting. They are also free of any pests. Most specimens have ticks, or other parasites, some specialised to the particular specimen. It is unpleasant to work with an infested specimen, and it is always possible to be bitten and infected by such pests.

Freezer burns

Specimens in deep freeze will last many months in good condition. If the specimen has been skinned down, it will be more prone to freezer burns or dehydration. To correct this, use either a damp cloth on the affected area, or submerge in clean, cold water. This will quickly restore it to normal.

DUCKS' WEBBING

The webbing on ducks' feet is prone to drying out, and many specimens are mounted by amateurs without correcting this fault. If the webbing is stiff, cotton wool wrapped around the foot and secured by cotton, then soaked in cold water, will allow the webbing to relax, while work continues on the skin.

FREEZER LIFE OF SPECIMENS

Frozen specimens do not spoil overnight, but will deteriorate gradually over the months. The finished mounted specimen is only as good as the original specimen. Small birds spoil quickly. The tendon in the leg quickly dries out, and on soaking, the leg becomes prone to 'scale-slip'. Up to three months should be classed as maximum, although I have done inferior specimens after three years. Small mammals such as mice are affected like small birds and have a similar life in the freezer. With these creatures, the tail becomes the greatest problem. Ducks and similar sized birds fair much better, and can last a year or two without too much dehydration. I have successfully mounted six-year-old birds, and mammals, but they have to be treated as a delicate skin, and are prone to problems.

BIRD FACE-PLATES IN WAX

Gallinules, moorhens, and coots, have a special problem in the fleshy forehead plate. Some of these 'outcrops' may appear quite firm and solid, but the underlying cartilage or gristle-like nature will cause the outer surface to buckle and shrink.

The first action to take is to photograph or draw the fresh shape, from various angles. Then measure the width, length, and thickness of the appendage, plus any oddities, such as 'overhangs', natural curves, inclines or leanings.

Coot

Let us look at one example; the coot. So many museum specimens do not show the white fleshy forehead that can be seen, even in twilight, at great distances.

Set up the specimen in the normal way. If you find it 'all feet', do it standing on one leg, as they often pause in that position. It also adds interest to the specimen. The face-plate will shrink to at least two-thirds to half its original area, and ripple as it flattens out. Allow it to dry; the longer the better, but not less than three months.

The amount of beeswax-resin mixture required to do such a head is small, and can easily be mixed with white oil-paint by hand, no other heating being necessary. It pays to allow the mixture to mellow for a week or two, to set the oil-paint, and prevent white finger-prints on the feathers. With the coot, the white can be as harsh as one can make it. If lesser shades are required, a translucent colour can be obtained by using only a little colour and blending in by hand. If re-heated in hot water, this will be lost, as this action seems to make the colours harsher (see also Beeswax Colouring). Warm the beeswax-resin by hand and roll out in a 'long worm' until it is approximately one third of an inch thick.

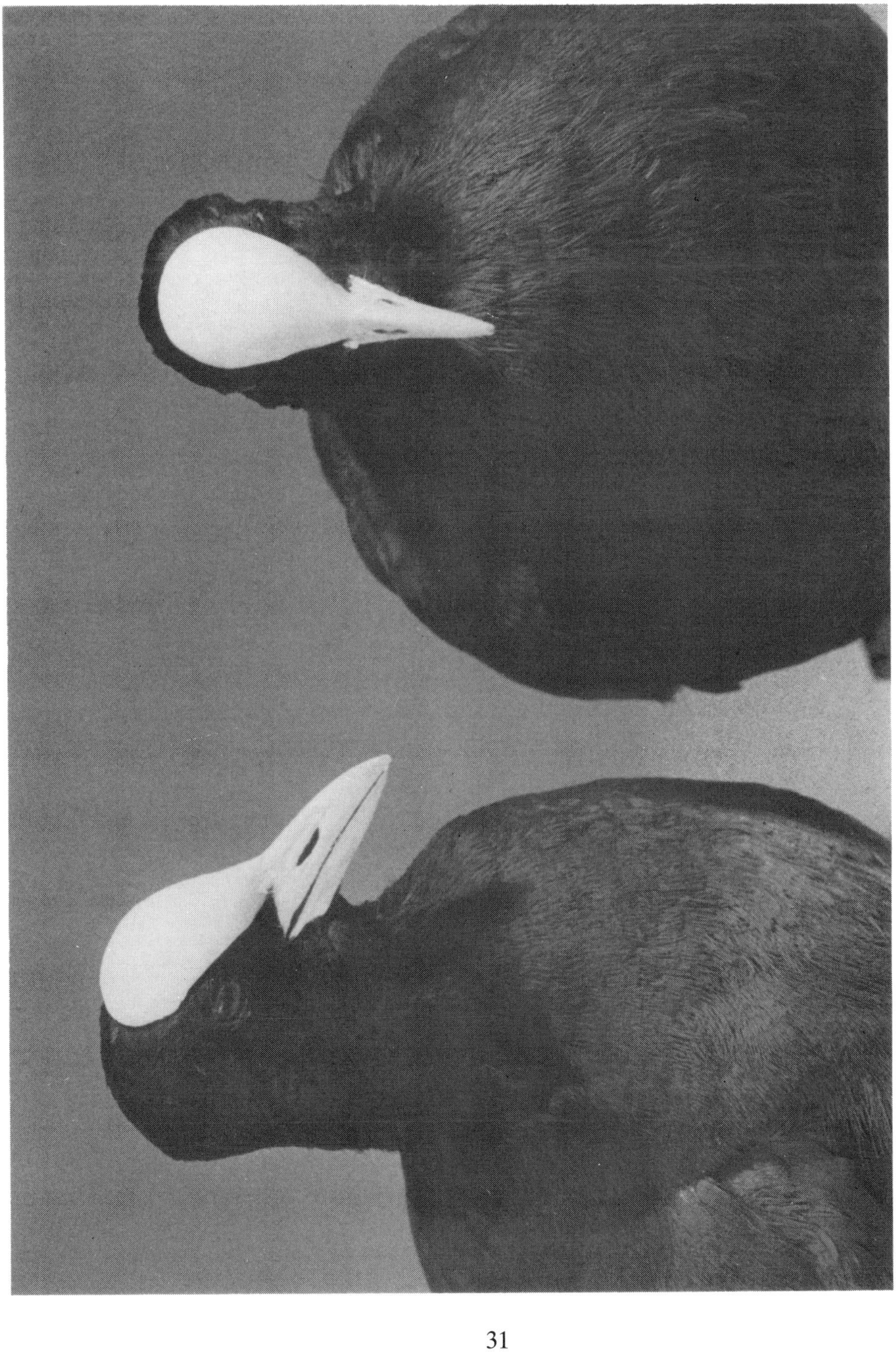

Figure 1.28 Coots, showing the face plates built up by beeswax resin techniques

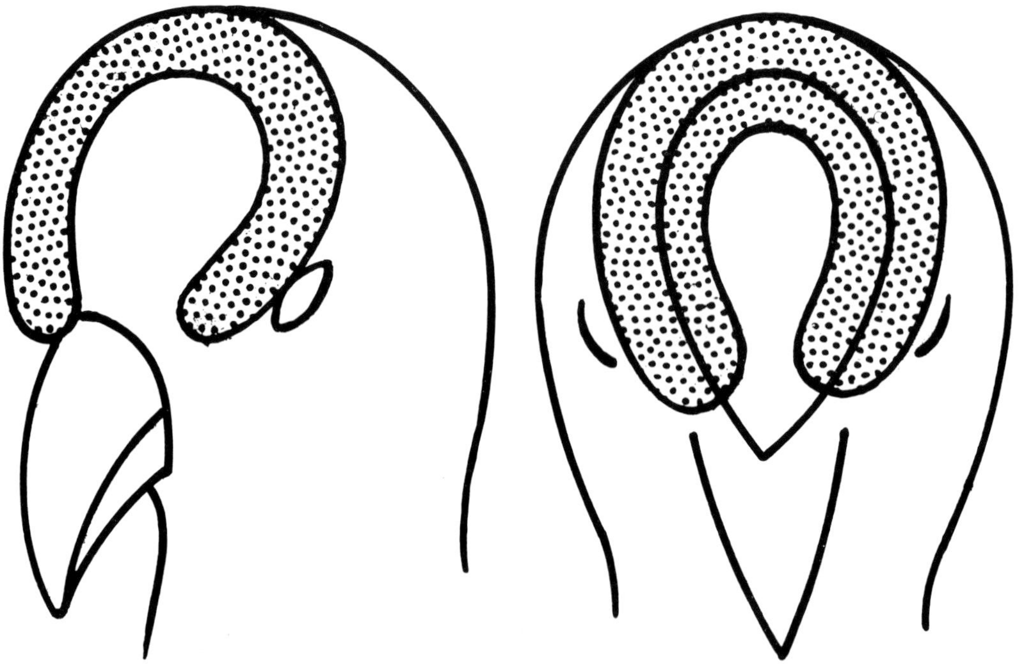

Figure 1.29 Building up the face plates

Loop it along the edge of the shrunken forehead, rather like an elongated down-turned horseshoe, and press lightly into position. Make sure to have a good overhang to make up for the shrunken area; see figure 1.29. Then press the inner side of the horseshoe hard into place, spreading it towards the centre. The object of this is to make a very firm anchor for the wax on the original base which may reject the wax, because of its slightly greasy nature, unless driven home hard.

Another shaped piece of wax is placed quickly in place, like a cap, and shaped and moulded to complete the final shape of the face-plate, as in figure 1.29. Once the shape has been achieved, the final touch is to blend it in with the beak.

The secret of most of these attachments is a good 'keeling', or anchoring of the first base wax. If poorly done, it is possible it will loosen over a period of time. Many taxidermists suggest dabbing with Formalin over the face-plate before drying takes place. If this is done, then it must be appreciated that the shrinkage will be more severe. In some cases, such as if one has limited time, this could be an advantage, but natural drying must be preferable.

The difference between the finished specimen compared with one untreated in this way, will be seen to be dramatic, and many an old specimen can take on a new lease of life with this technique.

CHAPTER 2

MOUNTING A FOX MASK

This chapter concerns the setting up of a fox head or 'mask' as it is known in the profession. The same principles can be used for most small and medium sized heads; from hare to roe deer size.

THE IDEAL SPECIMEN

First the specimen shall be of good size, with good fangs, ears and general appearance. A specimen that has been mauled by dogs or has had its skull shattered by a car should be left until one is more proficient.

Removing the pelt

The pelt should be removed with plenty of throat and neck, as one needs more neck skin than the amount displayed in the finished trophy. If it has a very short neck, then this restricts the angles or positions in which one can display the creature. I prefer to take the skin from as low as the sternum, between the front of the fox's legs, and up around the base of the neck, in front of the scapula or shoulder-blades. This gives me the maximum skin to work with and prevents any form of stretching. Stretched skin is unnatural, and besides causing possible warping, also thins the fur. Before skinning starts, plug the nostrils with cotton wool to prevent any blood damaging the mask and also wipe out the mouth and gums. Skinning and trimming of the skin will take between two and four hours. Take your time and leave any surplus tissue on the body, not the skin.

Work around the neck evenly until the cartilage of the ear base appears. Cut through the meat and cartilage of the ear as close to the head as possible; the remaining flesh can be trimmed off later. Continue towards the eyes and cut well back around the eye leaving all the tissue on the skin for later trimming; the skin is later split down to the eyelid; the reason will become apparent as we progress.

The mouth is cut as close to the bone as possible, leaving surplus skin and flesh again on the pelt. Free the lower jaw completely, then continue removing the pelt from the upper jaw until the cartilage of the nose is met. Cut through this near the bone, and the pelt will come completely away from the head. Note the colour and size of the eye, then cut the skull from the neck, and the tongue out.

Cleaning the head

The head is now ready for cleaning. Boil the head in a borax solution or a salt solution; a cupful of either is enough for half a gallon of water. The cooking time is approximately four to five hours. When cooked, all flesh can be easily removed and the brains washed out of the skull, taking care not to lose any of the teeth which will now be loose. Wash in soapy water, clean teeth with an old toothbrush, drain and allow to dry. The details of the head muscles should be recorded in a note book, together with your eye details.

Trimming the mask

While the skull is cooking, the mask can be trimmed. Starting about an inch back from the eye socket, split the skin carefully until one has a flap of skin adhering to the pelt only by the rim of the eyelid itself. The object of doing this is to enable one to put a little modelling clay between this flap and the pelt proper. When the skin has been set up and dried, it becomes thinner due to the loss of water content. With the modelling clay inserted and sandwiched between the tissues, the eyelids do not become thinner or distorted, as they are firmly held in place by the clay. The ideal tool to do this job is a Swann Morton scalpel with a number 15 detachable blade.

Lips

The same procedure is used on the lips of the fox with care being taken not to slice through the base of his whiskers. The lips under the nose are split through by burrowing in from either side, thus making a tunnel under the nose itself. The lower jaw can now be done, working from the corner of the mouth, under the eye, where the flesh is plentiful, towards the much thinner front.

Ears

The ears are split from the back, between the cartilage (which will remain in the specimen), and the skin holding the short black fur. The ear is turned completely inside out, and this can be done by pushing with a blunt instrument, once the initial flesh on the ear base has been passed; extreme care needs to be taken here as the skin at this point is quite weak and delicate.

PRESERVING THE PELT

Before we go on to the preserving of the pelt, I would like to say I normally freeze the heads as they come in for twenty-four hours, to get rid of any parasites, such as fleas, ticks and fly eggs, as these can make work very unpleasant, and that when I finally trim the skin, I normally keep it in a freezer until I wish to complete it. If you do not have a freezer available to you, don't worry; you have a choice of ways and most taxidermists have used them from time to time especially if they have done expedition or field work.

Methods of preserving

The pelt now needs preserving. This can be done in one of two ways, either complete immersion in a White Leather solution, or by rubbing a dry solution or mixture of Alum and Saltpetre on the flesh side; a four to one mixture by weight. The latter is suitable if the skin is

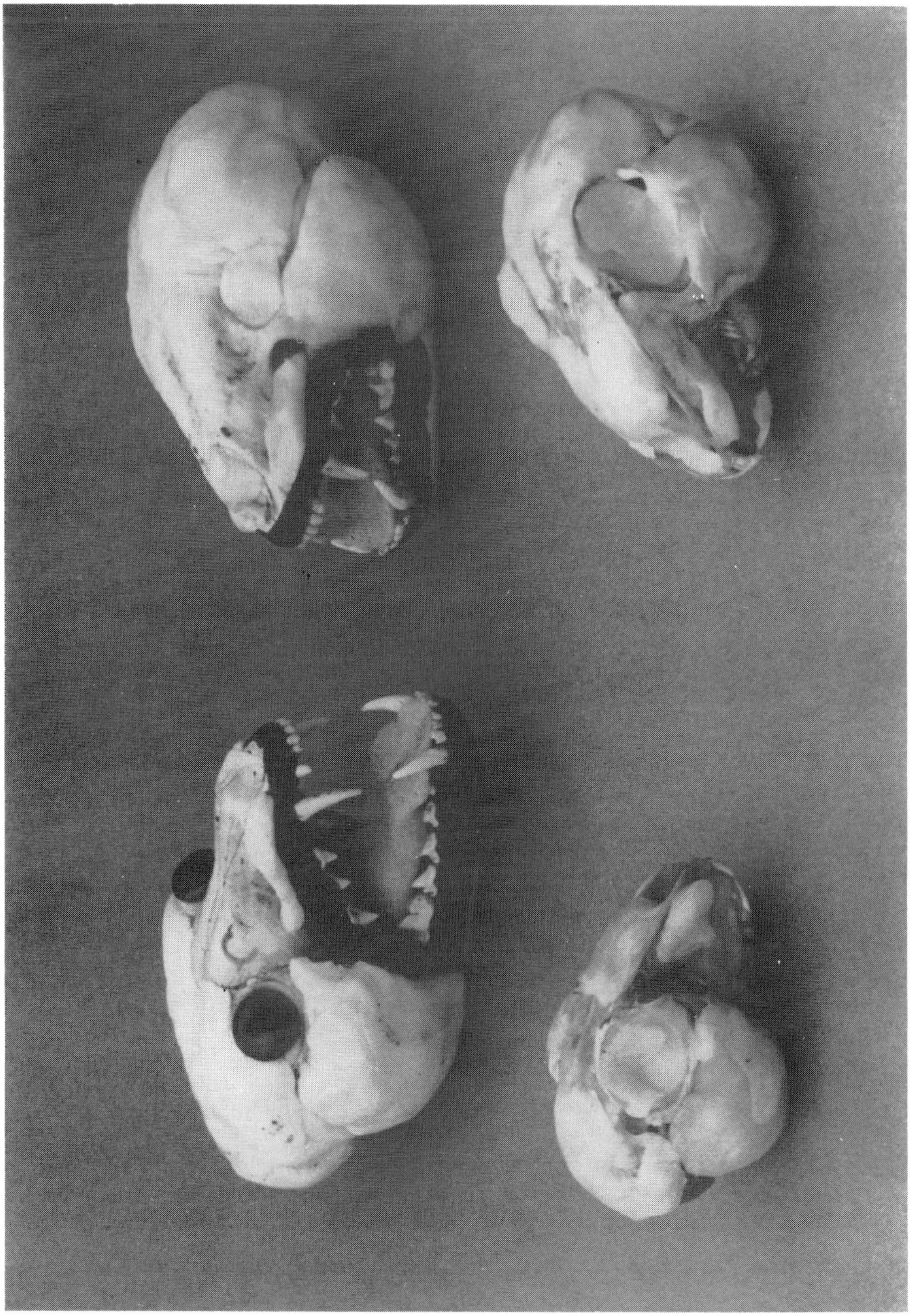

Figure 2.1 Skulls: *top left,* fox; *right,* badger; *bottom left,* rabbit; *right,* hare

clean, and pre-frozen i.e. removal of parasites on the fur side, and probably a little easier to work with for the beginner, especially when one comes to adjusting the features. With complete immersion, the pelt will shrink a little, but much of this can be recovered by stretching gently by hand. Larger, heavier skins must be trimmed and fully tanned to effect the best results, otherwise distortion can occur. The White Leathering process is suitable, provided the skin is suitably prepared. However, tanning is explained in greater detail in Chapter 4. The wet skin, once drained, can be wrapped in a towel and squeezed, then dried with a hair-dryer, but care must be taken around the eyes due to the intense heat. Absorbent paper wiped and pressed around the eyes will take most of the moisture from this area.

THE SKULL

I normally allow the skull to dry for a few days – longer if possible. The first stage in the build-up is the gums. For these I use black or grey Beeswax-Resin and place it where the gum was originally. This will hold the teeth in place. The lower jaws are waxed, then bound together with cotton or thin twine; this can be hidden in the dark wax by smearing over. A triangular wax spacer at the junction of these bones makes the whole structure quite strong. As you do this check the lower jaw against the upper jaw to see you are not making the lower one too wide. Wax the upper jaw and roof of mouth; on this can be drawn grooves with a scalpel to imitate the original.

The wax tongue is pressed onto the lower jaw, the jaws placed together, and the cheeks waxed in, making a solid unit of the mouthpiece. Snags to watch out for here are making the tongue too long; if this happens then there is a tendency for the tip of the tongue to keep rising from its placed position. Another very common mistake is to have the mouth open far too wide, so it is suggested that a gap of approximately one inch between the small front teeth be tried for the first specimen. The 'meat' for the rest of the head should be built up of either papier mâché or again beeswax, leaving eye sockets. These are filled with wax and suitable eyes attached by pressing against the soft wax, and adjusting them so they are not 'cock-eyed' (see figure 2.1).

The basic head is now complete. Wires for the neck can be added by using three wires approximately one foot long, these being hooked over at one end. These are inserted, hook first, into the brain cavity, which is then filled with Plaster of Paris, making sure first that any minor holes on the underside of the skull are sealed off with modelling clay. Allow time to harden off before continuing.

An oval disc of plywood approximately three by four inches is cut out. The disc forms an anchor for the wires and allows the head to be screwed to a plaque or shield later. Six holes are drilled near the edge of the disc. Of the three wires now protruding from the skull, two form the back of the neck, and the third is bent under the throat and follows the approximate line of the windpipe. The wires should be spread about two inches apart and run parallel where possible. The two back wires are threaded into the upper part of the disc, the throat wire through the lower portion; then thread the wire back through the remaining three disc holes, and bend and trim.

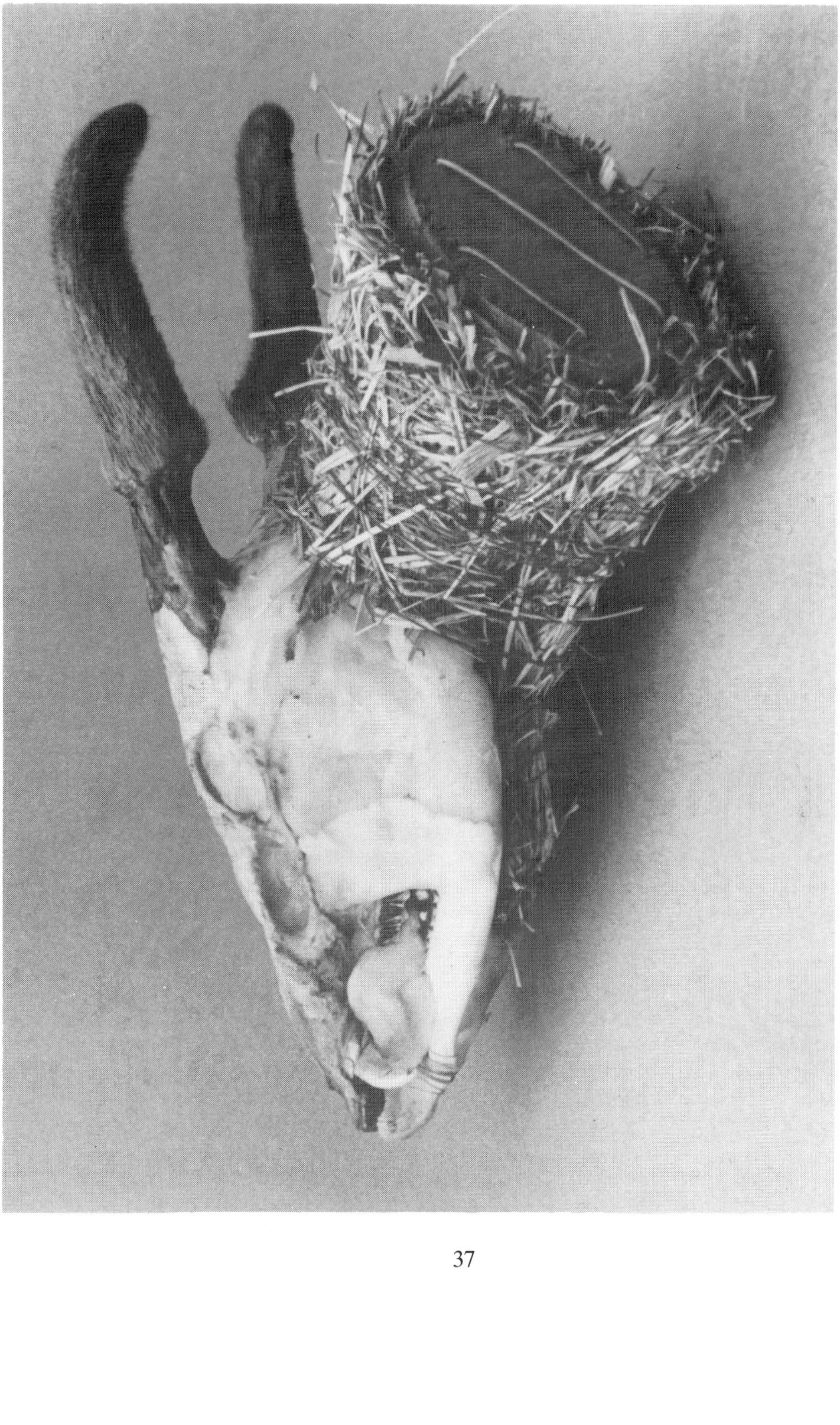

Figure 2.2 Muntjac head showing hay neck, wires, and plywood disc

The Neck

The neck is now built up with hay or wood wool, which is held in place by cotton. When the neck diameter and shape reaches correct proportions, a windpipe can be added. To make this, bend some hay in your hands and wrap with cotton. Insert in the throat hollow and down the front of the neck and bind into position (see figure 2.2).

The Nose

The hollow of the nose in the skull should be filled with wax, and a small ridge of wax can be pressed on either side of the upper jaw about half an inch above the teeth; this helps to form part of the snarl later.

SKIN

The false 'form' or manikin is now complete, so we can now return to the skin. With the skin turned its natural way, fur outside, take a drawing of the ear shape on a piece of cardboard and cut out. Produce two of these; I find a cigarette packet the ideal thickness, and if done back to back, gives one an idea which is the front. When the skin has been lightly dusted with preserves (if it has not been White Leathered), insert each card into either ear, between the cartilage and the back of ear and adjust until the card fits correctly. Make sure you have the right card in the right ear. Put modelling clay into the base of the ear to give thickness, and this also helps to hold the ear in the correct position later.

I pause here to state there are many ways of doing ears, and specimens for that matter, and we are only discussing one. Granted, it is a very good one, but that does not make the others wrong. In time you may well come to use another one or a combination of two or more, or even untried ways. It is well worth remembering that a taxidermist is governed only by two rules, these being firstly that **the work must look natural when it is set up,** and secondly that **it must remain so over the years and not become twisted or distorted.**

Use modelling clay to fill the tunnel under the nose. Force well in on one side to prevent any air pockets, then the other side; finally finishing by packing the nostrils from the inside. Use a thin roll of modelling clay to go round the edge of the mouth and fold the skin back to its natural position. Use small quantities of clay around the eye-skins and fold back to their natural positions. The clay used for all these items should be of a firm, pliable nature, like plasticene, as the dampness of the skin will render it much softer.

Fitting the skin to the manikin

Do the following carefully. Ease the manikin into the skin and, when in position, stitch the neck onto the back of the plywood frame, using the exposed wires as anchorage spots. A little modelling clay at the 'Adams' apple, or lower, can help with the final neck line.

Screw the head onto the temporary plywood backboard to prevent your final shield becoming stained. All that needs to be done now are the final adjustments, and if you are following this method blow by blow, the head now should look like nothing on earth, so do not be dispirited as the work is nearly finished.

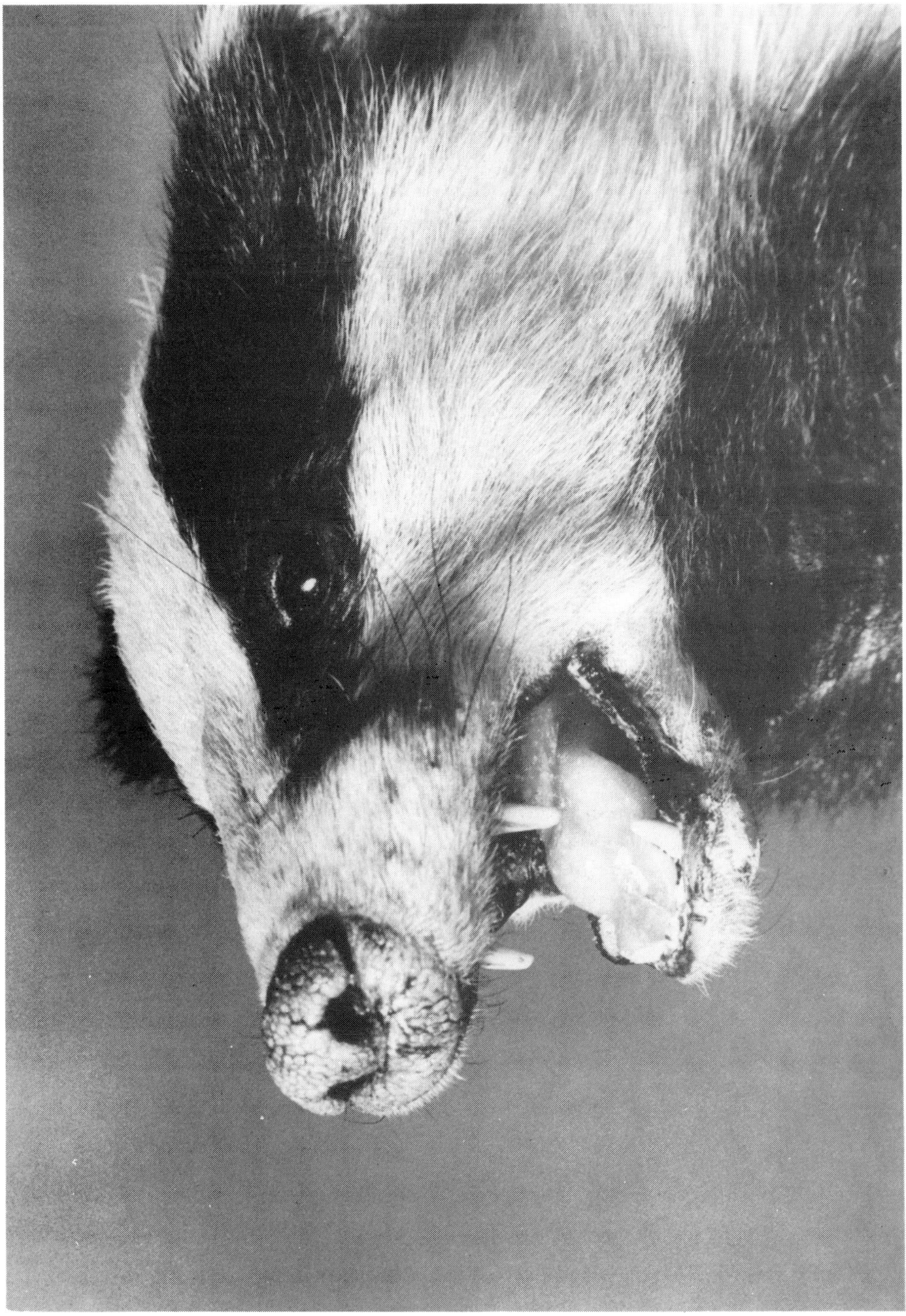

Figure 2.3 Badger head close-up

Final adjustments

First start on the lower jaw. Drive five pins into and through the skin and into the wax either side of the fangs and in through the front smaller teeth. Adjust and pin around the eyes. Lift nose and place a thin layer of modelling clay on the bone leading to the nostrils (this when grooved later will produce the final lines to the snarl). Replace nose and press to required shape, placing two wires up nostrils, and plug the outside with cotton wool to keep the shape, otherwise the cartilage will shrink and leave the nose the size of a small button.

Return again to the lower jaw, and pin along side of tongue. Smooth the muzzle and tuck mouth below eye in an attempt to make the mouth smaller; then pin into place. Use a forcep handle to make snarl lines or grooves on skin by pressing from the nose to the eye. Readjust the eyes. It is extremely important to have good photographs to consult at this stage. Pin bristles or whiskers at right angles with one pin each on each side. Adjust ears to required position and press clay at their base to help keep them there before pinning. Except for minor combing and adjustments where necessary the main work is finished.

Note there are glues that can be used to stick the skin to the head, but this is not necessary if the instructions have been followed, and can be very messy for the beginner. For the next ten to fourteen days or longer if possible, allow the skin to dry out. Drying time will depend on where you store the head; the place wants to be fly free and not too hot, as heat can cause distortion.

When you are sure the head has hardened, remove the pins, and brush and clean up the head, also removing cotton wool plugs. Look at the head closely; there may be a little extra wax to be added around the mouth to seal the pelt and the manikin together solidly. Darken skin around mouth and eyes with thinned down oil-paints, and I stress the use of these paints very sparingly and as thin as possible; then allow to dry.

There remains only the job of varnishing the nose and mouth with artist's picture varnish and then screw the finished head to a shield or plaque. Figure 2.3 shows a completed badger in close-up.

CHAPTER 3

MAMMALS

SMALL MAMMALS

For small mammals up to rabbit size, I use a wire anchor base of cork. For larger mammals up to small deer I rely on wooden blocks, usually of plywood, as it will not break up easily. The wire is run through the cork, then bent over and hooked into the cork, by pulling it hard, as in figure 3.1. The cork acts as a junction for wires, where the limbs are situated on the animal. Many taxidermists just wrap one wire around another, but I think this way is more positive.

The two corks are linked together first, as it is very important to get this spacing correct. The skinned carcass is laid into the position one intends mounting the specimen in. The wire with one cork attached and anchored, and the other attached but loose, is laid on the body and shaped into position, so the cork can be placed exactly where the limbs lie. The loose cork is then anchored (see figure 3.2). To this are attached a head wire, four leg wires and a tail wire. The latter may be thinner, as it has not a lot of weight to carry. Tow, or even plumbers hemp can be used to make up the body, although anything that provides a solid base, and allows a needle to pass through it, can be used.

Squirrel manikins

With reference to figure 3.3, the manikin on the left has not had the limbs built up. The skull is built up with beeswax. The head wire has been threaded through the hole in the base of the skull, and coming out at the nostril. This wire has not yet been trimmed, which is done prior to mounting. Note the tail wire is thinner than other supporting wires.

The manikin on the right has limbs. It is plain to see they are built up of three separate bindings of tow, the centre one being wound straight onto the leg wire. Then, with the hind leg, the second binding is looped onto the tail wire and leg wire. The third is then slipped on the leg wire to become the upper side of the limb. All are stitched together. In the foreleg arrangement, bindings two and three are reversed, so the second binding lies in the front and is stitched to the throat side of the neck. The third binding forms the back of the foreleg, and again, all three are stitched together. When prepared in this way, the round effect is avoided, especially in the hind leg.

Rabbit manikin

The rabbit manikin in figure 3.4 is built of cork blocks, wire netting, hay and cotton binding. Note the hind leg binding, made of one length of hay, bound, and the ends turned in, and again bound. The hay is folded in half and bound again. This makes a rear upper limb four

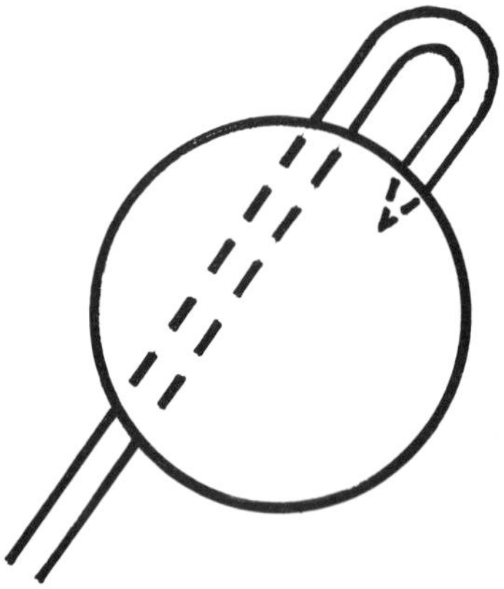

Figure 3.1 Anchoring the wire

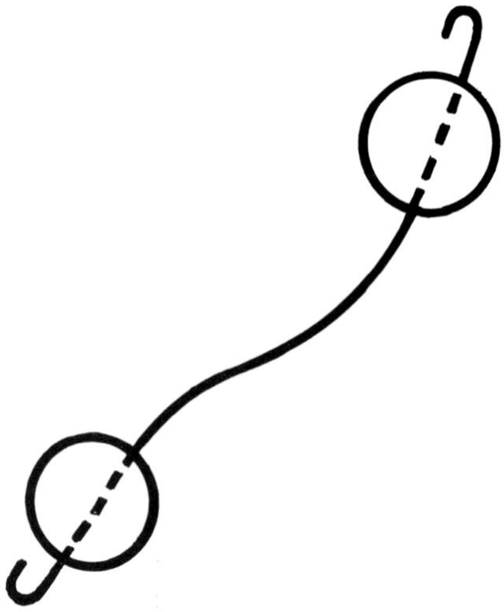

Figure 3.2 Linking corks to form the basis of the manikin

times broader than it is in width. The section is slipped onto the leg wire and secured by stitching. Care should be taken to see the wire comes out of this leg section, to lie, and run down the back of the lower leg section, when joined. If it does not lie in the right position, the leg will look unnatural.

The head is built from the skull and beeswax. Note the binding of the lower jaw in black thread for strength. The head wire is threaded through the hole in the skull base, coming out at the nostril. This is cut off before mounting. With this type of manikin, the leg bones below the knee are left attached to the skin. They are cleaned, and either tow, hemp or hay, used to replace the muscling. The tendons are cut at the toes, and all cartilage and sinew removed, and replaced with modelling compound; again what type is a matter of choice. The marrying up of the leg bones at the knee requires care. I find it better to work here, as there is more space, and the skin is stronger. It is also easier to hide the marrying up at this point, (see figures 3.5 and 3.6). Once the skin has been stitched into place, and the animal anchored onto heavy cardboard or a wooden temporary base, it can be pulled around, and adjusted. The toes should be individually positioned and either pinned, nailed, or bandaged until dried. A final adjustment, combing and brushing of the skin, finishes the work until fully dried out.

Using hay

There are numerous ways and materials used to construct manikins; this is only one way. What I like about this method is that it is simple and it allows for small adjustments to be made on completion, which can make the difference between just being a 'stuffed' animal, to one having a magic life-like appearance.

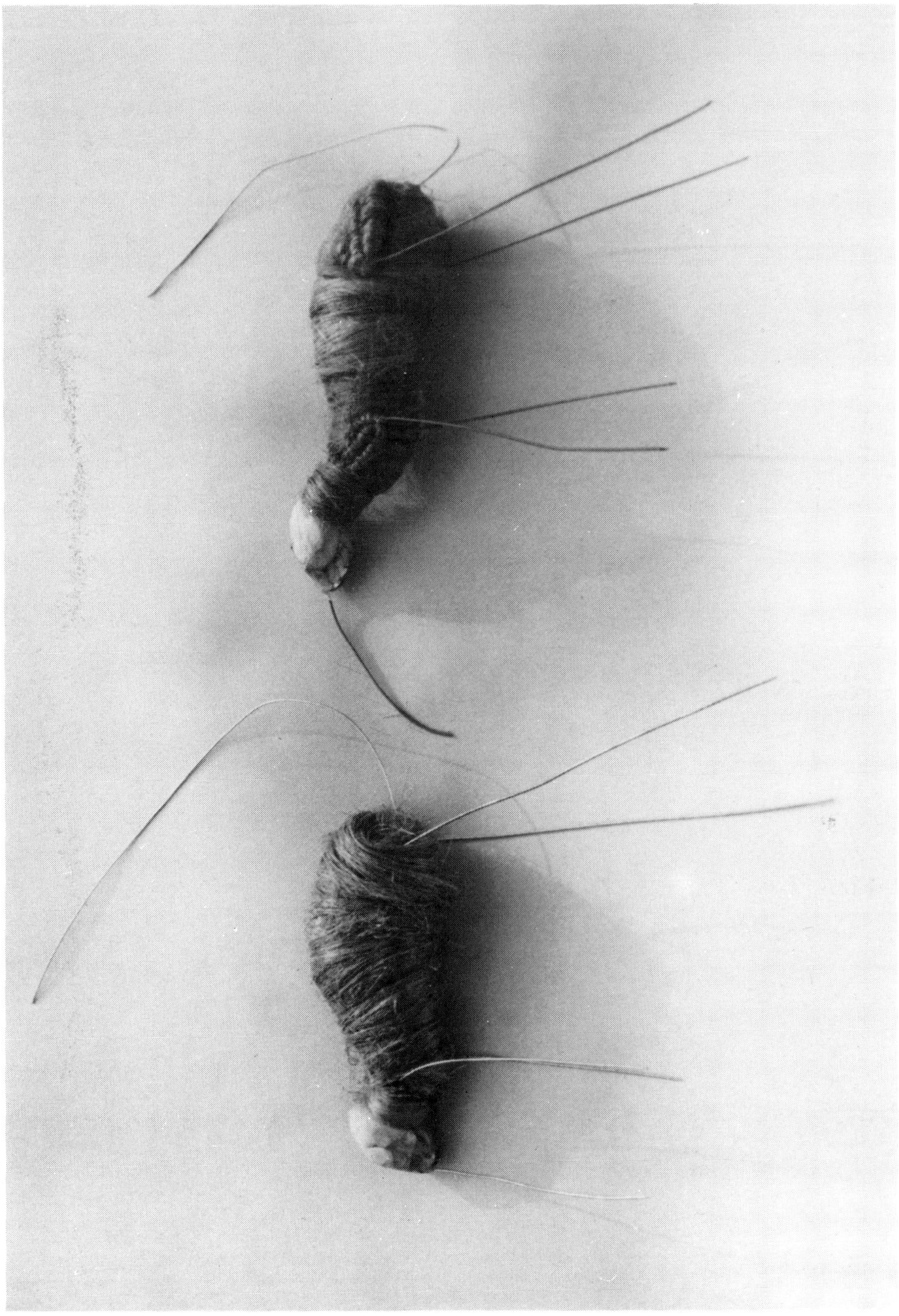

Figure 3.3 Squirrel manikins made from tow and wire; the one on the right has limbs added

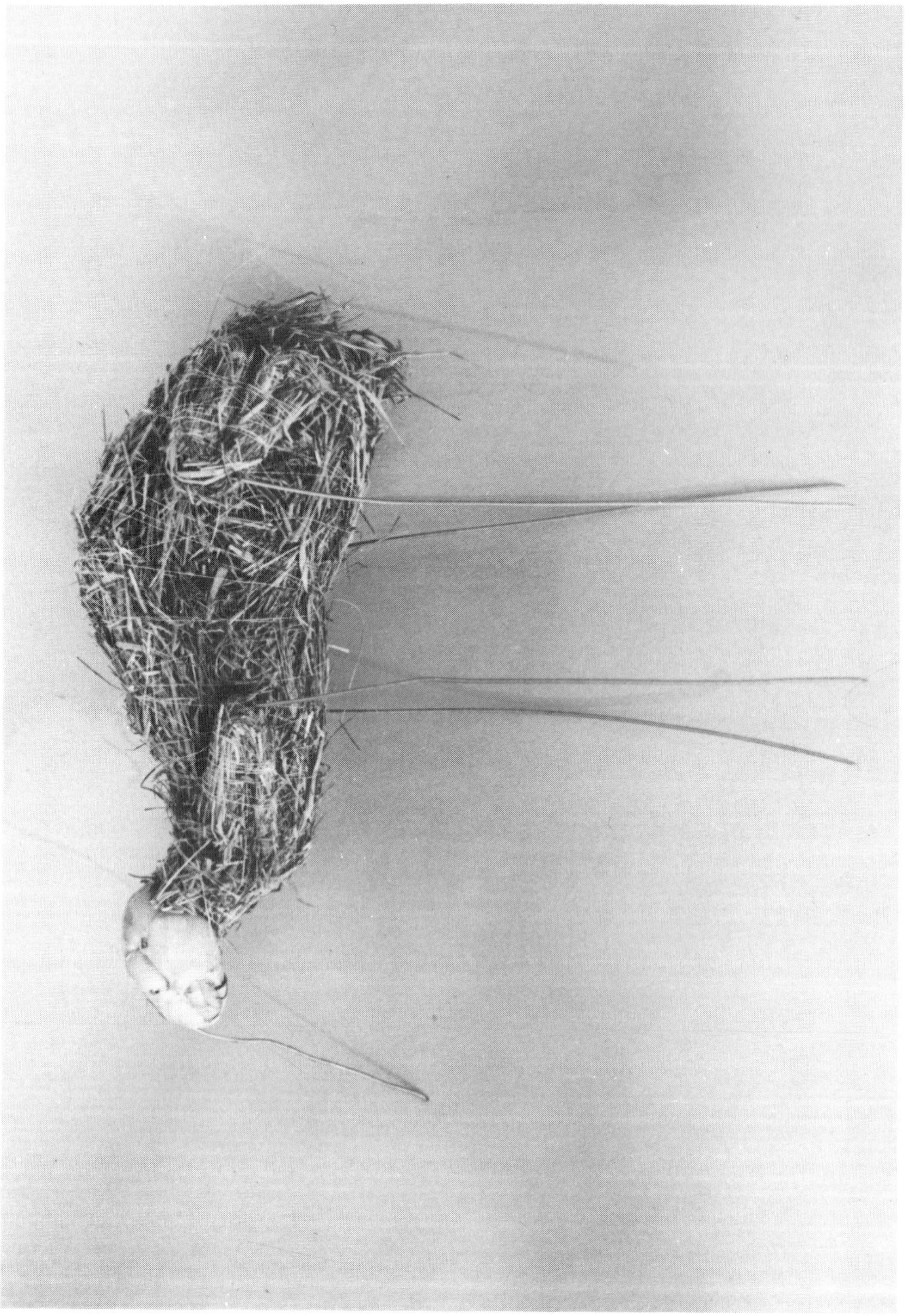

Figure 3.4 Rabbit manikin made from hay and wire

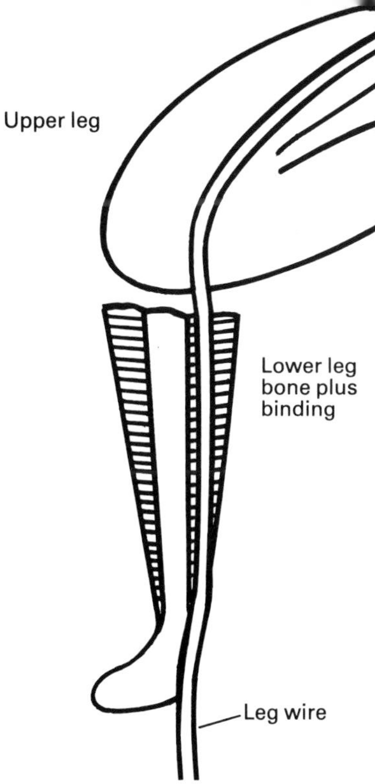

Figure 3.5 Setting up of the leg bones

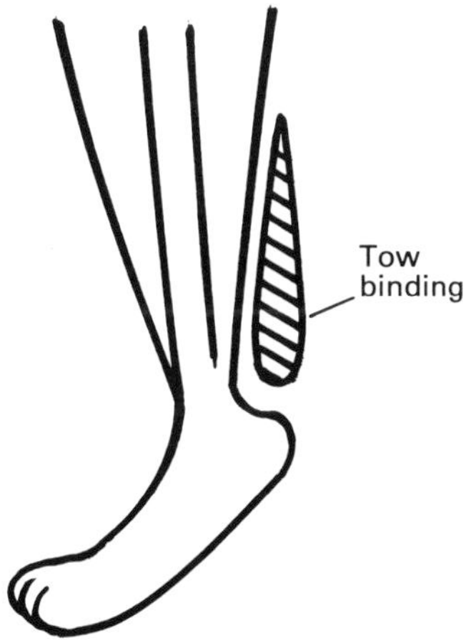

Figure 3.6 Tow binding replaces the tendon

I have stripped down specimens which were over a hundred years old, and made of hay, and was well pleased with their condition after such a period. It should be noted that some hay, especially if it has become damp, can contain very small, almost microscopic life forms. It pays to freeze the manikin for 24 hours, if possible, to sterilize it. If impractical, a box, or even a plastic bag containing some insect killing fluid should be used as a precaution. As a pest controlling device, some fly-killer, such as Vapona, can be inserted inside the manikin. This must be cut as soon as it is exposed to the air or else it becomes like old shoe leather.

MANIKINS FOR LARGE MAMMALS

Types of manikins and materials used for large mammals are numerous, and it takes many years of skill to be able to tackle such enterprises. Before a method is chosen, one must consider the size, and finished weight. A large animal will need a hollow centre to reduce weight, and minimize transporting problems. If the creature has a short pelt where muscle display can be put to good use, as with a rhinoceros, attention to the muscles would be all important to a good finish.

A fibreglass manikin could be considered for this. I do not intend to go in for a detailed approach to modelling in fibreglass, as there are many good books on working with this material, so we will deal with points that will help produce a taxidermist's manikin, which will not be in these books. Photographs of live animals, in the positions visualised, taken from as many angles as possible, are essential. Photographs or drawings of the skinned carcass, to show hidden muscling, are most useful. If any muscling and tendons have been cut, it may be deemed necessary to pull them tight and stitch them into a live position. Remember, too, that

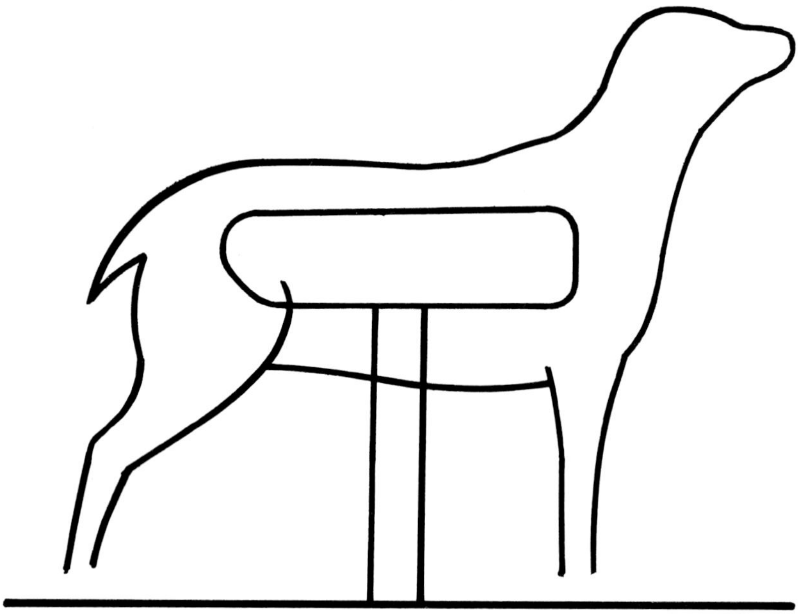

Figure 3.7 Supporting a specimen in an upright position

the carcass viewed is dead, and would not give the same view as a live animal, if it were possible to see it minus its pelt. The muscles are not under live tension, and the lungs are deflated. There may also be a characteristic mannerism peculiar to that species, that is also lost in death.

Casting a fresh carcass

If it is decided to take a copy from the carcass itself, heavy animals are better done lying on their sides, on a piece of ground where the contours of the animal's body can lie to even it up more naturally. Animals need to be skinned out completely down the limbs, to leave as much detail as possible on the carcass. It will pay to remove the surplus fat, but mark where it has been removed from, on a drawing, and the amount removed.

Smaller specimens can have a cast taken by propping them into an upright position. The entrails and organs are removed and a 'T' shaped support inserted into the cavity. This is to support the back evenly. The rest of the cavity is packed out and stitched up (see figure 3.7). Wires or rods driven into the neck and limbs will give the necessary support required to prop it into the desired position. Injections of formaldehyde into the body will tighten the flesh.

The eyes have to be removed, and partially filled, as does the throat, if the mouth is required open. The cast cannot be made in one section, and is usually done in two or more for upright specimens. They are known as the upper section, and the lower section, the latter containing the inside of the legs and belly. There are of course many variations to this. A point to consider is the size of the head in relation to the neck. One must decide whether to include the head, or take the cast to the top of the neck, or treat in a similar manner to a larger animal, namely, a cast in two large vertical halves, and four inside leg sections.

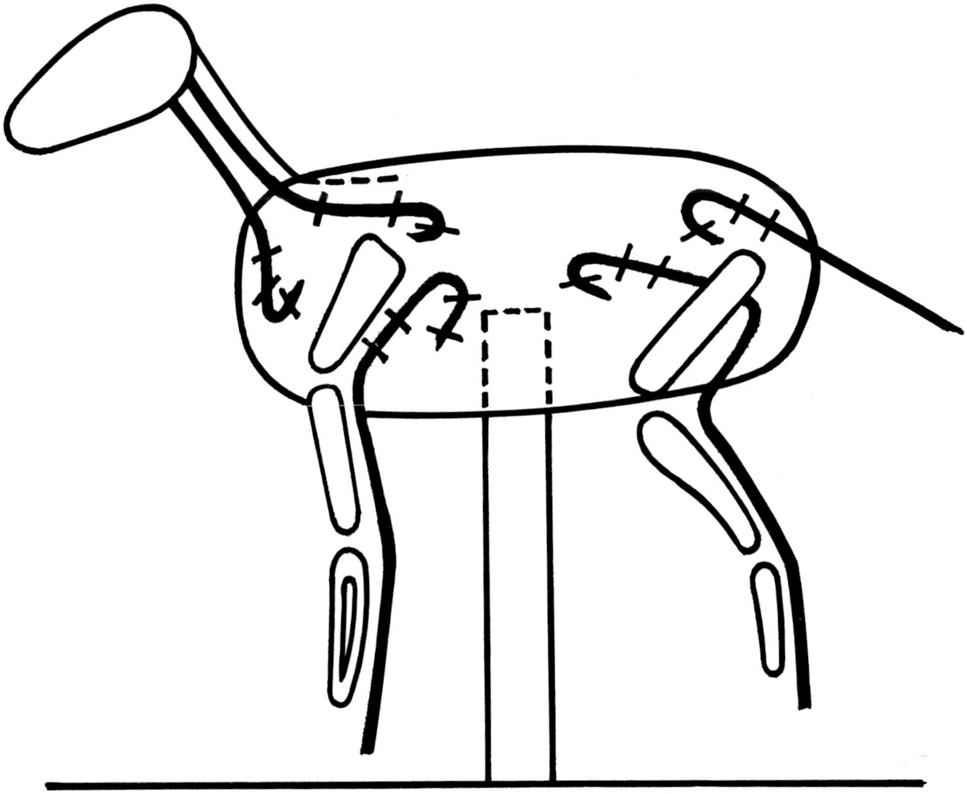

Figure 3.8 Casting using the bones

As just stated, large mammals are cast lying on the ground, positioned to the required stance, and the outside or upper sections done first, with the inside of the two legs closest to the ground. Pegs driven into the ground outline the position of the carcass, so when it is reversed its position can be matched exactly on nearby ground, by measurements, drawings, and photographs. Reinforcment of the cast is essential, and depending on the size of the creature, strength and thickness of the cast, etc., it may even be possible to turn the carcass over containing the cast. This would ensure a perfect match, and save much time.

Casting using bones

It may be decided better to rough skin the skeleton, or even just the leg bones, and construct the mould later. Drawings, photographs, and measurements will still be required. Whichever method is used it will be necessary to have a vertical centre board cut out of quality plywood to act as an anchor to the leg wires, and netting used to fatten the body into a realistic shape. The shape of this body, if the backbone is not used, needs to be like an outline of the specimen. The requirements are illustrated in figures 3.8 and 3.9. The leg wires need to be heavy enough to carry the weight, and bent to follow the shape of the leg bones. A strong hollow pipe slipped over these wires or rods will bend them in the right places.

EARS

Ears are cut off at the junction of the head, the flesh removed, and are skinned via the back of the ear. As soon as enough area has been cleared, the ear is turned inside out, and skinning

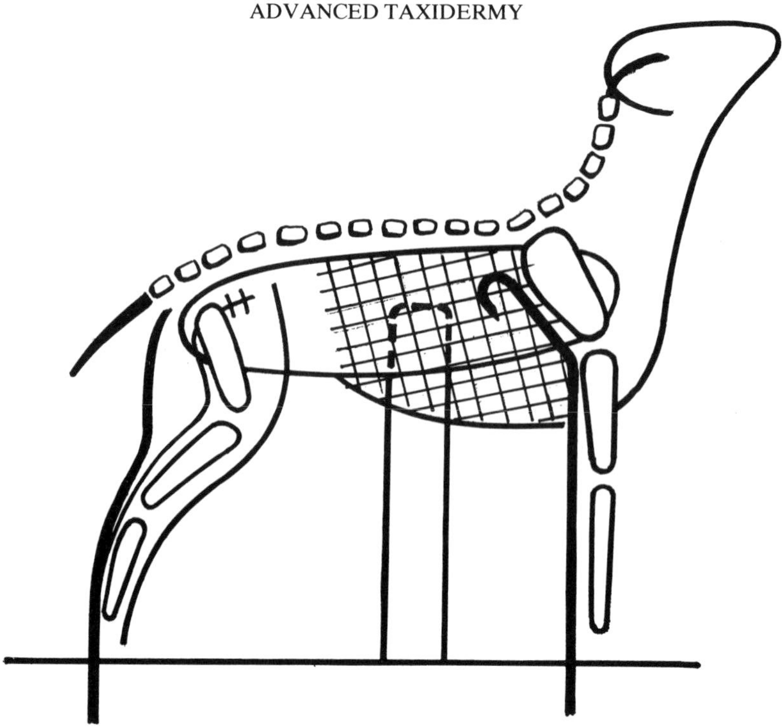

Figure 3.9 Shaping the body using the skeleton; netting is used to fatten the body into a realistic shape

continued. An indication that the edge of the ear is imminent is that the cartilage becomes very thin, and then its edge in many cases becomes broken and serrated. As the ears are very thin, in comparison to the rest of the pelt, I always alum them immediately. Some taxidermists think it is essential to remove the cartilage completely, but up to red deer size this is not necessary, and unless the skin has been tanned beforehand the cartilage removal can result in the damage of the fragile skin.

Ear liners

Ear liners can be bought from a taxidermist's suppliers. I prefer to make my own, and so do many of my customers. Anything made of plastic seems to lower the value to the owner. Craftsmanship is required by the trophy owner. The reason I prefer to do my own is that one tailors to the individual requirements of the specimen.

The shape of the ear is outlined on a suitable thickness of cardboard. Two pieces of cardboard are placed together and cut out. This way the ears are the same size. Splints are then inserted into any individual damaged ear. The cardboard is dipped in hot wax for waterproofing, or varnished.

The base of the ear, on mounting, has modelling clay added, to build up the removed flesh area, and can be pressed into shape with the final skin adjustments. Air bubbles can be a problem with ears, if one is not careful. I put a few needle holes in the top section of the ear, and expel any remaining air, on completion. A check during drying time is advisable. If one runs a hand over the ear, checking its shape, and hears crackling, then there is air present. It may be necessary to cardboard and pin the affected area. Another good idea, especially for a rabbit or a hare, is warm, not singeing, curling tongs. Hold in position for a minute or so, and the ears are immaculate.

Squirrels', rats', mice's, and very small ears can be done simply by shaping them from the outside with modelling clay, which is retained by a pin driven into the head, and covered with another small piece of clay. When the ear is dry the clay is broken away and the ear dusted.

Making ear casts

If one is to produce a number of ears over a period, of the same type and size of creature, then it is as well to make one's own casts for ear liners. The ear cartilages are removed from the specimen as soon as the skinning has finished, and are kept. If they dry out, soaking will spring them back to their natural shape.

To make your cast, lay the cartilage on a bed of sand for support, making sure it is fully supported; no hollows underneath. Mix a little Plaster of Paris, and apply a very thin coating over the inside of the ear, covering all the surface. Build up the thickness and allow the ear to harden before removing the cartilage. It can now be dipped in warm beeswax or have kitchen foil wrapped around it. It is now ready for making fibreglass ear liners.

A car body repair outfit (in fibreglass) will supply your needs. Cut out a slightly larger shape than required, and place on the back of the plaster mould. Hold in place with a few cotton loops if necessary. Mix the catalyst with the resin, and saturate the fibreglass 'bandage' or 'gauze'. Allow to harden before trimming and removing the mould for future use.

HINTS ON ANTLER AND HORN AREAS

A typical problem is that the skin shrinks down the stem of the antler, leaving a bare white area of bone showing. If this area is stained or darkened before the skin is mounted, and the skin only moves a fraction, it will be unnoticeable. The problem is caused by shrinkage, and the smooth shaft of bone, allowing no grip for the skin. One approach to overcome this is to make this bone rough and put some grip there. This can be done in a number of ways, ranging from a string, twine, or wire, lashing or coil, placed on the bone stem below the antler crown.

Glue and coarse sawdust would make an ideal medium for the skin to grip. Gloss paint and coarse sand could also suffice for more delicate skins. On heavier skins, one could use acrylic, as a glue, and short chops of galvanised wire to roughen the bone area. In figure 3.10, the oblongs are the galvanised chips, set in acrylic. The dotted line is cotton or twine to hold the skin in place until it shrinks enough to bite into the metal chips. If shrinkage has occurred, it can be invisibly mended by filling in the area with glue (No. 1 Bostik) and matched hair from another specimen.

HINTS ON DAMAGED EARS

Many tattered and damaged trophy items can be obtained from various auctions and antique shops. Usually the ears have had more than their share of damage. I have repaired tigers' ears by using badger hair. The tigers have a rusty patch behind each ear. The texture for both skins was roughly similar, and I was surprised to find that colour on a badger. If the colour is not

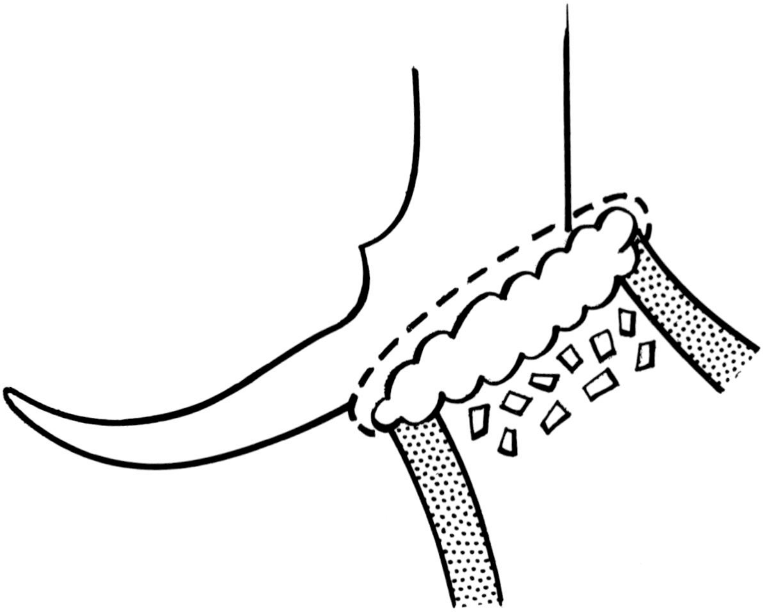

Figure 3.10 Method of preventing skin shrinkage around antlers or horns

correct, then it may be possible to dye the repairing piece to match. Another point relating to the tiger was the absence of most whiskers. Apparently the natives remove them to use as an aphrodisiac. The replacement to these items I found in a bass or garden broom. By careful selection, or trimming, one can make fairly effective ones.

If an ear is damaged on assembly, or skinning down, and the damage is in a very thin area, darken the ear liner around the area before inserting. Hold the damaged area in place with pins or paperclips and cardboard. Repair once the skin has fully dried, using glue carefully, and holding into place until dry.

DISTORTION OF SKINS

Many of the problems encountered by the advancing taxidermist are caused by skin distortion. This can be caused by a combination of a number of factors. Poorly made manikins that have the incorrect shape, or are not firm enough, can be an underlying factor. Another more likely cause is that of shrinkage in the pelt itself. This can be caused by the tanning or preserving process itself, or by not thinning the skin enough before mounting. Again, faults can arise by not giving enough strength to thin vital areas during the drying period.

A pelt is not just a skin. It has thick and thin areas, areas which have cartilage effect, and so on. The thin areas will dry out first, generally in their required positions. If nothing is done about the thicker skin area, it will act like a gigantic spring, over the months and years, to twist the weaker areas out of position and shape. Many books have been written on the handling and treatment of skins, and no doubt many more will follow. Unless one wishes to go into making rugs, leather, or fur coats, most can be ignored.

The problem is to even the thickness of the skin, where possible, or to put the stresses elsewhere, or try and even them over the skin, where practical. Shaving the skin down by the inexperienced can cause more damage than a shotgun. Generally, however, the more paring, the better. Another good practical approach, which I recommend, is a series of criss-cross cuts, not more than half an inch apart, in the thicker areas, forming a trellis-work pattern. This breaks up the power of the spring-like action, and keeps much of it in localised areas. It also allows easier penetration of preserves. The half inch pattern I would use for deer heads. Smaller specimens would have a finer pattern.

DISTORTION OF PADS

Another area where a great many beginners go wrong is in the area of the foot. The following is a method of setting a fox's front pads. On skinning down, the first 'toe' is reached fairly high on the ankle. It is cut off and skinning continues right down until the foot bones begin to show like fingers on a hand. The cartilage, or spongy tissue of the sole, must be removed, otherwise it will shrink at an alarming rate. Pack the foot hard with firm modelling clay which prevents the pad shrinking on drying. The pad, on assembling the full fox, will have to be shaped from the outside, toes positioned, and bound into place with a bandage. The bandage allows the skin to dry easily, and prevents the claws moving. Alternatively, they can be secured by pins or nails until dry.

COLOURING BEESWAX

This method is used both for beeswax and beeswax substitute supplied by Kerax Ltd. Experiments are continually being made as to what is the best of these substitutes, which go under the various code numbers. The most successful one I find is Coata CX1230. A letter to the firm's sales manager will confirm the best one being used at the time. The main difference with substitutes is their variable hardness, but all are workable and far cheaper than beeswax. To improve the quality of any purchases, add beeswax.

Warm the wax in a bucket of fairly hot water. When pliable, dry off and press out into an oblong shape. Sparingly, smear the colour of oil paint selected and fold over the edges of wings and press out into the oblong shape again. Continue doing this, again and again. The same technique applies as for making puff-pastry. The oil paint does not mix, so much as become laminated into thousands of layers. The shade of colour depends upon the amount of oil paint used.

The treated wax needs to be left a few days before using. If it is re-heated in warm water, the colour will become more intense. If the colour is too stark, or bright, more wax can correct the fault. It is ideal for tongues, gums, veins, and so on, used in animals and in combs and wattles in birds.

Beeswax modelling

Beeswax	3 parts
Resin	1 part

Melted together and used as required.

Substitute beeswax

Needs no resin reinforcing, as it is prepared to the taxidermist's requirements. See Colouring Beeswax for type in use.

VISUAL ASSEMBLY OF A SMALL MAMMAL

The following describes the assembly of a fitch polecat in nine stages. Reference should be made to the figures as indicated.

1 Figure 3.11. Specimen skinned down. Note the gums split to show base of bristles.
2 Figure 3.12. Specimen showing trimmed inside skin, and tow bindings on lower legs.
3 Figure 3.13. The skin being introduced to the manikin. Note the skin is not stretched while inserting leg wires.
4 Figure 3.14. Skin adjusted around manikin. Wires bent out of the way for easier stitching of belly.
5 Figure 3.15. Zig-zag stitching, and tidying up and adjusting skin and stitches in process.
6 Figure 3.16. Skin stitched into place.
7 Figure 3.17. Specimen placed onto temporary cardboard stand, and stance adjusted. Note: no attempt has been made to adjust head skin.
8 Figure 3.18. Head adjusted and pinned. Toes and claws adjusted and pinned.
9 Figure 3.19. Specimen on finished stand, one month later.

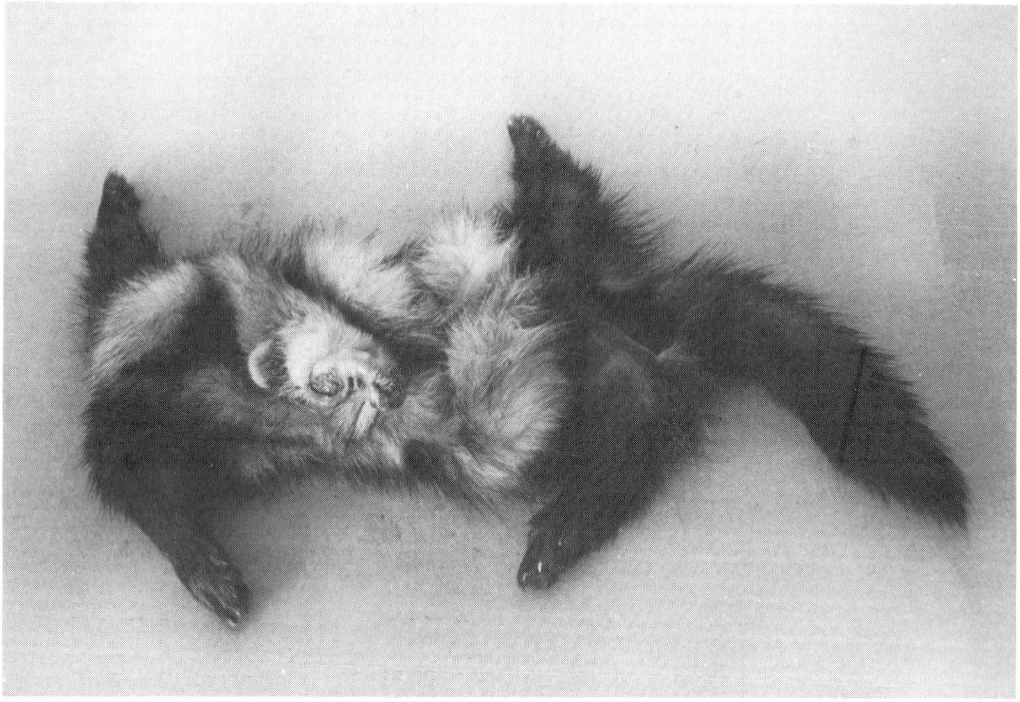

Figure 3.11 Specimen skinned down; note gums split to show base of bristles

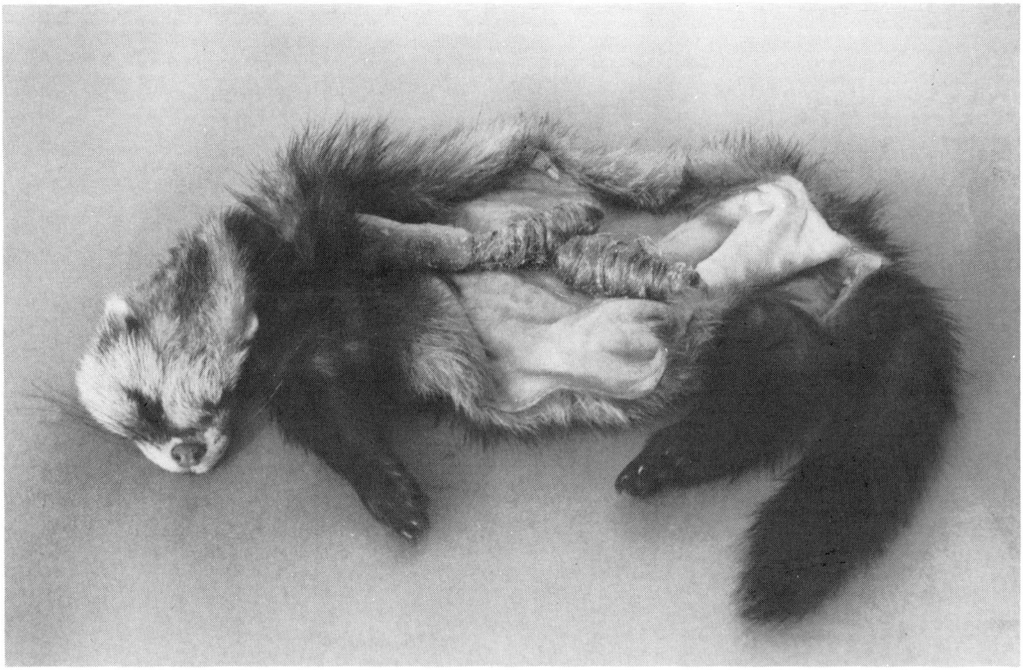

Figure 3.12 Specimen showing trimmed inside skin, and tow binding on lower legs

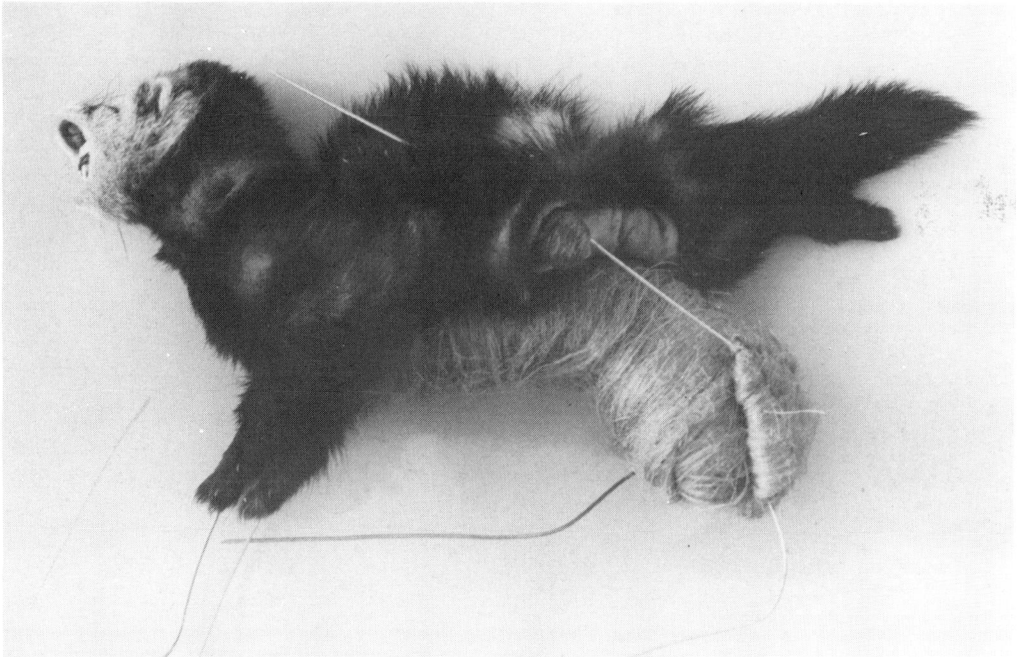

Figure 3.13 Skin introduced to manikin; note skin is not stretched while inserting leg wires

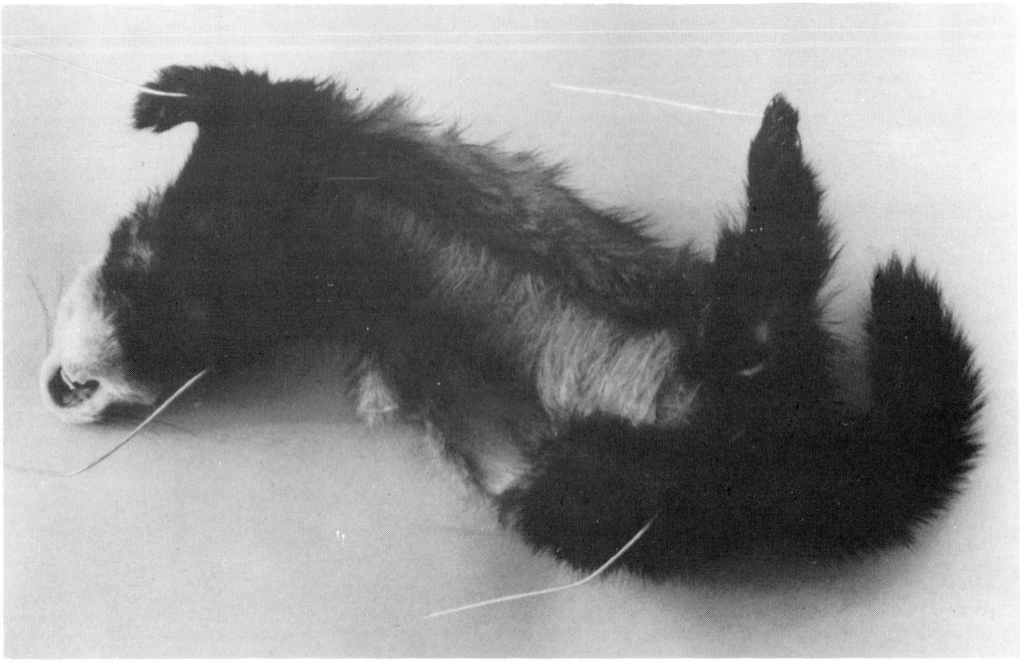

Figure 3.14 Skin adjusted around manikin; wires bent out of the way for easier stitching of belly

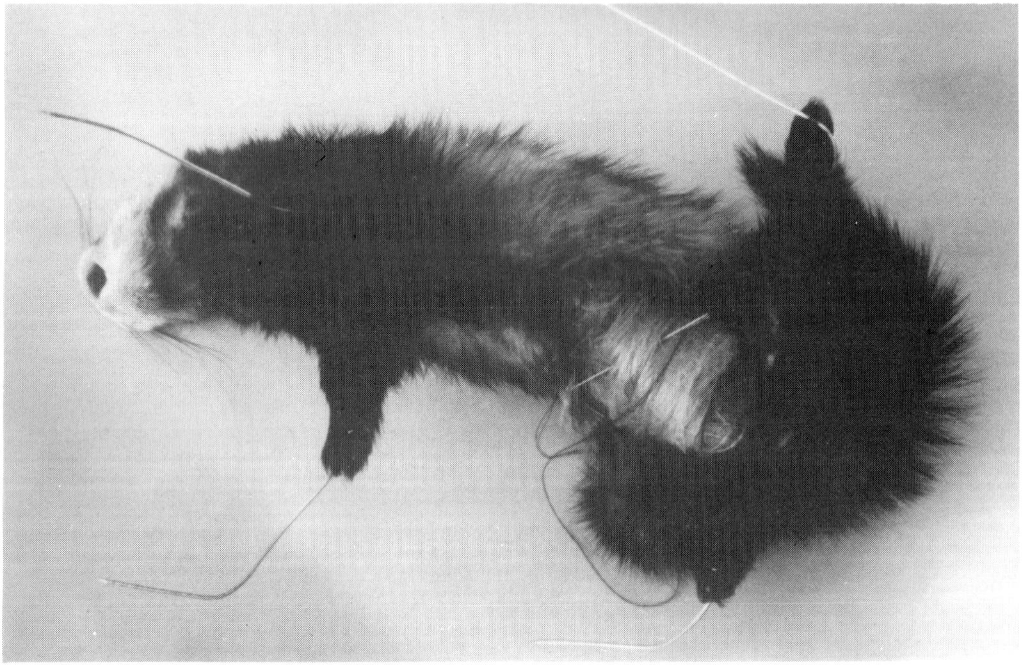

Figure 3.15 Zig-zag stitching, and tidying up and adjusting skin and stitches in the process

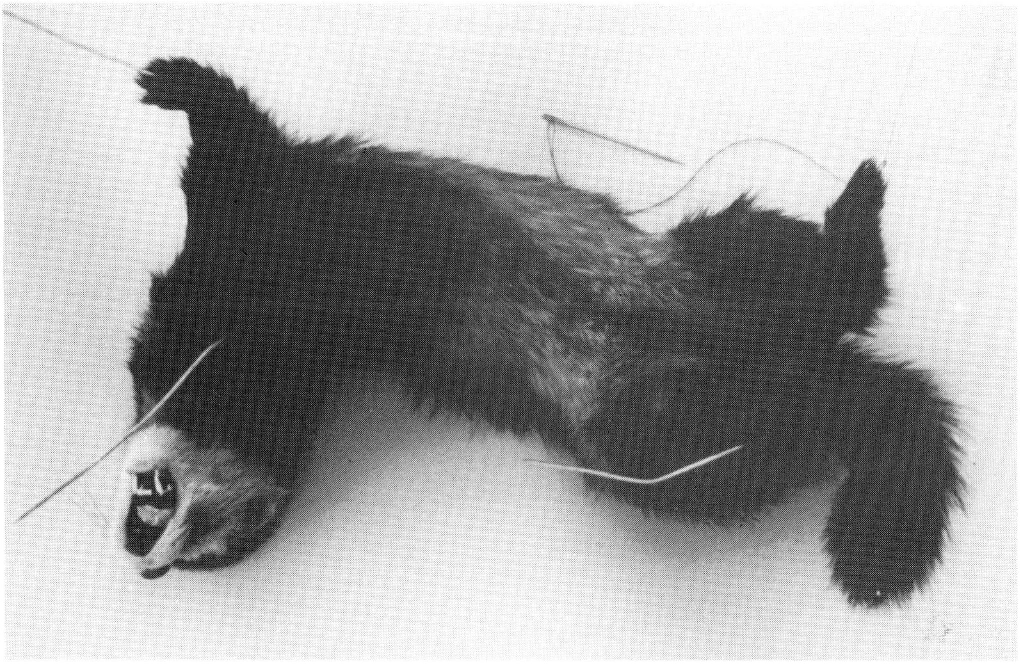

Figure 3.16 Skin stitched into place

Figure 3.17 Specimen set on temporary cardboard stand, and stance adjusted; note no attempt has been made to adjust head skin

Figure 3.18 Head, toes, and claws, adjusted and pinned

Figure 3.19 Finished specimen

VISUAL OBSERVATIONS ON HAIR-DRYING

1 Figure 3.20. The albino grey squirrel has all fat and flesh removed from skin. Gums etc., split, and skin washed and drained.
2 Figure 3.21. The skin has had as much moisture removed by absorbent paper towels as possible.
3 Figure 3.22. Hair-dryer in operation. Note how close the nozzle is to the skin, while on full heat.
4 Figure 3.23. Specimen now assembled on a temporary stand and allowed to harden.

Figure 3.20 The albino grey squirrel has all fat and flesh removed from skin, gums split, and skin washed and drained

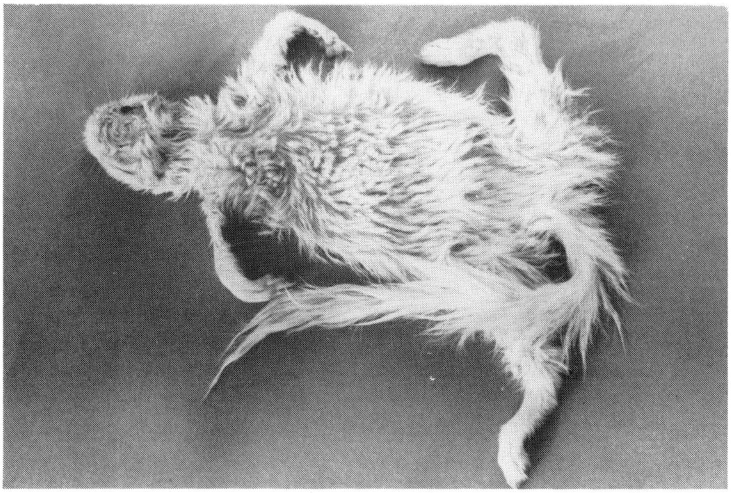

Figure 3.21 The skin has had as much moisture removed by absorbent paper towels as possible

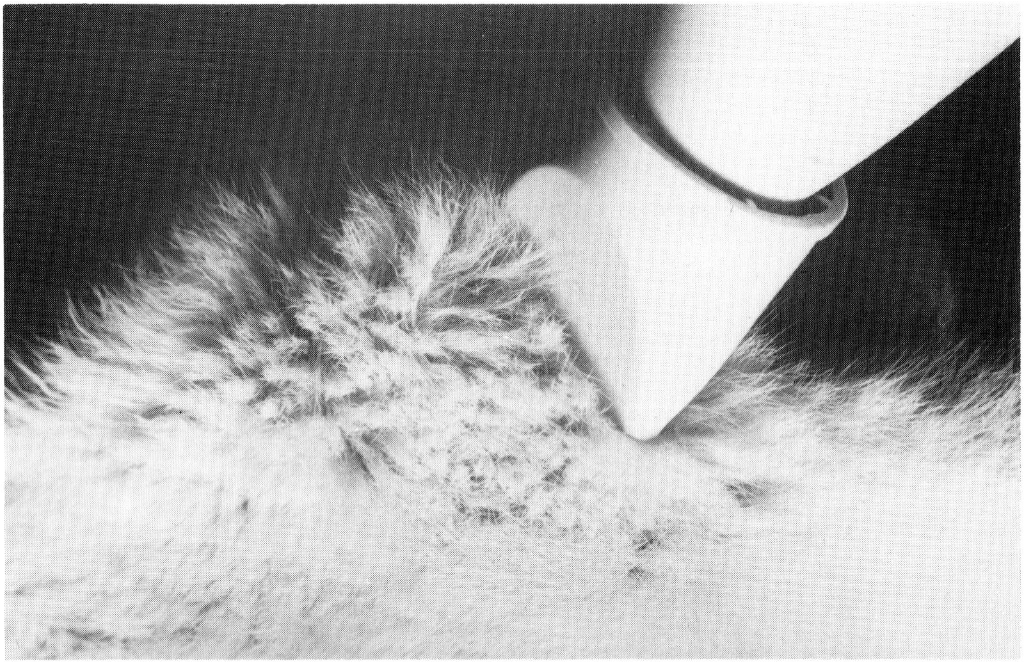

Figure 3.22 Hair-dryer in operation; note how close the nozzle is to the skin while on full heat

Figure 3.23 Specimen now assembled on a temporary stand and allowed to harden

CHAPTER 4

TANNING

There is no magic or secrets in the field of tanning other than good equipment, hard work, and patience. If there is a secret at all, it is in the preparing of the skin, and working it. Many taxidermists have their skins tanned for them, because of the expense involved in equiping oneself out, and the housing of the equipment, once you have it. However, if approached in the right spirit, a taxidermist can run his affairs from a suitcase, at a pinch. A vat, for instance, can be constructed from heavy plastic sheeting and a suitable sized hole dug in the ground, when one is on an expedition. Backwoodsmen will tell you any stream is a natural coolbox. Adaptability, improvisation and commonsense are needed when one is on a collecting trip.

REQUIREMENTS

The minimum tools needed for working skins are fleshing beams, large and small, and a selection of working knives and scrapers of various sizes. All of these are to make the job easier for the handler. I am sure the Eskimos never aspired to such equipment, but used what equipment they had to break down the fibre; namely their teeth.

As far as knives go, a scalpel is a fine tool. I have skinned down two mountain lions in succession using nothing more than a scalpel. That was from choice and not necessity. I mention this because many people become dismayed at the formidable array of equipment available. This equipment is for speed and comfort. Good fleshing and working beams can be made from hammering posts into the garden, and trimming, or using trimmed tree stumps in a similar manner. True, it is nicer to sit indoors, away from the elements, hence the array of equipment.

The different formulas one comes across can also be very confusing. Some go back to the beginning of modern taxidermy, and new processes are continually being added. All are pretty effective, and individuals swear by different techniques. I don't think I can emphasize enough that the results obtained by one's own efforts cannot be as good as a well equipped tannery, full of experts with years of experience. Tanning for oneself is a time consuming and laborious job. However, in Britain, most tanneries do not deal with much taxidermy work, and I would not consider sending one of my skins to one. My reason for this is that I care about the skin, and its condition, far more than anyone else involved. With me, it is under my care until completed. There is also the pleasure of producing something very beautiful, completely on your own. It is, in my opinion, essential for a taxidermist to produce tanned skins, to enlarge his skill and knowledge.

AIMS

The aim of the taxidermist is to get chemicals or preserves inside the hide, once it has been freed of any fat or grease. This allows it to become leathered, when dried, trapping the chemicals inside. Then the fibre must be broken up in all directions to allow it to become supple and useful. The thinner the hide is, the easier it is for the chemicals to enter, and to achieve this suppleness.

PREPARING A FRESH SKIN

This starts immediately the specimen is dead. Keep out of the sun. Skin down, removing all fat and tissue. Eyes and gums are split, ears trimmed inside out, and with heavy skins shaving or thinning the thicker areas should be started. A point worth noting is that salt has an effective penetration depth of approximately ⅜ inch. Remove cartilage from the pads, along with bone, leaving only the last joint holding the creature's claw or nail.

Give the skin a really good salting on the flesh side, be generous, and fold up, flesh to flesh and store away for a day or two in a cool, fly free place. An old refrigerator is an ideal place for the summer. In the winter almost any outdoor cool floor will do. Paring or thinning down fresh skins is extremely difficult, but it is far easier after they have been salted for a day or two. I prefer to get as much paring as possible done at this stage, and get this work behind me. I think it cheers me up to know that the worst job is reduced to a minimum.

However, paring and shaving can be done both before and after tanning. Now salt the skin well, and fold in flesh to flesh and store in a cool, fly free place, such as the bottom of the refrigerator.

Thinning down

Most skins are best thinned down a day or so after salting, and before tanning. It is very difficult to thin a pelt directly it has been removed from the specimen. The skin when salted, but not dry, is excellent. If the skin has hardened overmuch, it can be relaxed either in borax solution, carbolic solution, or plain fresh water. If the latter, inspect often, in case the fur starts to slip. I try to do all necessary paring and shaving needed at this time, the advantage being that the skin is thinner going into the tanning solution, which makes for a quicker and better penetration, and faster tanning time.

The fleshing knife is used to remove the bulk of the surplus skin in conjunction with a fleshing beam. Then continue the work with the currier's knife. The knife needs to be held at the correct angle otherwise it can cut too deep, and too low an angle will just slide over the skin. An adjustable guard keeps the knife at the right angle and smooths the skin ahead, giving an even, regular surface. These tanner's tools are very prone to rusting due to the salts and alums used, and must always be stored heavily oiled.

To give an idea how much skin can be removed, in 1898, John Rowley of the American Museum of Natural History records that the skin of a rhinoceros, weighing 270lbs, when pared and shaved down, weighed 27lbs. That was the wet weight of the full pelt, feet and all. In March 1886, a young mounted male elephant, called Ajax, was presented to Leicester Museum. Its initial weight was recorded by the Curator and Taxidermist Montagu Browne, as one ton, one cwt. He took 63lbs of chips and parings from the skin, mainly in the area of the feet. The skin when finished weighed 112lbs; 130lbs wet. The total weight of the elephant completed was 212lbs. He went on to cap it, by having two tigers fighting over the elephant's body, an ambitious project for any taxidermist.

TOOLS

Fleshing beam (heavy)

These come in all shapes, sizes and novel ideas, ranging from adjustable wall stowage types to heavy workshop types, some of which can be fitted, so they can be lifted into the roof space, when not in use. All have the same functions and basics. It is a hardwood plank, 5 to 6 feet long, 1½ to 2 inches deep and 9 to 10 inches broad, tapered and rounded at one end, ⅛ inch thick, to work heavy skins. This round end varies in height, for comfort of the individual worker. I find the ideal height coming midway between my belly-button and my groin. I believe the recommended height is two inches above the belly-button. The heel of the plank sits on the ground, while a trestle, or legs, keep the working end at the height described. The beam is used for main paring work on skins (see figure 4.1).

Fleshing beam (light)

This is also known as a bench beam or finger, and again is made of hardwood. From twelve to eighteen inches long, 2½ to 4 inches wide, and one to 1½ inches thick, again tapered, wedge-like to a rounded point. This can have a hole or two in it secured by a vice, G-clamp, or be permanently screwed into position, and can be the source of all sorts of accidents over the coming years. Used for areas such as eyes, ears, mouth, pads, and the difficult small places. I prefer mine made from oak, but that is only personal choice (see figure 4.1).

Fleshing knife

Heavy two-handled draw blade, which can be made from industrial hacksaw blades, but is cheap enough to buy. Comes in many styles but all are basically similar. Used for thinning and paring skins (see figure 4.1).

Currier's knife

Double edged bladed tool, with a handle at both ends. Works similar to carpenter's plane, and works better if fitted with a guard (see figure 4.1).

Staking tool

Cheap, simple tool, made of a five inch half circle of ⅛ inch steel set in a wooden handle, and having a blunt edge. Used to break up the fibre when used with force. There are many designs of this tool (see figure 4.1).

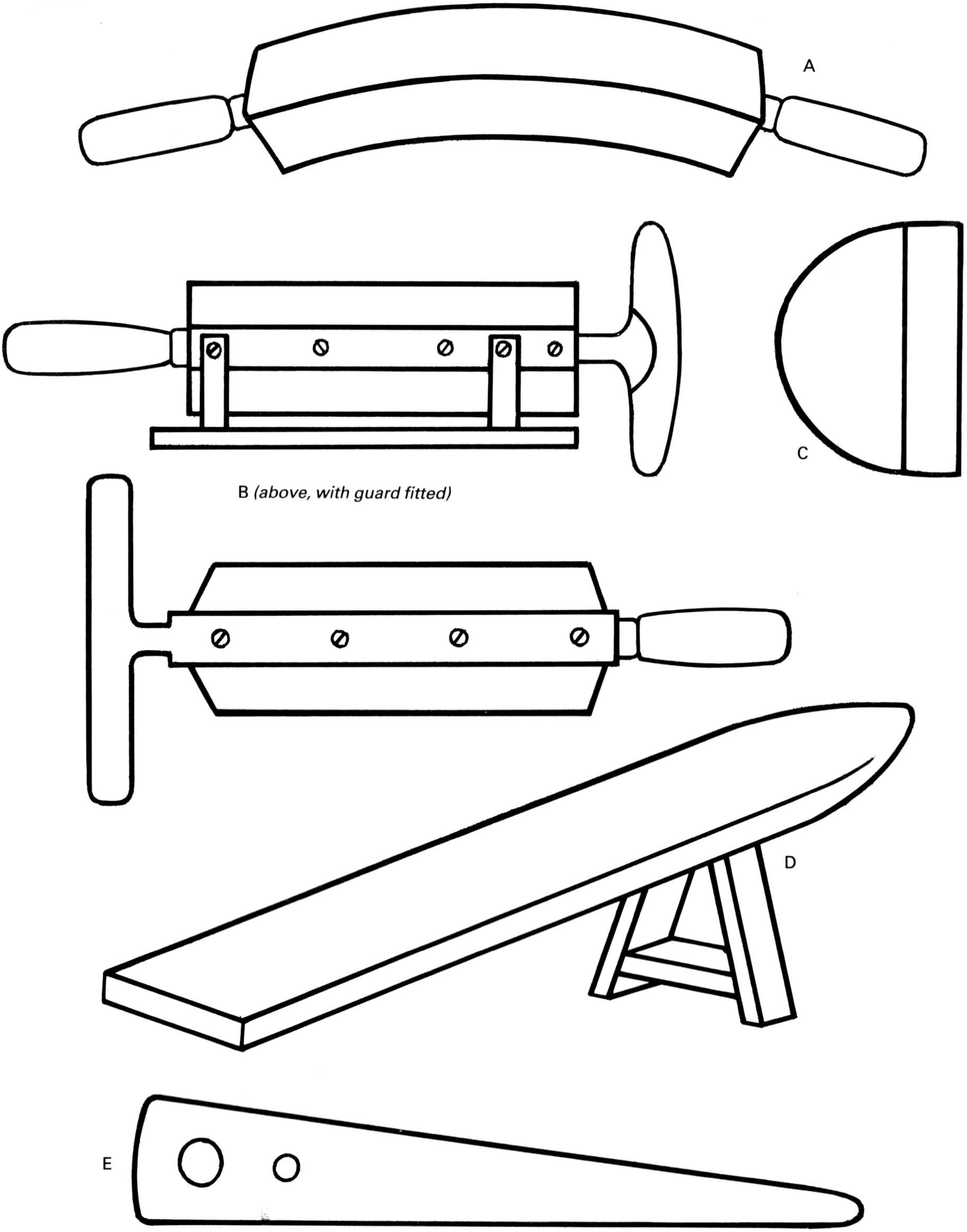

Figure 4.1 Various tools; A fleshing knife; B currier's knife; C staking tool; D fleshing beam (heavy); E fleshing beam (light)

PREPARING A DRIED SKIN

A dried skin will not accept chemicals or preserves, unless it has been relaxed to allow this process to happen. This can be done in a number of ways. Two recommended ways are set out below. The first I use as a prelude to white leather, the second for chrome tanning. The advantage of white leathering is it is safe to handle without gloves and has been used over a hundred years.

Carbolic Acid Solution

Carbolic-acid or Phenol:	1½ Tablespoons
Water:	1 gallon

Mix only as needed, and submerge skin into it until soft and pliable. This will take a few hours for a fox.

B-S Relaxer

Borax or Soda:	1 oz
Water:	1 gallon

With oily skins wash in a borax solution and continue with a fairly warm Sal-Soda Solution (Washing Soda).

WATER

It is important to mention that the best water for tanning is soft water. A person living in a hard water area could make use of rain water or water softening equipment, for the really best results. I live in a hard water area and use tap water for white leathering with good results but I mention it as an important factor for the perfectionist.

DEGREASING

Naphtha, a liquid by-product from coal is excellent, but difficult at times to obtain. Benzene again is excellent, but expensive.

Degreasing Solution

Benzine:	4 parts
Commercial Alcohol:	1 part

This mixture is highly inflammable. Grease settles on the bottom after use, and needs removing. Skins can either be immersed, or put on the flesh side only, out in the fresh air, and later in soapy water and well rinsed in warm water, and drained. Skins can either be fluffed with powdered borax or Plaster of Paris. This is removed by beating or blown out with a hair-dryer. They can also be dried by using absorbent tea-towels and a hair-dryer, excluding the borax and Plaster of Paris.

If one uses naphtha on large pelts, both sides, then warm sawdust, rubbed well into the skin, will remove both chemical and grease, to a large degree. Beating and washing will also be needed for final removal. Thinning the skin can continue over this period, remembering that the thinner it is, the easier will be the work later. Do not thin down to the hair roots, but the thin membrane of tissue that lies on the skin side of the body fat must be removed sooner or later.

WHITE LEATHERING

Once the skin has been degreased, washed, and well drained, it can be immersed in the white leather solution. It pays to stir it occasionally, as the chemicals near the skin are absorbed by the pelt, and stirring brings stronger solutions to its surface.

White Leather Solution

2lb	Salt
1lb	Alum
1oz	Sal Ammoniac
2 galls	Water

Mix together in warm water. I have used this formula without the Sal Ammoniac, and cannot see what advantages this has, and have since discontinued its use. The formula is well over 100 years old. Once the immersed skin goes white, it is ready to be pinned out, fur side down. A fox takes seven to ten days.

When pinned out, Neats-Foot oil solution can be applied warm to the skin side, brushed on, and allowed to sink in, as it dries over the weeks. This is, of course, if one prefers to add this oil. I would suggest that it is not used on the first few skins, allowing the worker to see the difference. I prefer not to use it at all, on light skins.

Neats-Foot Oil Solution

Water:	1 part
Sulphonated Neats-Foot Oil:	1 part

Salt and Sulpheric Acid Solution

2lb	Salt
1-2ozs	Sulpheric Acid (Concentrated)
2 gals	Soft Water

Dissolve salt in water, then **slowly** add acid to solution, stirring gently. On removal drain and soak pelt in a bucket with roughly ½ cup of washing soda to cancel the residue acid. Work skin while damp, until supple when dry. Suitable for small mammals.

Aluminium Sulphate Formula or Combination Solution

1lb	Salt
1lb	Aluminium Sulphate (iron free)
3ozs	Gambier or Terra Japonica
2 gals	Soft Water

Mix the Salt, aluminium sulphate and 1½ gallons of water together. Mix two pints of boiling water and the Gambier in another pan. Add the solutions together, and top up to two gallons. When cool, the solution is ready for use, and skins can be submerged into it, until tanned. Remove, drain, and wash in B-S relaxer made of borax; then rinse in fresh water. This produces an excellent leather, different from the previous two mentioned, with different qualities. Made from a combination of vegetable oil and minerals. Soft and pliable.

FINISHING HINTS

A very thin paste of soap spread over the skin-side overnight will help with the rub-down. If the skin is to be worked while damp, the ideal time is when lighter spots appear when stretching or folding it. Dampen if it becomes too dry. Rubbing with sandpaper may help even the skin thickness. The thin membrane tissue must be broken up. A blunt notched knife or scraper is ideal for this.

Dried skins, like white leather subjects, are easier to work if left out in the night air, sheltered from rain. The chemicals pick up the moisture in the air, and make the skin much better to work with. Alternatively, one can cover with a damp cloth and work when the lighter marks appear on stretching.

Work the skin as often as possible over a beam to break down fibres in all directions. Work the skin over any regular smooth edge, or even a ring or loop fastened to a beam. Some skins can be rubbed down using only hands and palms to break up the fibre. I refer to most British mammals, and deer and sheep, but not to cows or horses. If a skin is deemed to be unsatisfactory, the whole process can be repeated and the effect will be to have a far softer skin. There are no short cuts to tanning skins, as the end result shows it. Effort and patience are rewarded.

BUCKSKIN

This was first brought to the attention of the white man by the Crow and Navajo Indians, and was quite a messy affair involving brains and ashes, but the results were the soft buckskin tan famous for its durability and toughness. The only skins we have in this country to make genuine buckskin are the deer, calf, and perhaps antelope in the private parks. The Indians also used caribou, elk and wolf. To make buckskin, clean the skin in the normal way described for tanning. It now needs the hair removing by soaking in one of the following solutions.

Lime Water or De-hairing Solution

4ozs	Lime
1 gal	Water

Mix lime into a paste and add the water slowly and stir thoroughly.

Lye De-hairing Solution

¼ cup	Lye
10 gals	Water

The above formulas must be kept away from the skin as they are dangerous. Protective gloves must be worn.

If put into the lime water, it will take one to two weeks for the hair to come loose. Do not attempt to cut skin. Use only a blunt knife or scraper to remove hair. If any sticks, then return pelt to vat until later. With the lye solution it will only take a day or two for the same effect. When completely 'de-haired', wash pelt, and soak in boric acid solution for 24 hours to neutralize the lime.

Boric-Acid Solution

1oz	Boric acid
1 gal	Water

Rinse a number of times in clean water and allow to drain. It may now be tanned on any of the solutions already mentioned.

THE INDIAN TOUCH

The final flare and hallmark on the completed buckskin is achieved by adding colour and smell. The pelt is smoked, preferably in a proper curing or smoke house, but it can be done over a small fire heaped with damp shavings and wood. Indians preferred slow burning decayed wood, and continued the process until the light yellow to yellow-brown stain was obtained, both sides receiving treatment. It is important to note that the skin must not be subjected to heat, otherwise it will be ruined. Then it can be washed, stretched, dried, and then worked supple.

DEODORISING PELTS

Some pelts can build up an unpleasant odour in a room over a period of time, polecat and skunk being prime examples. Some people complain even of the fox.

Deodorising Solution

4lbs	Bar soap (chipped or grated)
4lbs	Soda
3-4ozs	Borax
1-2ozs	Oil of Sassafras

Boil the soap and soda together, and simmer until blended in. Then remove from heat and, while still hot, add borax and oil of sassafras. Ready for use on cooling. This is best used before tanning, because the sooner one gets rid of the smell, the better it is for handling. Swill the skin well in the solution, allowing the hair roots to get plenty of solution to them, and allow to soak for a short time. Rinse well with warm water, then cold, to remove all soap before continuing with tanning process.

CHROME TANNING

Chrome tanning is used by tanneries for the making of leather, for shoes etc., using de-haired pelts. A method using a commercial name of Krome Tan is suitable for mounting, and many American supply firms stock it.

TANNING SNAKESKINS

Remove head, and cut down to belly. Carefully peel skin off, and clean. Soak in warm lime water solution until the scales are easily scraped off. Then neutralize the lime by soaking in boric-acid solution; then wash in clean water, and drain. Then immerse the skin in the following solution for four days.

15 grams	Chrome Alum
4ozs	Salt
1 gallon	Water

Mix and add the following very slowly, stirring as you go. Take up to twenty minutes doing this. Stir the mixture daily, and leave for about a week.

5 grams	Sodium Carbonate
8 ozs	Warm Water

Remove skin to final solution of one part Sulphonated Neats-Foot oil to three parts water and leave it for some hours. Drain and peg out. When dry, work supple on a beam and finish by pressing with a warm iron. The condition of the snakeskin well depend largely upon its condition before death. Its colour and sheen will be enhanced by a coat of liquid celluloid or a suitable furniture polish. With dried skins, soak in warm water, until pliable, before commencing with this work.

CHAPTER 5

RUG MAKING

SKINNING

Unlike most authors on this subject, I will not say 'send it to a tanner', and then go on to explain how to tan it. The creature is cut from the throat to the vent and on until the tip of the tail is reached. The next cut is from the 'wrist', not the middle of the palm, up to the elbow, then across the centre of the upper arm to the chest. The aim is to keep the thickest fur of the arm (or leg) in the middle, leaving the thinner fur to become the edge of the rug, thus giving a balance to fur density and pattern. The hind leg cut is again from the 'wrist', following the back of the leg up to the back of the knee. The cut then moves slightly to end up between (in the male) his reproductive organ and anus. A matching cut is made to the other leg.

Skin carefully, leaving as much as fat as possible on the carcass, not the pelt. Skin down to the 'fingertips', leaving only the last joint containing the claw, or nail, attached to the pelt. Deal with the head in the same manner as one would a trophy head, splitting gums, eyelids, turning ears, and so on. Remove spongy cartilage from paws, any surplus fat from the pelt, and cartilage from the ears if one wishes to make ear liners. There is always much paring to do around the mouth, and care should be taken not to break through the skin at this point, as it is easily done, and quite weak when damaged.

The head

While the skin is receiving this treatment, cook the head, removing throat, tongue and eyes beforehand. If a pressure cooker is used, care must be taken, as, if overcooked, it will destroy the bone which becomes brittle, with no strength. Use saltwater or borax water. After cleaning and thoroughly drying the skull, build up in a manner described in the chapter on trophy heads. I normally keep my skins in the preserve or tanning tanks until mounting, only to remove them at times suitable to me for working the pelt on the beam.

Technique

From here on, as far as I can tell, I seem to be on my own as far as technique is concerned. When one writes on a subject, one reads all available work, some dating back over 150 years. One good reason for doing this is in case one misses out a vital factor. Another is to incorporate a good idea. All I can say is that I prefer my way, and I think it holds more satisfaction, than buying in bits, to save time. Good mounted rugs are a labour of love and job satisfaction. I only do them occasionally. To see a freshly completed job, well done, rather than a tatty tiger rug that has been ravaged by time lying in some antique shop, is

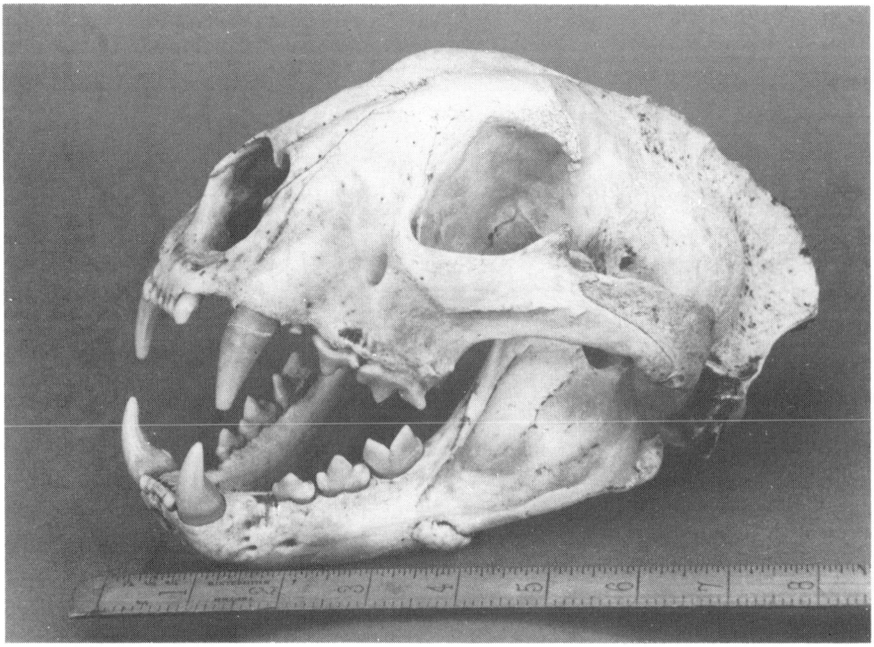

Figure 5.1 Skull of mountain lion, before wax buildings; note, it is completely free of grease

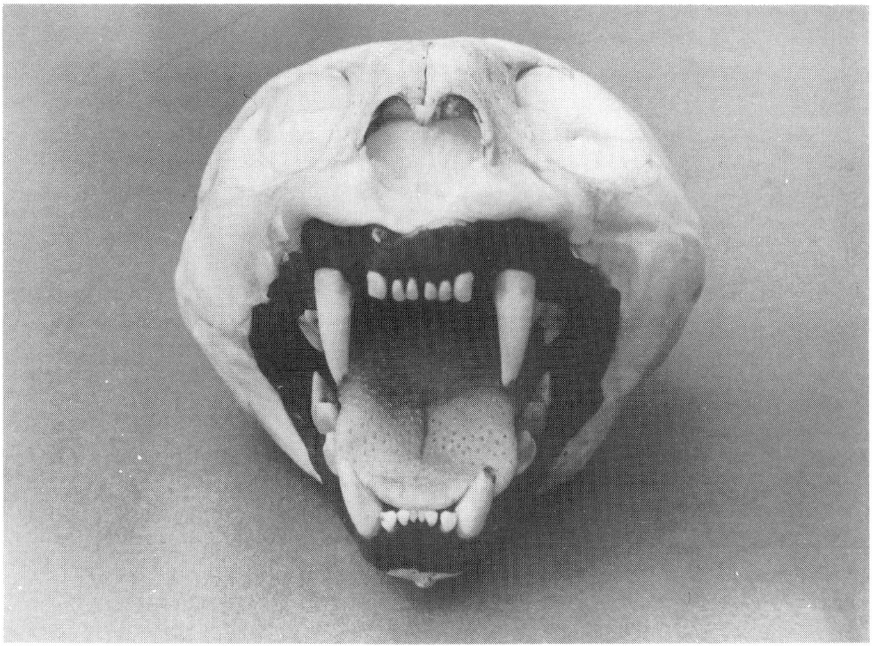

Figure 5.2 Skull of mountain lion, built up with wax tongue, gums, and muscling

breathtaking. The Americans, with their drive and very large commercial field are ahead of the British with opportunity, and have produced some great taxidermists, many of whom are alive today. We must produce Rolls Royces filled with older craftsmanship to counterbalance this.

Drying

The pelt is removed from the tanning solution, drained, and allowed to hang in the air, to get it as dry as possible. After two or three hours, press absorbent paper into the pads, gums, and ears, removing as much moisture as one can get out. The made up manikin is set up, exactly the same as a trophy head, completely ready to insert, eyes, tongue, and gums into place. Leather ear liners may be used, in case anyone falls over the head. If they are not used, continue as a normal mount.

The pads

These are filled with composite, or modelling filler, which is forced in hard. The advantage of not cutting the 'palms' can now be seen, as they stretch well and form bags to hold the filler. The skin at the wrist may now be cut, to allow the skin to lie completely flat, when pegged out. The cuts or nicks are small; in a fox, for instance, they should be not more than half an inch on either side.

PEGGING

The pelt is now laid on a board, flesh side down, and pegged out. I use large headed galvanised nails to do this. If care is taken, the head and tail will lie in a straight line, so there will be no need to correct such a fault (which can happen from a tanner's apparently). The pads or claws are laid out, with balance and symmetry in mind, and pegged. Do not overstretch the skin in places you do not want the skin in the finished rug. This will do away with excess trimming, and wasted pelt. The pelt will adjust itself within the area you have allowed it, as it dries. (see figure 5.3).

Leave until it has completely dried out, which will be a week or two. After this time it can be unpegged, and the pelt rubbed down, the fibre being broken down for the last time. I prefer to do this using only my hands, as explained earlier.

Staking tool

A staking tool can help at this stage. A handy one can be made up from a triangular paint scraper, if the corners are ground off. Lay the skin out and see if it lies flat – it should do. If it does not, then it may be necessary to cut a panel or wedge out of it to lie flat. Do not take too much out. Remember, it is easier to remove than it is to replace.

It is a good time to get rid of any thin or bald areas, like the armpit type areas, and this must be borne in mind when pegged out. If done correctly it can reduce the actual circumference, and edge carrying the trimming.

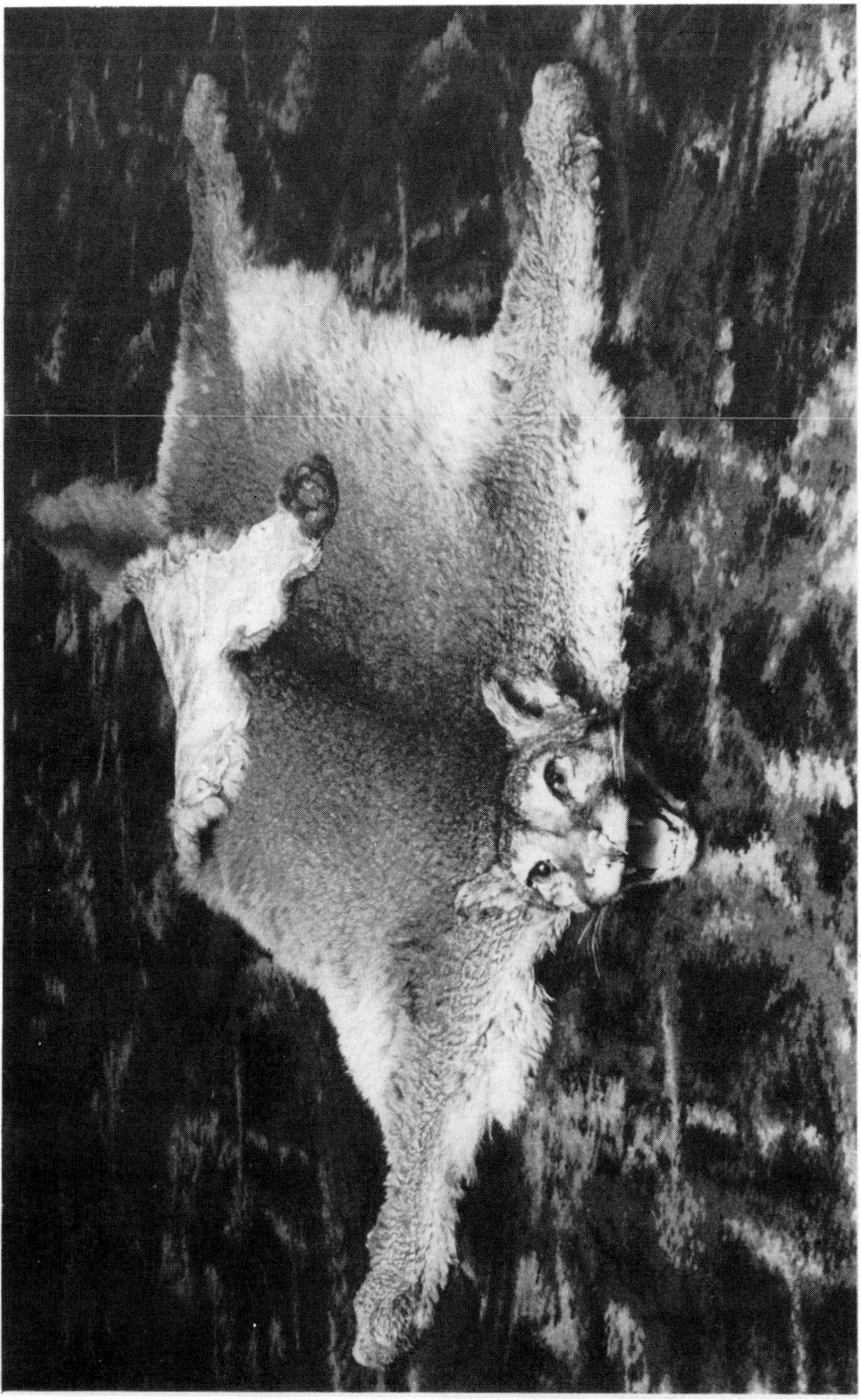

Figure 5.3 Note the added width of the rug by extending belly fur to forelegs, before pinning wet

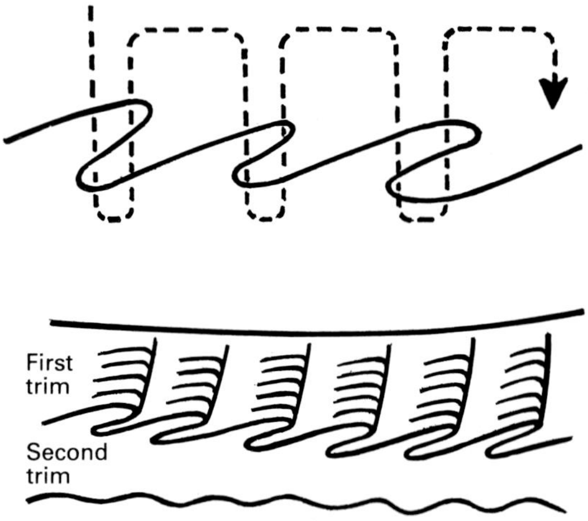

Figure 5.4 Edging the fur

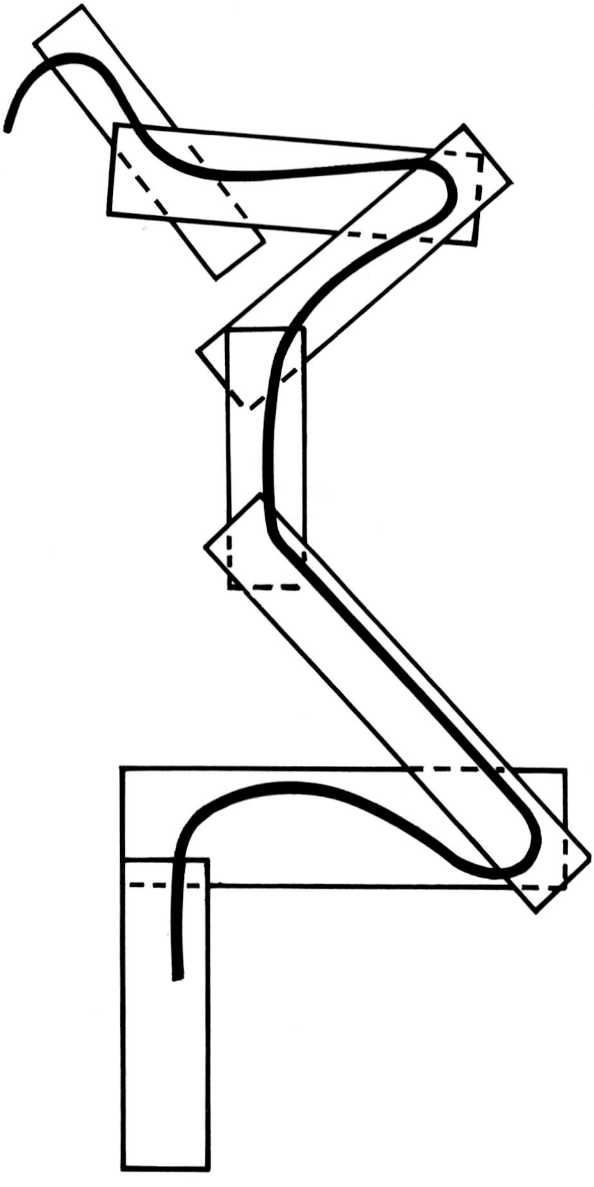

Figure 5.5 Stitching edges to form a symmetrical outline

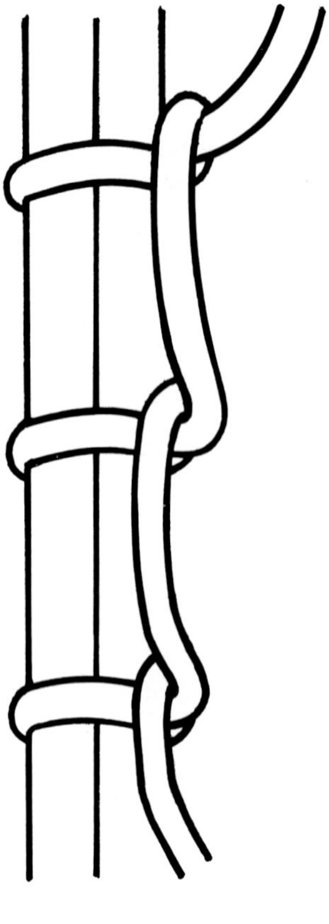

Figure 5.6 Stitching the underlay

PADDING

The padding of the interior puts a luxury touch to the pelt. A blanket can be inserted, but I prefer foam rubber carpet underlay, which can be obtained in varying thicknesses. Lay the pelt on the underlay and cut out the shape. If one wants to save here, pieces can be used for the legs, and bound together with carpet tape.

TRIM

Trim is made up out of felt and can be cut out in various widths, according to taste, two to four inches being suitable. Pinking shears should be used for this job, giving the edging a better finish. The first layer of felt attached to the rug I do in an overlapping way (see figure 5.4). It is surprising how much felt can be used this way. On a leopard with a 30ft (9m) circumference I used 120ft (36m) on initial trim.

The second layer of trim can lie flat and is built up of thirteen strips; edges again pinked (see figure 5.5). Stitching of these edges together to form one outline, should be done with a symmetrical view, with the joins at the same place to give balance.

The underlay can be tacked into position with a few loops and then stitched between the first and second trim layers. If a third trim layer is intended, then the underlay is stitched between the second and third layers (see figure 5.6). Waxed thread should be used for all stitching. A sheet of felt is placed under the rug and a rough outline cut out. This final backing can be lightly glued into place using Copydex glue, and the edge trimmed at a uniform distance around the rug. The claws are now varnished and the head finished off in the manner described in the section on head mounts.

CHAPTER 6

FISH

I intend to start on this subject assuming that the student is aware of the many ways of putting a fish together. We shall attempt to improve the final finish and discuss advanced mounted fish problems.

PROBLEMS

The greatest problem facing a fish taxidermist is whether he sets up a 'stuffed' fish or a model of fibreglass, plaster, or other material. There is no doubt that the trend is to produce model forms because of the more realistic finish of the two methods. The problem here is that the angler wants to see his trophy and nothing else in many cases. Each taxidermist must weigh up which path he intends to follow; either to express the best way to show a fish, or to pay attention to the fisherman, who is prepared to pay for his trophy.

Frankly, I believe that both approaches have merit and that the taxidermist must become a Jekyll and Hyde and put his heart into both skills of this field. On behalf of the angler the best efforts must be made to mount the fish skin or trophy. To the museum is owed the effort of reality, whether by skin, or faithful reproductions. At a later date science may allow us to bring both together again, but that I am afraid will be a challenge for our future brothers and sisters.

SOME SEA-FISH AND SCALELESS FISH

Having written the above, I must now say that many sea fish cannot currently be done by any method other than the 'cast' method. As a point of interest I tried 'freeze-drying' fish for two years to try to solve the problem, and get a perfect sea fish. I would have loved to have had the perfect fish to show Eric Hare that his skill had been overtaken by science. I regard him as the greatest British taxidermist among us today, certainly in experience, and his greatest love is fish. Having said that, he is also responsible for the finest African Elephant I have ever seen – but that is Eric; a grand master of the craft. The point I emphasise is that there is no challenge to the craft in this field by recent science so it is well worth learning.

Dogfish – freeze-dried

Figure 6.1 shows the results of freeze-drying a dogfish. It has a glass eye. As sea-fishes go, its skin allows it in part to be an exception to the rule, and it is shown in a position very difficult to obtain by classical methods.

Figure 6.1 Dogfish, freeze-dried

Red piranha

Figure 6.2 shows a cased Red piranha, which was finished by colouring with nail varnishes ten years ago. The finish is as good now as the day it was finished.

FISH FINISHING

Once the fish is dried and almost ready for painting (i.e. tinting), small faults can be found on close examination, such as hollows around the base of the fins, scales missing, shrunken lips and barbels, damaged fins, coarse patches, and so on (see figure 6.3).

The hollows should be filled in with beeswax-resin mixture, or a similar non-shrinking material. Missing scales; this area can be painted with hot beeswax, and the scales marked in with a hot needle later (see figure 6.3). Shrunken lips are built up with beeswax, and so are the barbels. These have a wire core for strength, which allows them to be pinned onto the lips (see figure 6.3). Damaged fins can be repaired by sticking sellotape or gauze behind them and sticking in position. Make this repair patch larger than required, and trim to size when dry. Even polythene could be considered for this (see figure 6.3).

Fish rays, or even fins, can be made from beeswax, and pressed against the finished backing. If done carefully it can become almost invisible in the completed fish (see figure 6.3).

Open mouthed fish need the back of the throat filled in. Cotton wool dipped into hot beeswax mixture and placed into the back of the throat, can greatly reduce the amount of beeswax required. It can also be dipped and allowed to harden before pressing in place. Coarse patches need to be smoothed, by using fine sandpaper **carefully**.

The eye sockets are filled with beeswax, similar to the fish throat and a suitable eye pressed into place; any surplus wax is then removed by scalpel.

Final touches

One now finishes with a very odd patchy looking fish; smooth and shiny in some places, with a matt finish in others. This will be corrected as soon as a coat of shellac is painted or sprayed over the fish. Any paint shop sells suitable aerosols for this. However, before one does this, if the fish has been done with a hollow body, it would strengthen and improve the fish to spray the inside first. It should also be noted that fish like salmon and trout have very small scales, which can easily dimple, unless reinforced from the inside.

When I use the sand filled method, I strengthen this type of skin with soft toilet paper and polycell paste on the display side. Three or four layers are enough. On drying, if this paper is sprayed with shellac, it greatly strengthens this wall (see figure 6.3). Heavy scaled fish like the common carp do not need this treatment. Once one is satisfied the fish is ready for painting, then it can be shellacked on the outside and allowed to dry.

COLOURING FISH

Although the colour fades completely from a fish, the markings remain faintly in many places, to show where the colour originally was. Individual fish in any species vary a great deal, and fish books only show the 'type' or general standard fish. It is, therefore, important to make detailed notes, if possible, of the fish as soon as one is able to, noting particularly the colour of the eyes.

RED PIRANHA. Serrasalmo nattereri
deadly Amazon shoal fish who can grow to 11
and reduce an animal to a skeleton in
This fish hunts near the bones of a
small
of Europe Peter O'Connor
Tele. Luton 53158

Figure 6.2 Cased piranha

Figure 6.3 Fish finishing; A hollows around the base of the fins; B missing scales; C scale painting; D spraying with shellac; E fish rays made from beeswax; F repairing damaged fins; G shrunken lips

Many magazines, cards, and books, contain fish photographs or drawings, which are completely useless for the taxidermist's requirements. One book I can recommend is *Freshwater Fishes* by Holcik & Mihalik, published under Spring Books in 1969 by Hamlyn.

Oil paints

The method used a hundred years ago was exclusively oil paints, using square ended bristle brushes for stippling and fine pointed sable brushes for finer detailed work. Oil paints take time to dry, and this is one of the greatest drawbacks in using them. Linseed oil, refined, and turpentine, help to reduce this drying time.

To save time on many fish, it is an advantage to paint the sides and belly white with a quick drying paint (Titanium White for one), and allow it to dry before proceeding further with the fish. The use of metallic powder can be considered, if required. This can be applied after the paint, and before the finishing varnish, mixed with a varnish undercoat. The pearly effect is achieved by use of a liquid celluloid called 'Pearl Essence' and 'Essence of Pearl'. This can be purchased in paste form or as a liquid; with either it can be thinned with a lacquer thinner before use. A number of coats are needed. If one is aiming at an iridescent effect then a little colour or dye can be added to the essence. This must only be a hint of colour, because later it will appear stronger. Brush marks can spoil a fish, so stipple where possible to avoid this.

Learn from others

Examine other fish that have been set up by others, and note what you like and dislike about them, and try to imagine how they achieved these effects and act accordingly. One salmon set up at the British Museum, South Kensington, has each scale painted, or stippled, in three colours. Close up it is unimpressive, but seen from a few feet away, it has great effect. It is well worth a visit (see figure 6.3).

Nail varnishes

Some years ago I experimented with various coloured nail varnishes to bring the lustre and sheen into fish scales, and was fairly satisfied. This is a useful technique with some fishes, and the varnish has stood up to the test of time.

Acrylic plastics and paints

In modern times, new materials have become available to us, and are used by many professionals today. The trend is to spray the fish, and touch up small detailed areas with a fine brush. The cost of the equipment is the greatest drawback, unless one intends to do a large number of fish. There are a number of air sprays on the market, which are cheap and operated by cartridges, or pump-up, which would allow the amateur excellent results at a modest price.

Dyes and lacquer

This is another method that is superior to oil paints and is very useful when working in transparent or semi-transparent areas such as the fins, where efforts should be made to prevent them becoming heavy and solid looking.

Milky finish fault

This is caused by working on the fish with too much moisture in the air. To remedy, spray pure lacquer thinner at the damaged area and dry with a hair-dryer immediately.

Brush v. spray

The spraying of fish is the best way to deal with the large areas of fish, but the fine detailed work still has to be done by brush.

FISH DISPLAY

Here are some ideas for fish display, rather than the old method of casing. If the old method is wanted, then there are some tips under the section on swimming ducks. A contemporary way of casing is to fit the fish to the back of the case in the normal manner. Then make a netting frame under the fish, of chicken-wire, and cover with papier mâché; leaving hollows for the fins, for effect.

When dry, paint with a gloss paint, dust with silver sand, and again allow to dry. This method allows for an all glass case, rather than a wooden base. Grasses can be added by making holes in the papier mâché and gluing them into place. If the backboard is painted in an emulsion paint in three shades, lightest at the top and darkest at the bottom, and blended in, the effect is modern and very effective (see figure 6.4). Gravel can replace the sand if required.

Picture frame

Another modern display method is to use a picture frame. The backboard is covered in hessian, and sprayed any colour from light blue to black, and the fish mounted without glass. A more elaborate picture frame display may be achieved as follows. Replace the backboard with a frosted blue or greenish glass, and bond the fish onto the glass. Place a low wattage strip light along the bottom, hidden by the picture frame. An inch wide wire frame is added behind the frame to allow the heat to escape (see figure 6.5). The final effect is a normal fish by day and a silhouette by night.

Other methods of display

With the price of casing, many fish are displayed on slices of log, cut diagonally from the trunk, or without a plaque being visibly displayed. The approximate area of balance for this type of fish can be found by laying the fish horizontally on a broom handle, until a balance is reached. The pivotal point is then marked on the back of the fish (see figure 6.6). Fish can also be displayed on stands for the sideboard, built either from mock rock of papier mâché, or simply by using a piece of artistically shaped, varnished tree root.

SMALL WAX FISH AS PREY ITEMS

Study figure 6.8. All the fish shown are made of coloured wax, in two tones, and blended together. The small fish are approximately one inch long, and without heads. The fins are made from celluloid, and the scales scratched on with the point of a needle. They do not look very impressive on their own, but placed in a bird's bill, they can add dramatically to the effect of a specimen. The focal point of one's observations are drawn to it, rather than the other end of the specimen holding it.

Figure 6.4 Fish display; cased in, backboard painted, with gravel or sand

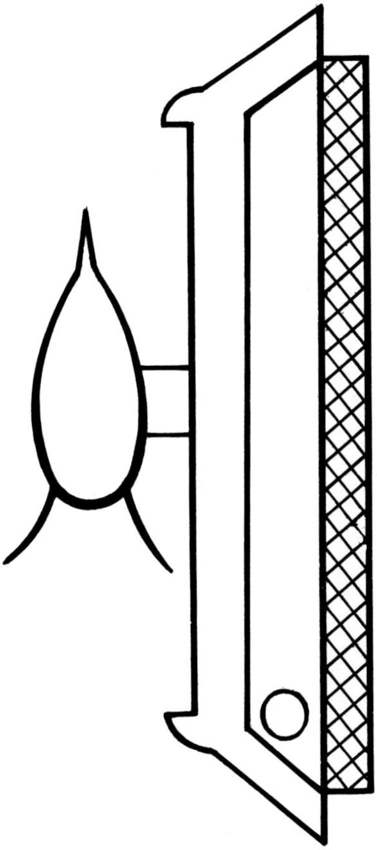

Figure 6.5 Using a picture frame for display

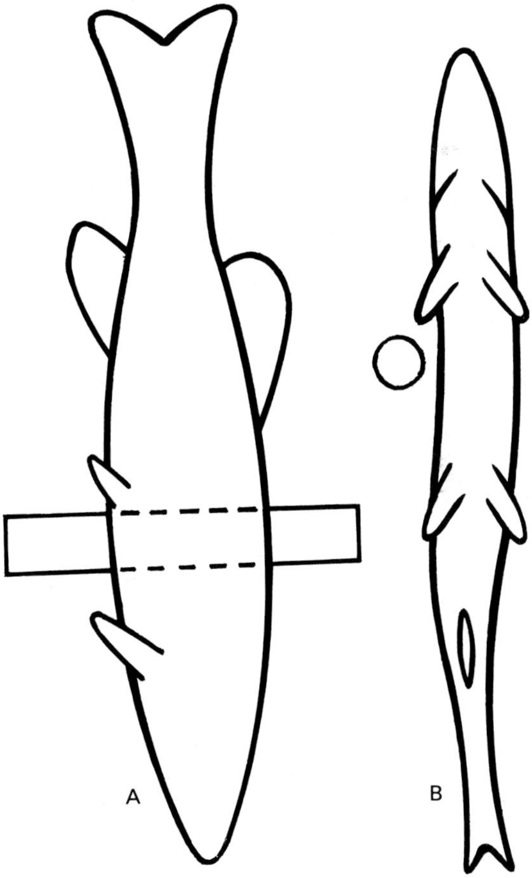

Figure 6.6 Finding the centre of balance

Figure 6.7 Tench, using freeze-dried techniques

Figure 6.8 Model wax fish to be used in birds' beaks

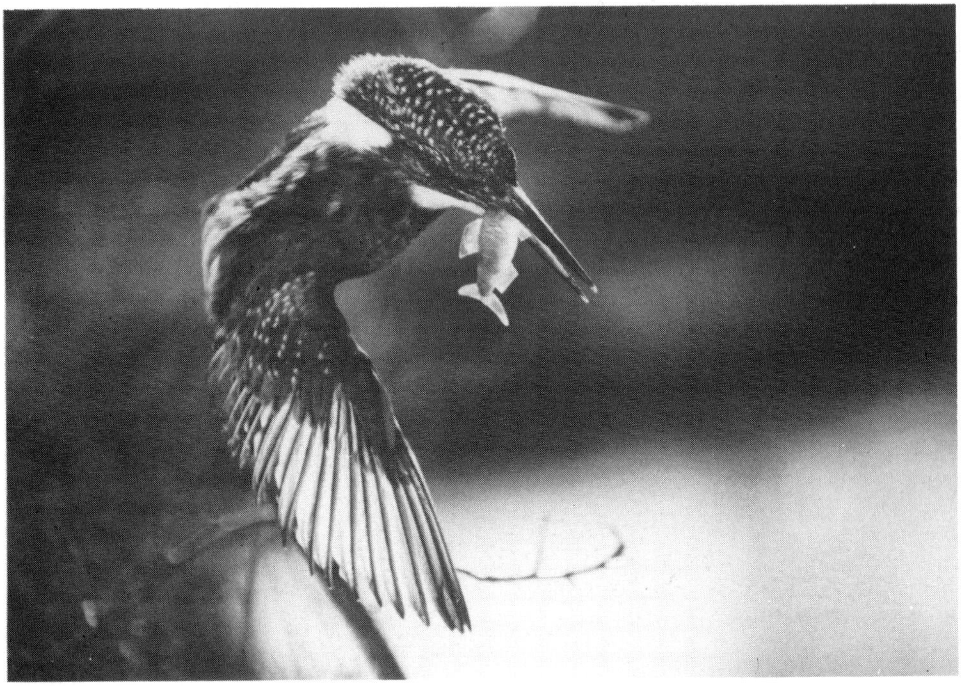

Figure 6.9 Kingfisher, using freeze-dried techniques, with a wax fish

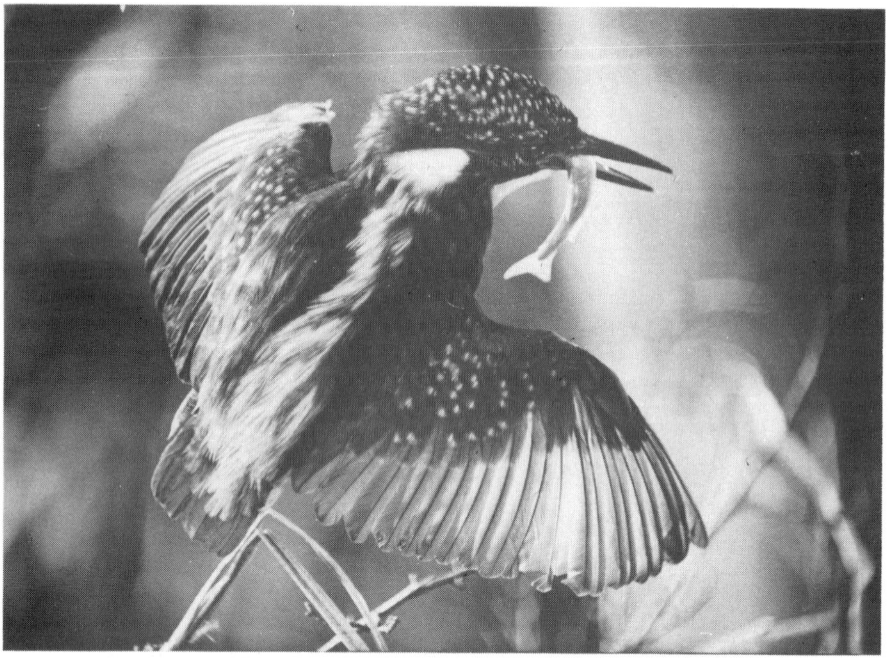

Figure 6.10 Another angle; the wax fish adds greatly to the effect

Figures 6.9 and 6.10 give an example, using one of the fish from figure 6.8. The flying kingfisher is supported on a single wire, hidden by the bird's body, and a grass stem. The focal point of attention, initially, is what the kingfisher is doing, rather than how it is doing it. Specimens that give this initial impact on the observer, leave a lasting impression.

When I was a young child, I was taken to a city museum. One of the glass cases contained a pair of ringed plover, plus a nest of eggs and one of the chicks, among many pebbles; a beach scene. To the untrained eye, suddenly discovering item after item in what appeared to be an ordinary case, was like magic. Years later I had occasion to see this case again. It was nothing special; all could be seen with a glance. The standard of taxidermy was professional, but not brilliant by any means. I mention this case because it was special to me. It caused itself to be remembered in a young boy's mind. It causes a point to be pondered on. We do not all see the same thing at the same time. Age, personal knowledge, tastes, experience, and so on affect our appreciation of a given subject or setting.

It is worth bearing in mind that, when one does scenes and casings, the impressions and opinions of youngsters are as important as adults and can often be painfully truthful, to a point of embarrassment. Specimens that are doing something concerning their daily routine, seem to hold far more interest than one just standing or perching to display their general shape and colouring. Part of the magic of a lasting impression, I am sure, is to have your specimen doing something.

CHAPTER 7

WAX LEAVES AND VEGETATION

We are not talking of the grotesque effigies that adorned Victorian houses. Those were composed completely of wax, which when hardened, became brittle and damaged easily. The colours too, were not 'fast' and soon became faded.

We are talking of the skill of the talented Mintorns, and Mrs. Mogridge, whose work completely fooled the Queen into raising one to smell and who also fooled Montagu Browne with some Golden Rod. He knew the family well, and was a worker in this wax field, and yet was deceived. I raise these incidents to show the quality of craftsmanship obtained. Since that date, one of Mintorns' secrets has been lost. Mrs. Mogridge would not allow the preparing of one process to be known, even to her students. She allowed them to buy the material prepared. I think with today's materials available, this should not be such a problem to overcome.

As the work has never been equalled, I have included the old methods briefly, together with what we know and what has been concluded by her students.

CASTING LEAVES

Basically wax leaves are made using a plaster cast, having a surface layer of thin wax, a backing of wax impregnated material for strength, and a stem built up of wax coated wire. Sifted Plaster of Paris is mixed thickly, then thinned by water, rather than adding extra powder, as that can produce lumps.

Place the selected leaves in water. Then remove and shake excess water from the leaf and cut off stem. A spoonful of Plaster is poured over the top or face of the leaf, and blown into every cranny on the surface. A second spoonful is added to it, and the leaf is placed on some old newspaper, plaster side up, to dry.

The flatter the leaf, the easier it is to get a wax impression. Variation is needed; some will have to be laid across bottles, plasticine, and so on, to obtain natural curls. These are best done by applying a single coat and allowing to dry, before adding more weight. The casts have to be built up to a thickness of half an inch, even to the edge. Clean leaf edges of plaster that has run onto the exposed underside before it has hardened. Allow to harden. Remove leaf and tidy edges up (see figures 7.1 and 7.2).

Hardening casts for wax

Make sure the casts are completely dry before proceeding to harden them for reproduction work. Put into very hot paraffin wax until they have ceased to bubble and wipe clean using absorbent paper.

Figure 7.1 Plaster casts of leaves

Wax for foliage casting (upper leaf)

Beeswax:	1lb
Paraffin wax:	4lb

Blend together in a heated pan set in a water dish (water bath), and add 8 ozs of hot melted resin, and mix, using sand bath (A sand bath is a pan within a pan, the outer one containing sand, at very high temperatures).

This wax produces the finest impressions and detail. Why another formula? Beeswax is tougher but one cannot hide 'join' lines of overlaying wax. Paraffin wax is apt to form air bubbles.

WAX IMPREGNATED CLOTH (FOR UNDERSIDE OF LEAVES)

In the old days, a fine transparent silk called 'Crêpe de Lisse', was used. Today we perhaps have a larger range of suitable materials to call on. The material was cut into strips three to four inches wide, and ironed smooth. When the wax was heated, the cloth was rolled up and completely dipped, in the fashion of a toilet-roll, so both sides received a coating of wax. It was then hung up to cool to remove wrinkles, and any unsuitable areas later scraped. It would keep up to a year if unused, and scraped after that time.

The formula for this was as below, and of course it had to be coloured before use. The underside of the leaves are lighter than the topside. Colour varies with different species, hence the matching before use.

Wax for impregnated cloth

Bleached Pure Beeswax:	2lb
Canada Balsam Gum, by measure:	3ozs
Resin, by measure:	2ozs
Boiled Linseed Oil, by measure:	2ozs

The wax is melted in a water bath and the balsam added. Melt the resin via a sand bath, add the oil, then both to the wax, stirring well, **Note: when hot, highly inflammable.**

STEMS

Examine a leaf. The stem radiates out, on reaching the leaf, into many veins or ribs. A support for an artificial leaf should be made up of a number of wires. This way they can fan out, and give a realistic tapering effect. The wires need to be cotton coated, and covered with wax and smoothed with the fingers, or they can be bare wire covered with long wedge shaped strips of the impregnated wax cloth. It is as well to note that the stems are normally lighter than the underside of the leaf, and darker on top, or even a different colour altogether. Observation of fresh leaves, if possible, is required for colouring.

ASSEMBLING A LEAF

Wet the mould by licking it. Lay a sheet of wax onto the face and see it is well pressed into every cranny, by using your fingers. The stem is now placed in position, fanning its fingers out,

Figure 7.2 Close-up of leaf moulds

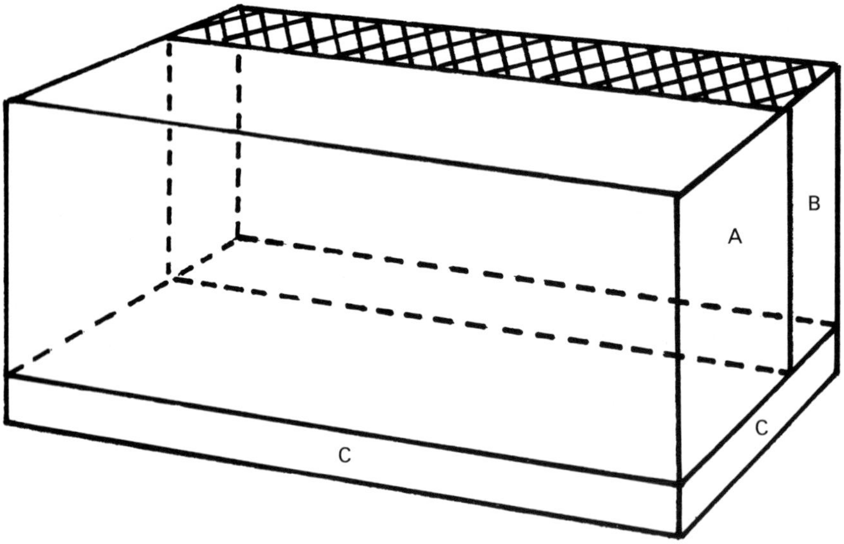

Figure 7.3 Display case (see page 90)

if it is a sizeable leaf, or if only a single main vein, put the point well up the leaf. Cover with wax cloth, and weld into place with fingers, avoiding the stem, and its movement as far as possible. Finally pin the stem firmly on either side and remove from mould.

The edge of the leaf is trimmed and notched with fine scissors. Make certain the leaf and stem base are firmly welded. If the gloss of the wax is not required on the leaf, press between two sheets of turpentine soaked blotting paper for a minute or two. When it dries off, there will be a matt finish.

A velvety surface can be achieved by stippling the leaf with dry dextrine and pressing on a dry mould. Parasite holes in leaves can be made with a red-hot needle or wire, and the edges tinted in oil paint.

The wax is allowed to cool into a block, and then is very thinly sliced, after it has been suitably coloured. One way this was done was by a device that had a planing or spoke-shaving effect. The tool was a carpenter's plane, called a 'trying plane'. I would think a bacon-slicer would suffice today, perhaps with the blade warmed a little with a hair-dryer, or warm water. One method to obtain small quantities quickly is to pour thinly over dampened glass, or even brush it on. It can be peeled off. It pays to heat the mould up in warm water for a few minutes before using it. If the wax is too hot or the mould too cold, the wax leaf can be spoiled. Expect to see a number of your leaves spoilt, so do more than required. If you are copying a branch, number your leaves, as size difference can spoil good work.

Moulds for large fleshy leaves are not boiled in paraffin, but merely allowed to dry. They must be placed in hot water for about 15 minutes before use. These moulds can even be dipped in the hot wax. If this is to be considered, then a wire handle should be built into the mould before completing.

Clover

Clover has a light pattern on its leaves. If a piece of cardboard is placed at the leaf centre paint can be stippled onto its edges. When removed, this will give the clover pattern.

Grasses

Grasses come in many sizes. The material for the impregnated cloth can be heavier. Cut to size and dip in hot wax quickly, the tip coming out first. This allows a greater concentration of wax down the base than the top. If the length is grooved, its strength will increase, and its appearance will be more natural. The grooving will give the waxed length a paper-like appearance, the base of which can have a waxed wire wrapped in it, and protruding (to anchor it in a setting), while the upper part can flatten out into a grass blade, or may be rounded, depending on grass variety.

All tools used when working with wax should be kept damp, and they should not be allowed to become sticky; that goes for fingers as well. Grasses have cellular walls which grain the grass, making it appear angular in places. A comb of finely set needles on a wooden block or handle can 'comb' some of this detail in. Heavier grasses grow on a long stalk with many blades coming away from the main stem. These blades are very flat, and need to be supported internally with a wire. A blueprint for the shape is made by stencilling the outline of a blade on clean paper, so the clean shape cut-out may act as a tracing for the grass' characteristics. Extra length has to be added for embedding in setting, and varying sizes as one progresses up the stem should be remembered.

The thinnest of the impregnated cloths is used for this because it will be used double, with the supporting wire sandwiched in the middle. The pressing of the two parts together should be done lengthwise to keep shape, and tapered from the wire in the middle to a thin outside edge on both sides. A blade of grass is shaped like a broadsword; tapering in its length, and from its middle to its edges. Combing also helps the effect.

Construction of the plant, should be achieved by copying the specimen or specimens itself, aping characteristics where possible. This relies very much on acute observation.

CASING AND PRESENTATION

Foliage and decor reached a peak for the unbelievable, besides fine and good representation, in the Victorian era. Today in Britain, very little serious casing is done commercially. Customers who will willingly pay to have their specimens mounted, become very reluctant to pay anything for interior decorations of a case, so it is no wonder that cases have become very spartan and contemporary. Time is money and a great deal of time can be spent producing a good case. Storage again, for variation of plants, can be a problem. Commercial taxidermists I have met, would sooner not case, than case. This will be the situation, until public requirements change and they are prepared to pay for labour and skill. This problem has been going on for many years now, and the commercial taxidermist almost became extinct and many of their skills have.

Stands

Museum requirements today are for uncased specimens, on simple stands or even no stand at all. This makes a specimen very prone to damage. A simple effective stand I use for such purposes is a plywood stand, cut out on a jig-saw, painted with olive gloss paint, which is dusted with silver sand. When hardened it produces an acceptable and cheap base.

Another striking stand for the drawing room is made from selected tree roots, which are more interesting in their shapes than branches. These are bleached, washed, thoroughly dried, then varnished. When finished, they are screwed to a polished, hardwood base. Felt is attached to this with Copydex glue. If the specimen is fitted directly to the base, the wires go through and are anchored on the underside. This can have a better appearance and stand more evenly by having the wires countersunk in a groove in the underside of the base. Once the wires are anchored, the groove can be filled with a wood-filler or modelling composite and levelled off. These grooves are again hidden by felt.

Cases

A striking case for the more adventuresome can be seen in figure 7.3. The back of the case lights up, giving a silhouette of the specimen in the 'A' compartment. This case is really made up of three parts. 'A' compartment is the true case containing the specimen, twigs and other decoration, the back of this case being a reeded or frosted type glass. 'B' compartment has a low wattage strip light fitted across its bottom length. This has to be lower than the decoration or ground level of compartment 'A', as its light is to be a weak floodlighting of the back; not a glare. The top of this compartment is fitted with a metal mesh grill. This is to allow the air heated by the strip lighting to escape. If one can fit another to the bottom, so much the better, as it gives a continuous flow of air, and cooling effect when the light is on.

When the light is off, the case is a normal display case. When on, there is the silhouette effect. Compartment 'C' can just be the base, or it can house a recorder of a song range or characteristic call ranged at intervals along the tape.

Picture frame or wall models can also be made. The frosted glass in this case is coloured or sprayed (if sprayed, overlapping paint marks must be watched for). The paint also has to be tough enough to stand up to a fairly warm environment. A heavy picture frame with fish or flying birds, fastened directly to the glass by a powerful adhesive, produces eye-catching results. The fish, of course, are supported by a wooden support bar, as normal. This is attached directly to the glass, thus pushing the fish away from the back of the case.

Lighting can again play a very effective roll if the case is lit from above. In this case opaque glass should be used in the lighting area, and the strip lighting should be fitted to the front of the top to do away with shadows. These can be used to an advantage, but not if it hides the subject's features, and points of interest. If a heavy top is put on the case, then it should be balanced with a heavy base. The other framework should be kept to an absolute minimum, or even done away with; using heavier glass with polished edges. Great strides have been made in glass adhesive. The local aquarium or pet shop is the place to find out the latest improvements.

With the introduction of marine fish as pets, and seawater being so corrosive, frameless tanks have arrived. Tanks up to six feet long, containing seawater, are held up by no more than glue. Modern technology now gives the taxidermist far more scope than his earlier counterparts. Whether his environment will is another matter.

DRIED GRASSES AND PLANTS

Silica gel is the agent for drying out plants, rather than pressing them. The specimens are packed in crystals in an airtight container. The crystals, which absorb moisture, can be used repeatedly. This moisture is removed by spreading them in a tray in an oven. When not in use, they should be stored in a plastic bag or airtight container, or else they will absorb the moisture in the air of an apparently dry room.

Dried flower arranging and technique books are available with all the up-to-date and new ideas of the subject. These, coupled with identifying specimens in old cases that have stood up to the test of time, are the examples one can safely use. Other must be classed as suspect.

Effects with dried painted grasses can be good, even if incorrect. The short, rounded, wiry grasses stand up the best. I have seen these dried and painted at their tops and stems. I have also seen them painted and dyed below, where the new growth comes from. Both, I would say, add to a normal average case.

It should be noted that grasses and plants can absorb colour by standing in dyed water while fresh. Vegetable dyes should be used.

FREEZE-DRIED GRASSES AND LEAVES

This is the most modern way of dealing with vegetation. The results at the time of writing are frankly disappointing, and far more research work has to be done in this area. The main problems are fading colour and fragile or brittle leaves. Colour improvement can be made by standing them in chemicals before processing, but personally I think dyes might be a better answer, or perhaps even a combination of the two. Reinforcing leaves on the underside, before processing, again may prove to be of value. It is a completely new field for a taxidermist with an inclination for research or a pioneering spirit.

COMMERCIAL GRASSES AND VEGETATION

By commercial grasses, I mean grasses that do not have to faithfully represent their own species, but rather create a general vegetation background, where large quantities are used, at reasonable cost. If we are relieved of the need to produce exact likeness, then grasses of one species can be dried and shrunk, to appear similar to those of another. Reed grasses, when dried, will lose between two-thirds and three-quarters of their width, creating in appearance, a smaller, lesser grass. Some Meadow grasses, when dried, twist limply, and give the impression of water-weed and, if laid horizontally, can be used to effect in fish case decor. Other uses seem limited.

Grasses and plants most suitable for dying and drying, have similar characteristics, regardless of their shape and size. They are usually extremely tough, coarse, wiry or leathery to touch, and normally found in very windswept, exposed places, such as moors, coasts, and swamps. If a grass is soft to touch and easily bruised, it is not much use to the taxidermist.

Collecting of grasses should be done when the plants start to reach maturity, but are still green to their tips, (for best dying results); this in the U.K. is about mid-May to early June. Gathering should only be done on dry days, long after the dew has gone, to reduce the diluting effect on the dyes, and personal experience has shown this is important.

Some common useful plants

Hair-Grass	*Aira caespitosa*
Wavy Hair-Grass	*Aira flexuosa*
Purple Moor-Grass	*Molinia caerulea*
Mat Grass	*Nardus stricta*
Cocksfoot (main seed stems only)	*Dactylis glomerata*
Gorse	*Ulex europaeus*
Reed	*Arundo phragmites*
Reed Grass	*Digraphis arundinacea*
Sedge, Common	*Carex goodenovii*
Sedge, Carnation	*Carex panicea*
Heather, Bell	*Erica cinerea*
Heather, Ling	*Calluna vulgaris*

The above plants will give an interesting number of combinations, especially if mixed with twig undergrowth and papier mâché rockery. Most mosses are suitable and readily accept and hold dyes used on them. Most sedges are also suitable.

AUTUMN AND WINTER VEGETATION

This type of vegetation requires very little or no dying to produce attractive settings. Investigate the countryside in mid-winter, to see what plants have resisted the elements best;

those species will most likely be suitable for case-work, where dampness and frost is absent. Ripe cereal and stubble scenes should also be considered.

COLD DYEING VEGETATION

Using Dylon Cold A15 powders. Use as instructed, allowing the plants to soak for an hour per batch, or longer if practical. Care should be taken to ensure the water content from the plants themselves does not weaken the solution, which will eventually happen if too many plants are processed. A guide to the strength of the solution will be given by the ease of removing it from one's own forearms.

The colours should be over-done, and appear too dark at first, because once the natural colour and chlorophyll dies out, the final result will look vastly different from the freshly dyed specimens. Sunlight, even indirect, fades the green dye at an alarming rate. Vegetation successfully dyed and stored in darkness for over a year, with excellent colour, rapidly faded to a soft shade, which remained. Other samples placed in direct sunlight faded completely within weeks. The most useful of the Dylon colour range in greens, were from emerald to the dark bottle greens.

VEGETABLE DYES

Vegetable dyes, much used by bakers and the food trade, are useful but costly. The advantage with this type of dye is that the plant will draw the dye into itself, besides staining the outside. However, it suffers from similar problems to the Dylon, although more promising if it becomes cheaper.

COMBINATION FLOWERS

Experimental research work indicates a big future here. Combination flowers are basically dried or freeze-dried, and the petals replaced by artificial ones. If one takes a tulip and freeze-dries it, the petals are removed, and the fine detailed head, with its delicate parts, are coloured by use of an air-brush. The petals are replaced by artificial beeswax-resin ones, or by using waxed crêpe paper.

This is a completely new field as the tools to do such work have only been in existence a short time. Anyone planning to experiment in this field, should start with the larger bulb based flowers, such as daffodils, tulips, etc., and then down to crocuses and snowdrops, before attempting the more delicate petals of other plants.

Tackling the problems this way, one will achieve good results, while training one's hands and mind for the production of the gossamer type flowers. Wax impregnated cloth, mentioned earlier for the production of leaves, was also used to produce flowers and petals, and could well be used with great effect, for some types of flowers in this range.

CHAPTER 8

FREEZE-DRIED WORK

HISTORY

Freeze-dried work on Natural History specimens is a fairly recent development in taxidermy. It has a terrific range and future, so it would be as well to record its short past.

In the 'sixties, Reg Harris, the Senior Experimental Officer at the British Natural History Museum, South Kensington, London, began experiments into freeze-drying Natural History specimens. He constructed a machine he called EF1. This consisted of a vacuum chamber, set inside an ice-cream deep freezer, and a high vacuum pump, running continuously to maintain a vacuum in the chamber. The appliance worked and led to the development of EF2, and later EF6. The main differences between these appliances, from a taxidermist's point of view, are the size of the vacuum chamber, and their prices, the latter costing twice as much as the former.

When I met Reg Harris in the late 'sixties, he produced a common shrew, which beat my work easily. The muzzle, feet and tail, were almost perfect; only a loss of colouring marred the perfection. The body was not so good, but he was the first to admit that he was not a taxidermist. To a taxidermist, he is akin to Merlin, for he has given a magic wand to taxidermists. The appliance, though, is expensive, and the main sales were, initially, to museums. Many people who were unskilled in mounting specimens, became instant taxidermists, and tried to set up creatures using this appliance, and failed miserably.

This is a new science, and as with the old classic form of taxidermy, each species has its own requirements. Having set up more than five thousand specimens, I have run into a number of these problems, and will deal with them shortly.

TECHNICAL DATA

The following is a brief description of EF2. It has a cylindrical vacuum chamber 15½ inches (39.4 cm) deep, with a diameter of 12 inches (30.5 cm). This is set into a larger vacuum chamber, containing a metallic evaporator coil. A sealed refrigerator unit is mounted beneath this chamber. Its refrigerant in the condenser coil produces a cold temperature of minus 45 degrees Centigrade (−49°F) at the evaporator coil, at atmospheric pressure, and minus 15 degrees Centigrade (5°F) at the vacuum or drying chamber's centre.

A two stage rotary vacuum pump is situated beside the refrigerator and is driven by an electric motor, having a displacement of fifty litres per minute. It uses normal household voltage and the maximum power consumption is 750 watts.

The appliance has a control panel which contains a Torr gauge for chamber pressure, a temperature gauge, with a two way switch, for coil and chamber readings, plus valves

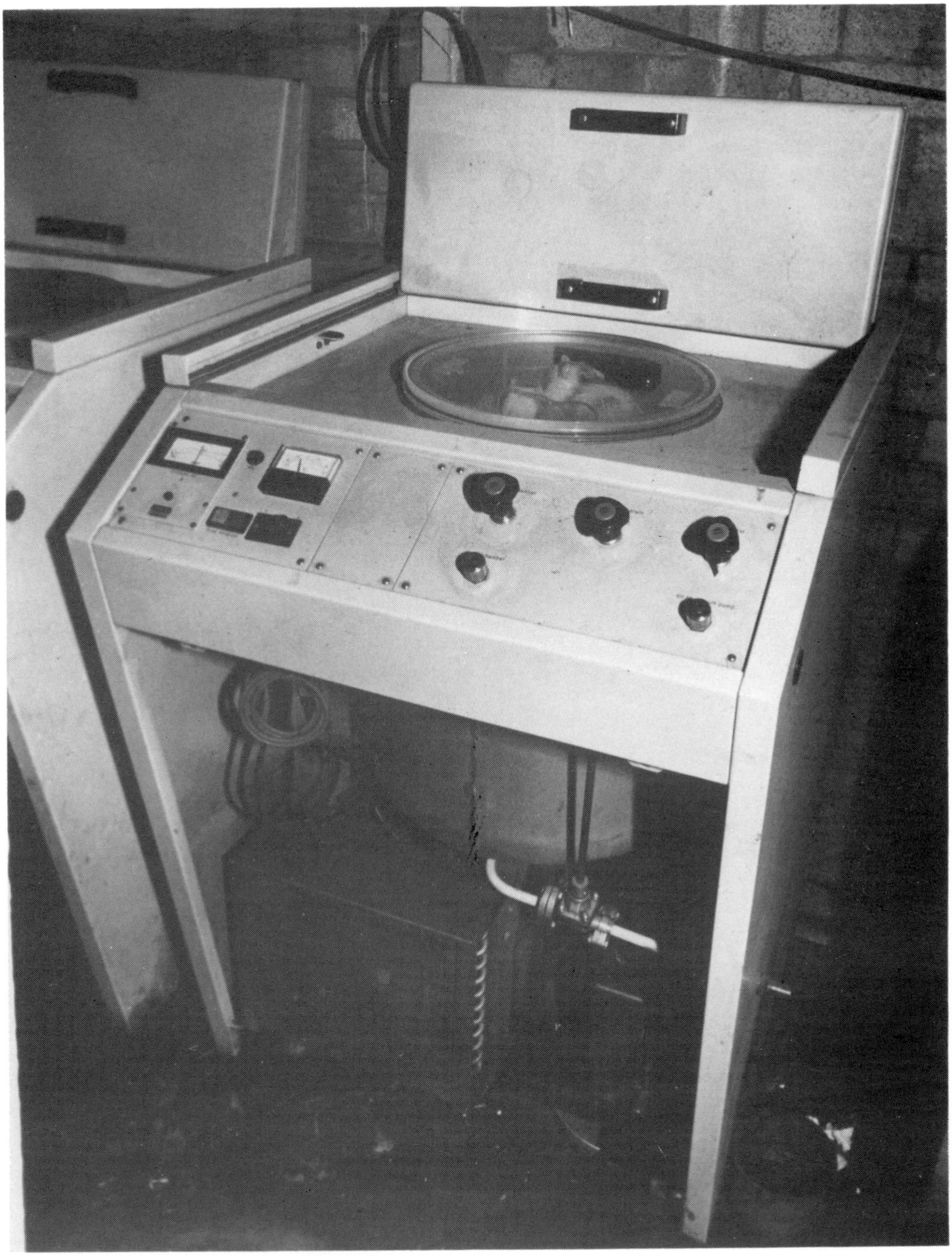

Figure 8.1 EF2 freeze-dryer in operation

Figure 8:2 Close-up of the EF2's gauges; the left gauge is showing an ideal reading for a commercial load; the right gauge is showing the temperature of the specimens; the coil would read −45°C

and fuses. The overall cabinet size of the EF2 is 31½ inches (80 cm) wide, by 33½ inches (85.1 cm) deep.*

Method of operation

Specimens to be freeze-dried should first be mounted into a suitable position, and then frozen in a household freezer at −10°C (14°F) for twelve hours, although I prefer a minimum of twenty-four hours. They can, of course, be frozen up in the appliance, but this stops it doing its job, if you have other specimens already in it.

Once sealed in the machine, and a suitable vacuum reached, the water content in the specimen is sublimed away as vapour. It is a slow process, and the number of specimens in the chamber, and their positioning makes a difference to how long they take. Eventually, all the moisture is taken from the specimen and it is ready. If a slice of the body was placed under a microscope, one would see, while it had retained its shape, it would be honeycombed.

Range of applications

The appliance is capable of preserving many life forms out of the taxidermist's scope, such as microscopic life, fungi, plants, insects, invertebrates, mosses and ferns, and so on.

***For the more technically minded, a leaflet is supplied, on request, by Edwards High Vacuum, Manor Royal, Crawley, Sussex.**

Figure 8.3 Inner and outer chambers of the EF2; the outer container houses the freezer coil; the black inner container is removable

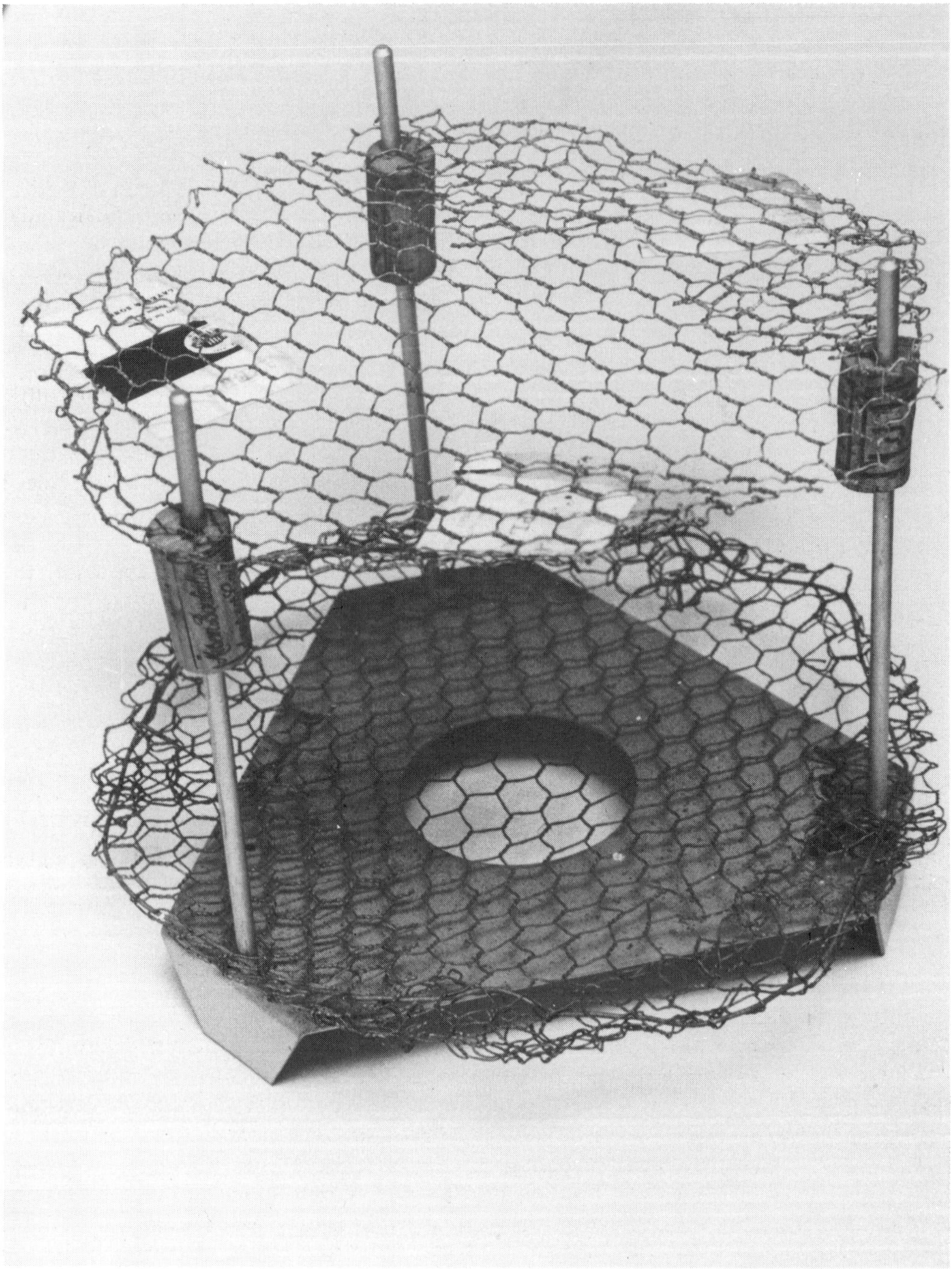

Figure 8.4 A useful stand for an EF2; this allows maximum use to be made of the chamber by creating two or more floors; the level is adjustable by moving the corks

As this book is for taxidermists I will concentrate mainly on the accepted lines of specimens expected from a taxidermist's workshop. We will also look at a few new possibilities open to our profession.

Hints on use

As a commercial taxidermist, the first snag I ran into was that of finding out whether the specimen was ready or not. The accepted way of doing this had been by using scales, and very fine weights, until the weight became constant. To do this, the specimen was removed into normal atmospheric temperatures, which quickly thawed its extremities, especially in specimens like mice. The ears and tail were immediately affected, and had to be refrozen before continuing the process.

I found that a thin, steel knitting needle, if pushed into the body, had a double effect. Firstly, one could feel the crispness of the creature's interior, and the needle met little resistance, if ready. If it did run into resistance, then it was ice, and not ready. Secondly, the hole left by the needle assisted the sublimation process. With smaller specimens even sewing needles can be used. If the needle or probe is used intelligently, no hole is visible. I normally used this probe via the vent, or followed the lie of the hair, or perhaps in a natural hollow or fold of the skin.

Over a period of years, one can get a 'feel' for specimens done. This is probably the relative lightness of the item, for its size, and a certain dryness in its texture. That, together with a time range chart, built up over many specimens of the same type, is normally enough.

BIRDS

The initial wiring for birds done at the British Museum, was external. A half circle of wire, with the ends turned in, acted like a spring. These ends were placed at the bird's vent or forehead. This gave the bird no future support when finished, and was very wasteful of the chamber area. The method set out below is one I finally decided on, and has been adopted by many museums. The advantages of this method are that it is simple, and gives full control of the bird's stance.

Removal of the eye

To begin with, the eye is removed with a needle. If the needle is pushed carefully into the side of the eye, it will come out easily, without shedding any of its contents. A thin roll of absorbent paper put into the socket will remove remaining moisture. If any liquid is spilt, remove immediately with absorbent paper. Care should be taken not to damage the eyelid by a careless needle or overstretching the eye longer than necessary.

The eye is far smaller than the eyeball, so packing is required. Modelling clay is too messy when working on the outside of the bird. I find that cotton wool, rolled into very small balls, is ideal. Place them into the socket carefully using two forceps, one to lift the upper eyelid, and the other for inserting the cotton wool balls. Arrange these balls, leaving a shallow hollow for the glass eye to rest in. Insert it and close the eyelids, to prevent it falling out. Do the same to the other eye.

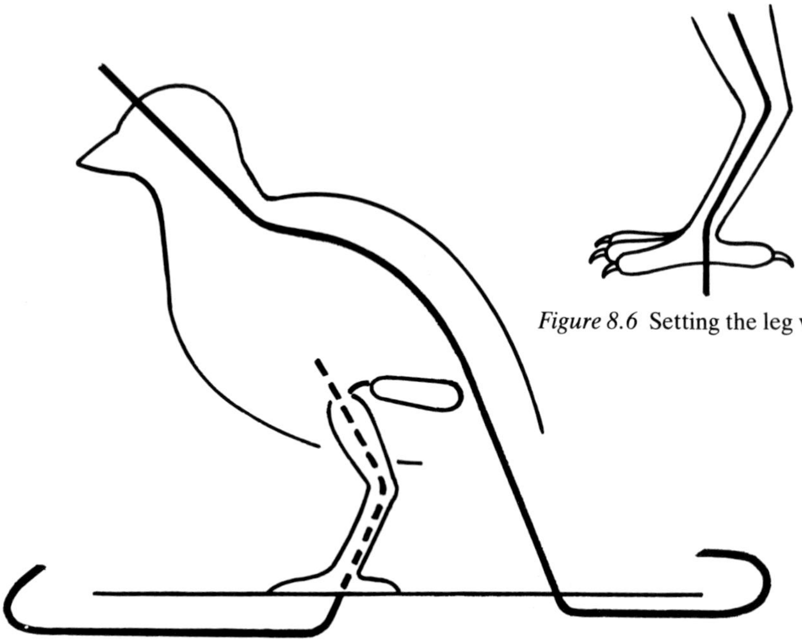

Figure 8.6 Setting the leg wire

Figure 8.5 Wire down the spine of a bird

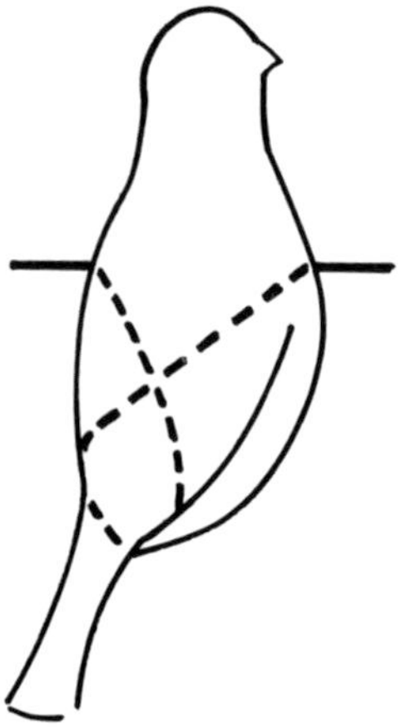

Figure 8.7 Wire or cotton used to hold the position of the wings

Wires

Cut three wires of suitable weight-bearing gauge, bearing in mind that two of them are to be passed up the bird's legs; these should be at least as long as the bird's overall length. The other wire should be twice its length. The wires must be filed to smooth points to prevent tearing.

The longest wire is used first, and is driven through the forehead, close to the beak. If it is pushed in higher up, control of the head position will be lost. Push it through the back of the skull, and down the neck, following, but not into, the spinal column. Then push into the body and out through the abdomen in the region of the vent. Leave a couple of inches protruding from the skull (see figure 8.5).

Place the bird on its back and push one of the shorter wires through the sole of the bird's foot, and follow the tendon up until the hip joint is reached. The leg is then bent into a natural position, locking the wire in place. The wire at the foot is bent at right angles to the claws. The other leg receives the same treatment (see figure 8.6).

Stance

A piece of cardboard is needed for a temporary stand. A four by two inch (10×5 cm) piece would be suitable for a greenfinch size bird. Pierce two holes one inch (2.5 cm) apart for the leg wires, and another two inches (5 cm) behind for the vent wire. Insert bird and bend the three wires passed through the cardboard and lock them into it. The bird will now be standing, but its head will be too far forward. Give the neck an **S** bend and adjust its stance,

Figure 8.8 Holding the wings

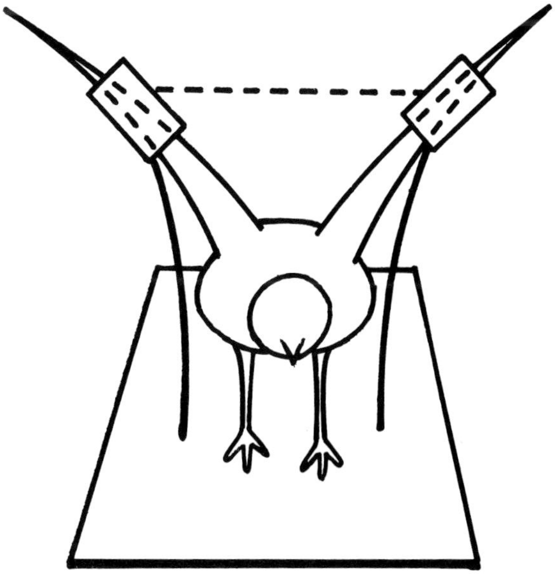

Figure 8.9 Additional support for the wings

and feathers. The eye can now be opened, and adjusted with fine forceps, and the bird is ready for freezing.

After trying one or two in this stance to gain confidence, try different postures, such as feeding, head under wing, preening, and so on. The triangle of the wire anchorage to the cardboard gives an excellent secure base, while allowing the specimens a good range of positions. Although many of the birds set up this way will have no difficulty in retaining their wings in the closed position, with no drooping, some will refuse to stay in position.

Securing the position

It will be necessary to drive a single, sharpened wire through both wings and the body. This may be enough to hold their position. If not, then cotton passed from the wire on one wing, across the back, under the abdomen and back up to the other wing, and repeated a number of times, will cure it. This 'figure of eight' cotton, can stay on the specimen until it has been freeze-dried. The wire can then be cut off flush to the body, or entirely removed (see figure 8.7). The tail can be protected by a fold of this cardboard, and held in place with a paperclip. This helps give a clean knife edge to the tail feathers. The tail feathers can also be spread and retained in this manner, if desired.

When it has finally been freeze-dried, the wire at the forehead is cut off. Before cutting the other end off at the vent, the wire should be pulled a fraction of an inch, so the wire at the head is flush to the skull; the remaining leg wires allow the bird to be mounted in the conventional manner.

VARIOUS BIRD POSITIONS

Birds whose final display positions are to be linked to twigs, such as perching birds, must be placed directly onto twigs before freezing. The three wires are again used as an anchor. The claws may then be curled to grasp the twig, and held in place by pins, or plasticine, this retaining material being removed when frozen into place. It may be an advantage to cut the tendons to the claws through the sole of the foot, before mounting.

Birds with raised wings are first anchored in the described way using the triangle of wires. The wings are simply lifted to the required height and angle, and held in place by another wire, a piece of cardboard (folded), and retaining paperclip, as in figure 8.8. To give this wire strength, it should be anchored into the cardboard. Figure 8.9 shows an additional support can be added, by the use of cotton, between the paperclips, if both wings are raised.

Care should be taken to see that the wings do not take on a lopsided stance. Once frozen, the wing supports can be removed, and feathering checked out to see that it is lying correctly. If any need rearranging, then the heat from one's fingers can thaw the area in seconds, and the correction made. This work of correction is best done with the species remaining in the freezer, as the wing in normal room temperature quickly thaws.

A number of birds often stand for long periods on one leg. Specimens to be set up may have a defect, such as claws, toes and even legs missing. A one-legged stance can make use of these birds. Three wires are used again. The wire used for the supporting leg must be far stronger than normally used, as it will be the only wire left to support the whole specimen.

COMBINATION WORK

Combination work is where there is more than one specimen to be set up, connected to one another in some way, for example, two hamsters fighting, or a python crushing its prey, or a bird pulling a worm from the ground.

It is easier in most cases to set up one of the specimens completely first, as with the case of the worm and the bird. The worm I would have freeze-dried first, then add colour to it, probably by the use of various nail varnishes. I would also add a wire the full length to give it strength. The worm, to be realistic, would have to be stretched before freezing and processing.

The bird is set up in the described fashion, and placed roughly into position, before introducing the worm to the beak. The wire containing the worm is pushed through the back of the bird's skull base. Both specimens are then frozen and freeze-dried, although one has already been completed. This way allows the bird's throat to lock firmly onto the worm, and become one unit, as can be seen in figure 8.12.

With items such as birds holding or catching moths, spiders, and so on, it is perhaps better to do the bird first, then add the insect. The advantages in these cases are that the insects require no further treatment and, as the bird is already freeze-dried, the time needed to complete the combination is very short. This saves appliance spaces.

Three lion cubs

A typical example of combination work, which I have at hand, is that of three lion cubs. The photographs (figures 8.10 and 8.11) show the completed group, and how the cubs can be

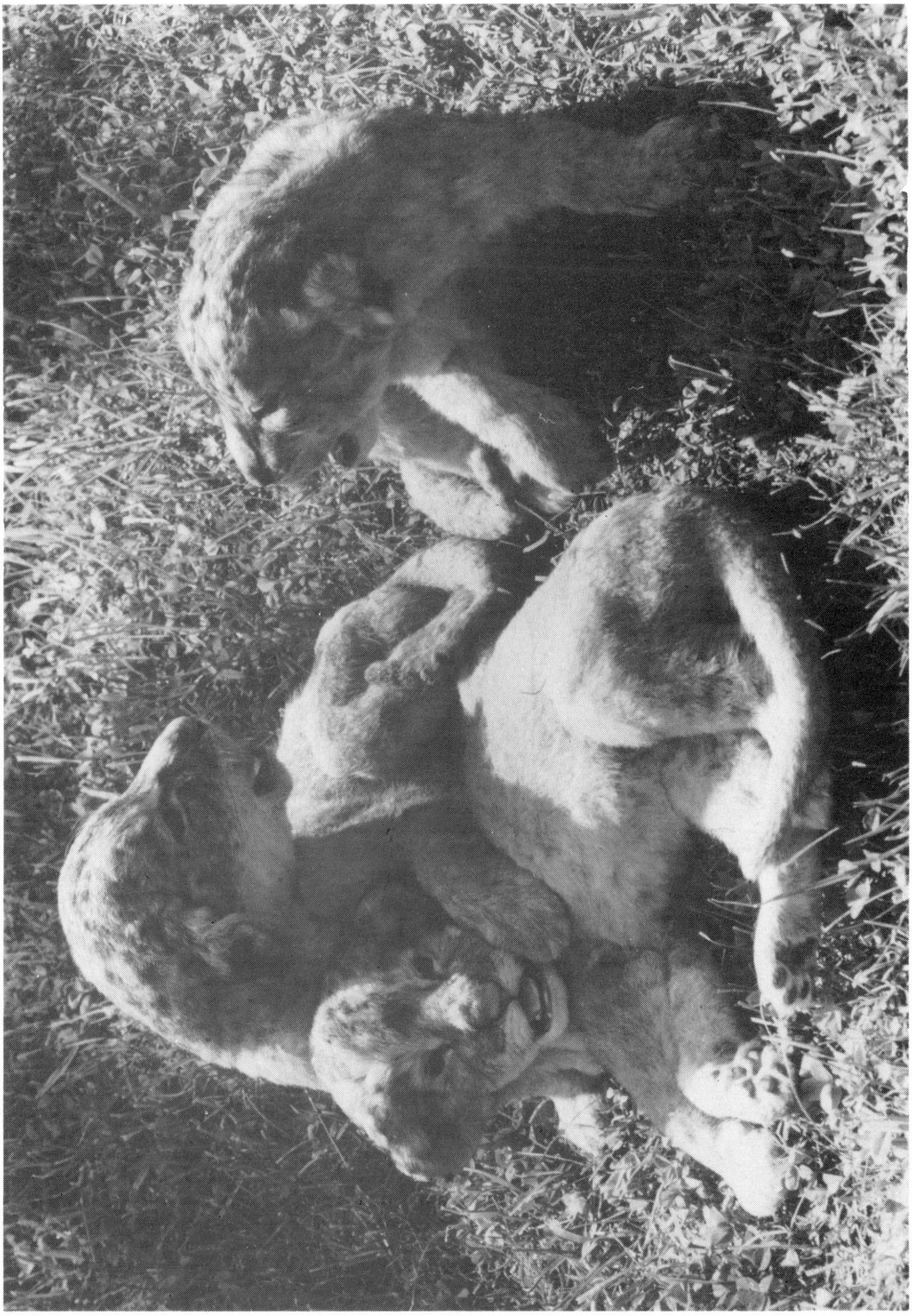

Figure 8.10 Lion cubs set up by combined taxidermy methods

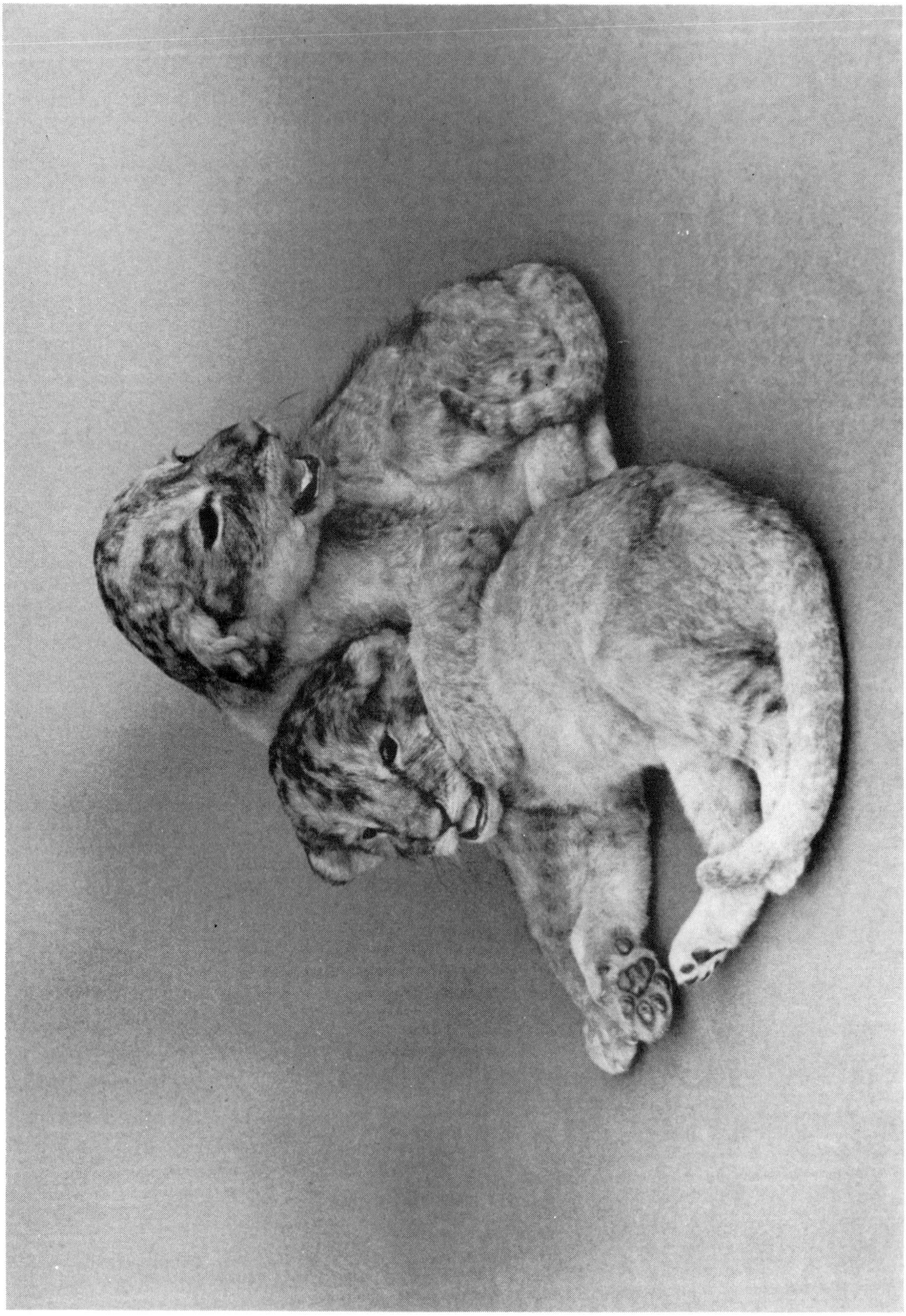

Figure 8.11 Two of the lions set up using combined taxidermy methods

parted. The initial cub was the central one lying on its side. The sitting cubs were added at different times. The completion time for the group was over 300 days. The work, although being combination work, is also done in combined taxidermy style. This style of work is expensive, but gives great scope to the museum workers, who have access to this equipment, and with the right mental approach, can explore this field more fully.

Many museums are disappointing from their display angle, relying on their past masters of display. This situation is caused, I feel, by tight budgets, and the secrecy of many past masters, as well as some present ones. A vast new horizon is appearing to the present day taxidermist. Specimens beyond his grasp and skill a few years ago, now present themselves; as do the questions of how best to display them. The stagnation time is over.

WATER WORK

Any freeze-dried bird considered for swimming on a water surface, should be set up in a swimming position, then, if to be set on a glass sheet, cut horizontally along its 'waterline'. The thickness of the glass used must be cut from the lower half of the body, otherwise the body size is distorted. The lower portion is fixed to the glass first, using a suitable adhesive. I use No. 1 Bostik. Once dry, the upper section is added.

If scenes such as sparrows bathing in shower puddles are envisaged, freeze-dried birds and acrylic (a form of clear plastic), are ideal. **Great care should be taken with the acrylic.** In its liquid form, it is highly inflammable, and almost as dangerous as petrol in a confined space. Once set, it is harmless. It also has a melting affect on a number of modern materials, such as polystyrene. A scene containing a hollow for the puddle needs constructing. If papier mâché is used, then it must be watertight. The acrylic is used, following the directions on the can. No more than a quarter of an inch (6 mm) in depth should be used until hardened. The birds are placed in position, and the waterline built up to the required depth. With a little practice and experimentation with this material, even droplets of water can be added to the bird's wings and feathering, achieving some interesting effects.

FREEZE-DRIED FLYING BIRDS

Before we go into true flying birds, it should be mentioned that birds alighting or departing from twigs can be done simply by combining methods previously mentioned. The thick single leg wire of the bird standing on one leg, and the method of raising wings on others, can be used on such specimens.

The true flying bird must be supported by **only one wire.** This wire, again, must be heavy enough to support the specimen. The wire is used through the head and body length, as previously described. The difference this time is that this wire is load-bearing and must **not** be able to slip out of the body, but must be locked into place somehow. This is achieved by a simple loop placed in the wire after it has been pushed through the bird at the abdomen or vent end.

The abdomen feathers are parted, and a slit cut into the skin, large enough for the wire loop to be inserted; then the skin is sealed by stitching. The bird is now firmly attached to the wire, as in figure 8.13.

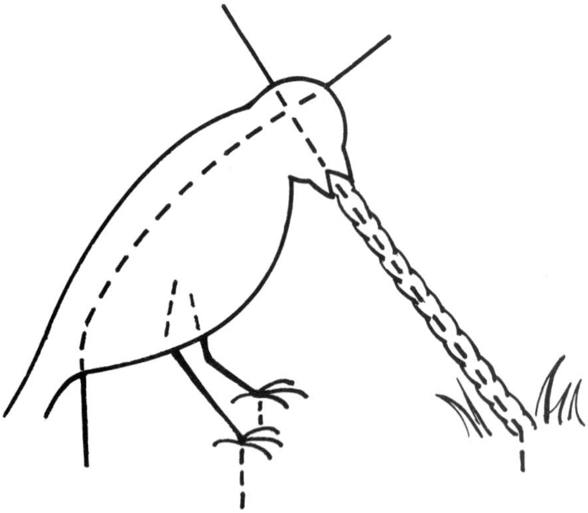

Figure 8.12 Fixing a worm in a bird's throat

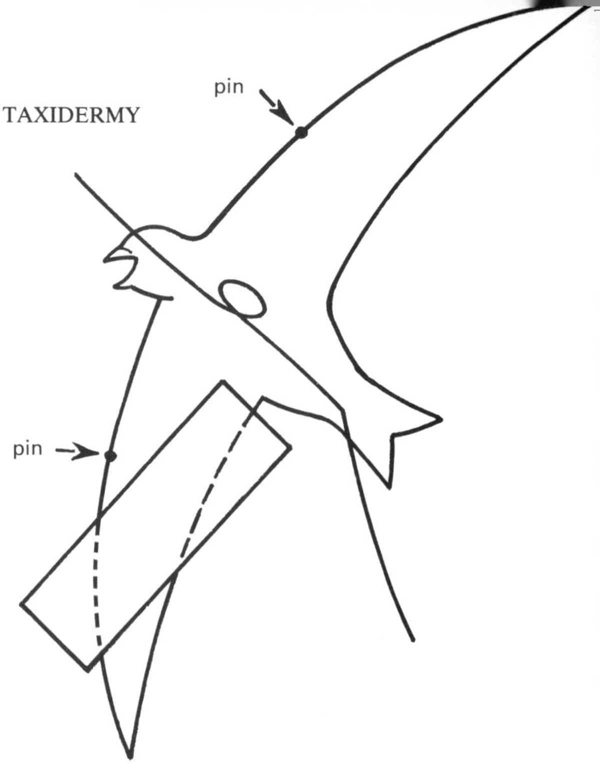

Figure 8.13 Inserting a wire loop into the specimen

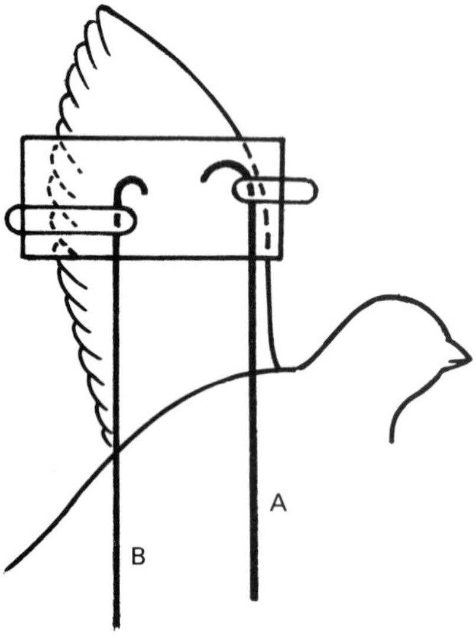

Figure 8.14 Pinning the primaries

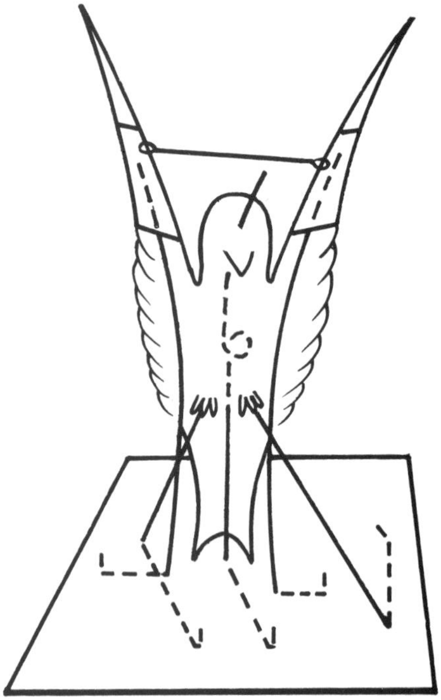

Figure 8.15 Clamping the wings in the required position

One could have removed the body organs completely before inserting the wire. This allows sexing, and assists with the freeze-drying process, as much of the water content is removed with these organs. The remaining space is packed with cotton wool, and stitched. The bird is placed on cardboard of a suitable size, and the abdomen end of the wire secured through it. The wings are spread out and held by a pin in the thumb area, to allow cardboard strips to be placed over the primaries, which are secured by pinning (see figure 8.14). The legs should now be adjusted to their required position, and the head twisted into the desired position.

I find in the case of swallows, martins and swifts, it is more interesting to have the head twisted slightly to one side, and the mouth open, to show detail. It can be kept open until frozen, by placing a small piece of cork in the mouth, held in place by a pin being driven in under the throat. Once the specimen is frozen, remove cardboard, and check that all feathering is correct, then re-secure it, this being done at the deep freezer. This method is suitable for some of the positions of the birds mentioned, and for plaque type display, but not for a great many species.

Before we move on to other flying birds, it should be noted that if wires are to be invisible, then the bird can have them removed, and simply be stuck onto a glass background containing a wire fork glued into place earlier. Another simple method is to fold the wire in half and push both ends through the abdomen, from the bird's interior, spacing them an inch apart. When they are anchored to the back of a case, perhaps on a block of wood, they are completely hidden by the bird's wings. The angle of the bird's flight is adjusted, once fixed to a twig or plaque, by twisting the wire, not the specimen.

Advanced methods

The flying methods dealt with so far have been simple, requiring the minimum of wiring, and should be tried out before becoming more ambitious. The next method, which is suitable for all small birds, can be very trying on one's patience.

The head and abdomen wire containing the loop is inserted, as with the previous specimen. Two long, light wires are inserted, one to each leg, and locked off, as explained in the section on simple mounts. The body wire is mounted onto a cardboard base and secured, when the specimen is at least two inches clear of it at its nearest point.

The angle of the bird is then adjusted, and that of the legs. The leg wires are now anchored to steady the bird as far as possible. One of the wings is now raised, and another wire, which has been anchored to the cardboard, is needed to support the wing from the underside. Clamp the wing and wire together with a cigarette packet and paperclips. Do the same to the other wing (see figure 8.15).

It is now possible to ease the strain on the wing wires by tying the wings together with cotton, using the paperclips as tying off posts. This may cause the wings to twist in an underside manner. To correct or prevent this, another wire per wing is used. This supports the rear of the wing, as in figure 8.14.

The head and neck are now adjusted, and then the tail spread and held with cardboard and more paperclips. The bill is next, and may be either open or shut. Then, finally, the eyes are adjusted. Once frozen, all feathers should be checked and corrections made if necessary. All angles of a bird's upward stroke can be covered by this method.

Figure 8.16 Angle of wire through a bird in a flying position with the wings on the downward beat

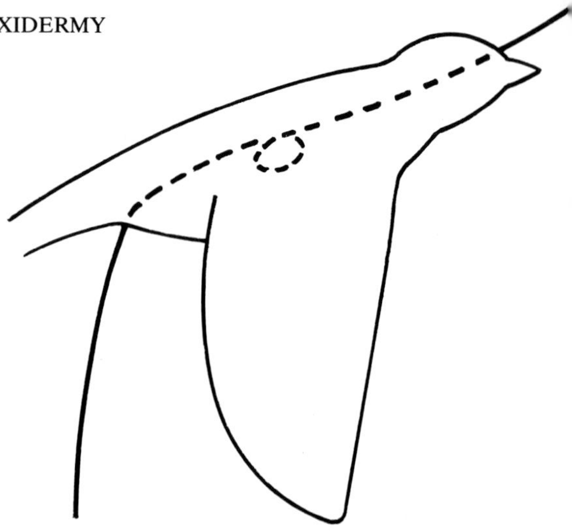

Figure 8.17 Side profile of bird on downward beat

Birds required with the downstroke of the wing are easier to do. The main difference to the wiring is that of the forward wing wires. Using thin sharpened wires, I drive them first into the fleshy part of the wing, then on, completely through the body, to anchor on the cardboard below the other side (see figures 8.16 and 8.17). The wings are then clamped onto them with cardboard and paperclips. The height and angle can be adjusted with the use of plasticine or cotton wool.

When completely freeze-dried, I do not pull these wires out, but cut them off, leaving an added strengthener inside the bird. Once a number of specimens have been attempted, this idea of internal wing wiring should be carried out on birds with the wing in the raised position too, for added strength.

I would like to add, however, that I have never had a bird break its wing with either method. To my experience, they are a far tougher and superior model to that of a classical mounted specimen. If a number of similar type and sized birds are to be done, I have found that balsa wood shaped to the bird's wing shape and mounted on a cardboard base, can speed the production of these birds.

Freeze-dried bird organs

Bird's sexual organs are hidden within the bird's body. I have done specimens with these organs uncovered, and freeze-dried. They come out well, and if set in a block of clear acrylic, they are ideal for teaching in colleges and schools. Many other delicate parts can be displayed in this manner.

FREEZE-DRIED REPTILES

Reptiles range farther from water, because they have a water retaining pelt. That is a known fact, and possibly significant for freeze-drying purposes. We will start with snakes, an example of which is seen in figure 8.18.

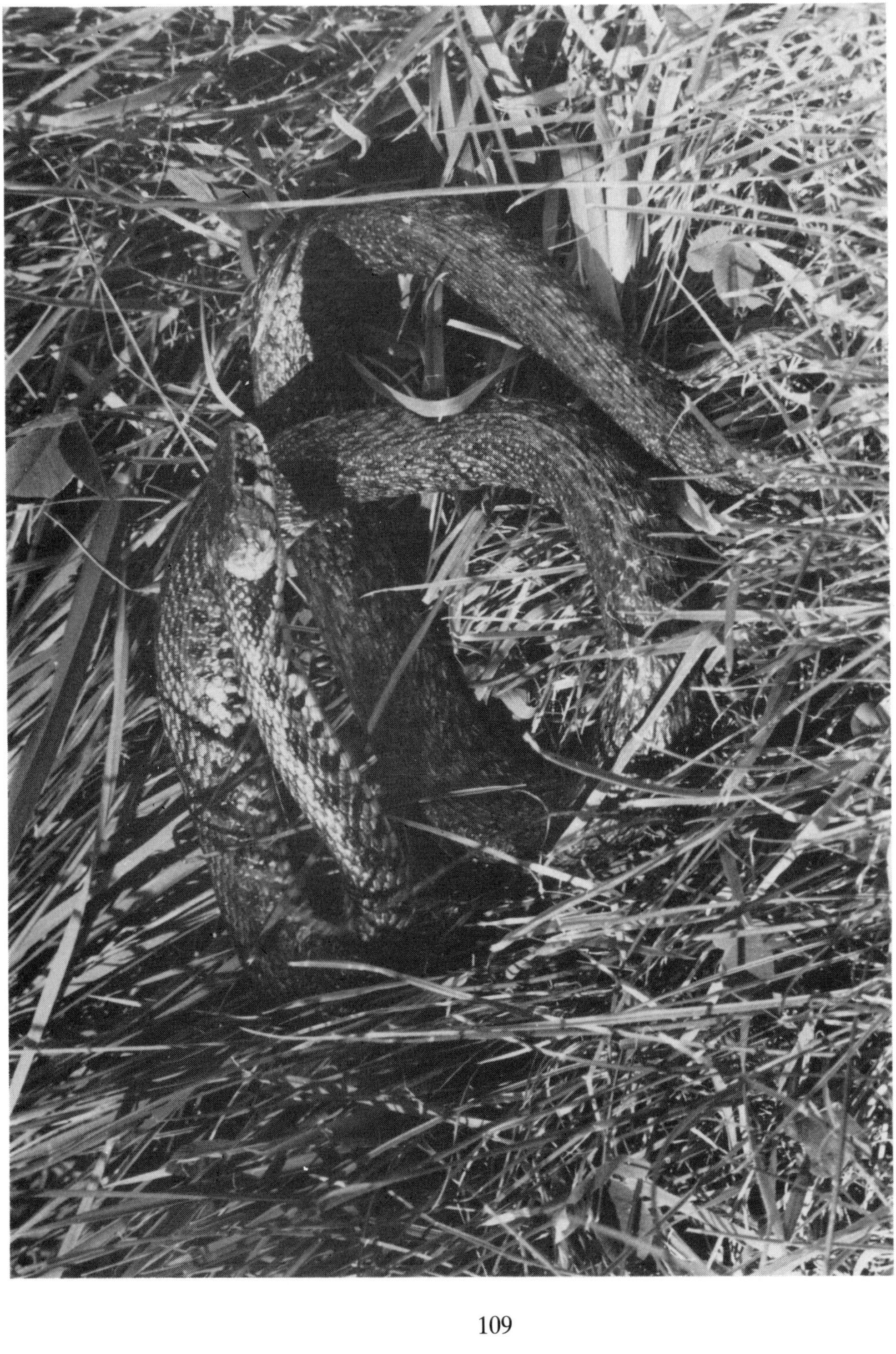

Figure 8.18 Grass snake, freeze-dried

Snakes

This is a large family, and most of the snakes in Britain to reach taxidermists are not wild, but more likely to have been in some form of capitivity, such as zoos, wildlife parks, or in private collections. They could be rather fat, which would make them unsuitable, at present, for normal mounting. However, this is the exception, rather than the rule.

I have set up a few hundred snakes, ranging from all parts of the world, some being venomous, and some harmless. My remarks are based on this background.

Condition

The snake must be in prime condition, particularly the skin. If it is near the shedding time, the skin is loose. On freeze-drying, this dry outer skin becomes opaque, hiding the true colours below. If this skin is removed after freeze-drying, the colour will be revealed. The texture of the weak underlying skin will not be. It takes a little time in the air for these scales to become hard, and useful. The skin under the opaque film is eel-like, and without good scale definition.

Observation

It pays to see some living snakes. Recently, at Leicester, I saw some local club specimens at the Entomologist's Fair. It was hard to believe the colour was natural in some, as it was so brilliant and harsh. They looked completely unnatural in their livid colours; their condition radiated from them. Personal contact with good healthy specimens is life blood to any serious taxidermist.

Many snakes have camouflage, even the eye is camouflaged in some. Unfortunately we are let down here by the eye producers, and there is not a great deal we can do about it, other than complain at every opportunity and challenge their skill. For those who are perfectionists, careful application of nail varnishes, and combinations of them, can help fill this present gap, to some extent.

Preparation

Now to work. If a snake has had a meal before death, then one should see the body lines distorted. Check the size of the bulge and then remove it via the mouth. The lump can be replaced with a wax replica, or better still, one shaped from balsa wood. This should be placed in the original position of the one removed, if required. The danger of leaving the original 'lump' is that it could well be a tame mouse, containing unwelcome fat, which would give the specimen a greasy area later on in its 'life'.

The snake is laid on its back, and a series of holes made, with a darning needle, about one inch apart for a grass snake. If it has a greater girth, then one should do a double jabbing across its width. Continue past the vent and to the end of its tail.

Remove the eye, noting it is necessary to cut away the scale protecting it with scissors. Insert a little cotton wool packing and position the glass eye. **Extreme care should be taken on poisonous varieties,** as even the moisture in the mouth of some can attack your system, but more on that later. No wiring is needed. If one visualises the snake on a rock, it is necessary to prepare that first. Lay the snake on it, and hold it gently in position with pins.

Figure 8.19 Chameleon, using freeze-dried techniques

Positioning

The head is propped up with plasticine until frozen. If I do a snake in a striking position, then I do not put any needle holes in the visible area, relying on the other holes to do the job, and perhaps an open mouth. Freeze and check the snake has not moved. Remove plasticine but not pins. The snake and stand or base must be freeze-dried together, otherwise the snake may alter its position. This is again true of a snake set on plain cardboard.

If the snake to be set up is in a very collapsed state, as some tend to be, an injection of water or air into its bladder region can improve it. I prefer the water.

Snakes such as cobra and rattlesnake, people expect doing the dramatic; namely hood up and fangs ready to strike. This type of posture needs a wire pushed down the snake's body, and out through the base, in the area of the raised body only. The fangs can be sprung forward into the strike position by careful use of the forceps, and retained in position by use of a cork, suitably wedged. Springing these fangs or hollow teeth forward can put pressure on the poison sacs, releasing venom. It is also extremely easy to get hooked up in a snake's mouth: **a poisonous one could kill you.**

Do not think a dead snake cannot bite you. It may be dead, but its venom is not. I once had my fingers trapped in a large python's mouth, while pushing 'balsa bombs' down it. The teeth, that point down its throat, hooked me, and in the shambles that followed, the snake slid off the work bench. The teeth opened my fingers like razor blades.

One cannot be too careful, even to the point of finding out if there are any antitoxins available at your nearest hospital. Find out what first-aid measures are available before you start, because seconds are important. I know because I have also been bitten by a live one.

In a setting

If a snake is required in a setting and needs to be wired to it, there are two ways, after it has been freeze-dried.

Firstly, mark out where the snake intends to lie. Then drive sharpened spikes into the board. These should be sharp at both ends. Make sure that none of them are higher than two thirds of the snake's body height. Then press the snake onto these. It will hold very well, even to a fair amount of abuse.

Secondly, a wire can be passed into the snake's underside, and out again a few inches along. The two exposed ends can anchor the snake. If two wires are used, the snake is absolutely rigid. Avoid the tail. This is the snake's weaker area, and has very little flesh.

Freeze-dried slow-worms

Slow-worms are the only lizards that need pricking on the underside, similar to snakes. There are two varieties, the normal common, and the rarer blue spotted form.

On freeze-drying, the spots will turn into colourless patches. This can be rectified by a nail varnish of suitable colour, and careful application. They are unsuitable for wiring, but can be spiked into settings, or stuck with a suitable glue, or a combination of both. The eye is 2 mm, and there is no special problem placing them in position.

Figure 8.20 Gerbil and youngsters, freeze-dried

Lizards

These can be split into two groups for freeze-dried work: medium and small. All British species are classed as small. These have black 2 mm eyes inserted, and are set up as for the newt. If required to be wired, then the body is better used, passing a loop of wire down the chest and coming out the vent, as described for snakes. The legs are also fine for wiring, and better stances can be made easier this way. Medium lizards can be wired the same as freeze-dried mice. A specimen three to four feet long can be done quite easily in the chamber, by either spiralling it on a false rock, or merely by curling its tail and body.

Crocodiles and alligators

These reptiles, if small, present no problems. Medium sized ones can be set up and frozen. Then a circle of scales removed from base of tail, and the tail cut through. The tail is then freeze-dried as a separate item. When completed, wires are driven into the tail, glued, and the tail pressed back into the original position. Any cavities are filled with beeswax or household filler, and the scales replaced with Bostik type glue. Large items are still better done by hand.

FREEZE-DRIED AMPHIBIA

Newts

The skin condition is very important. If they are not in prime condition then their shedding effect can make them look rough and faded. The two smaller British newts are too small for eye sizes. The crested, however, present no such snag.

They can be pinned down onto cardboard making sure that the skin remains unbroken. The cardboard needs a layer of muslin over it, to prevent a fading of the belly colours.

Females come out better than males as, once clear of water, the crest lies flat on the male's back. Setting in acrylic, or clear plastic, helps the colour and texture. It also helps to allow a very fragile specimen to be handled well. The wiring of newts is impractical, except for the larger crested.

Frogs

Again, the specimen must be in absolutely first class condition. The skin goes off so quickly, unlike toads. Frogs living in ponds have a weaker skin compared to one toughened up by living in undergrowth. The frog's eye is removed and a glass one inserted. The eye needs to be 'sprung', as frogs, in life, have eyes protruding high above the head.

Positioning

First it needs pinning onto cardboard. I get them roughly into position, then pin the hind legs, through the webbing. The head is held by plasticine, both holding it up and pressing it back on its haunches at the same time.

The eye now has a pin inserted under it which is levered slightly downwards; this pushes the eye upwards. Some plasticine added as a blob on the pin's end, assists, or maintains, this

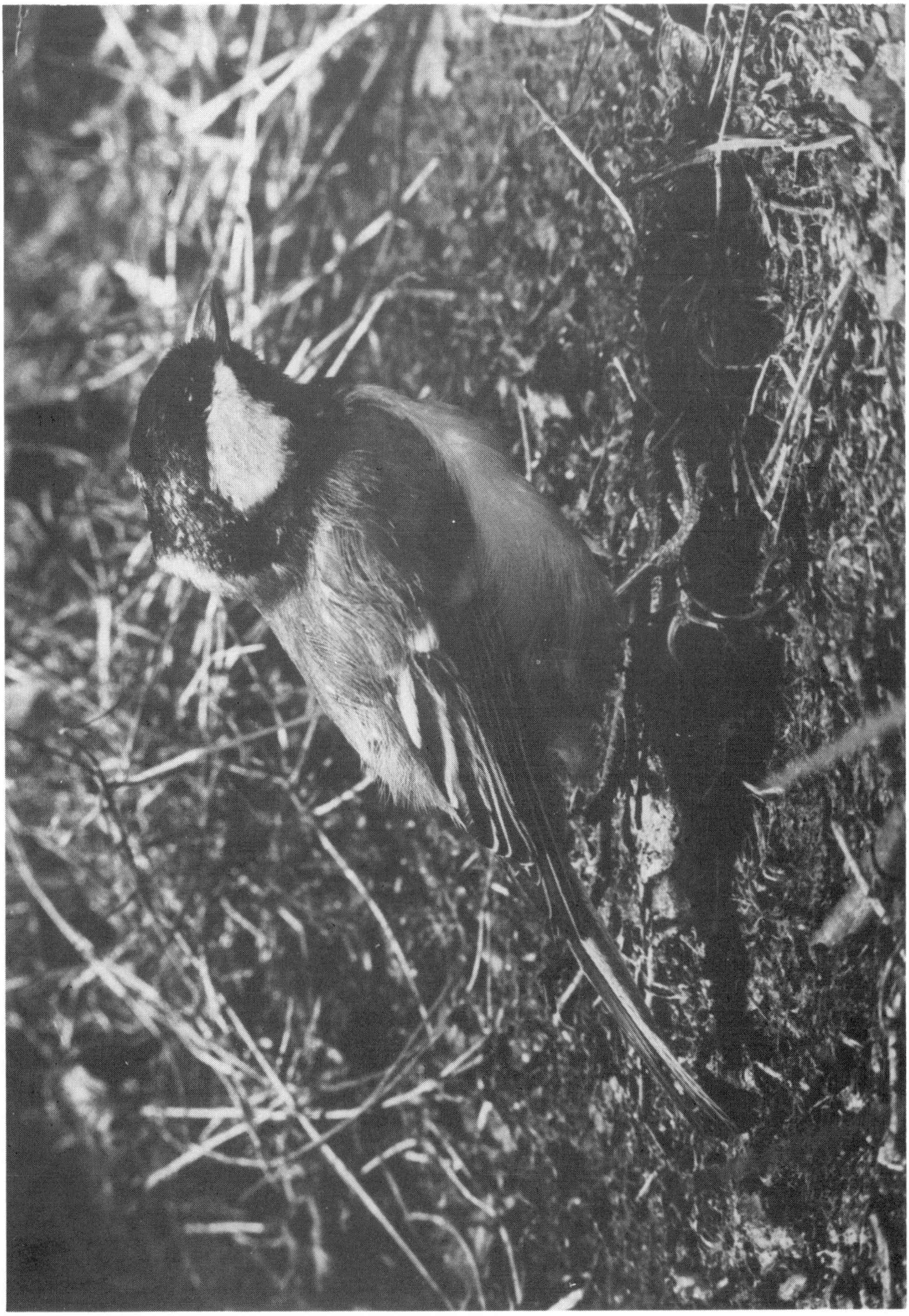

Figure 8.21 Great tit, freeze-dried

pressure. They are frozen into position, and the plasticine and pins removed. Any marks can be removed by the heat of one's fingers, and refrozen. For frogs, I cover the cardboard with a plastic bag, but remove them completely from it before freeze-drying. One can also leave the original eye in, giving it the same treatment as above, but replacing it with a glass eye after 'drying', using beeswax filling.

Toads: combination

Toads are done in a similar manner. Both of these creatures are the exception to the rule in combination work, and can be set up to better advantage by doing them as a unit in one go, the wrists of the forelegs being tied around the female's neck until frozen. The unit welds itself together, into one. Make certain the thumbs are in the correct position. Frogs are to be found mating a few days either side of March 17th and toads usually March 26th.

Doing research work into the age grouping of female toads on one site, I came across a male frog on one's back. I thought, even if he was short sighted, the mildly poisonous skin would have upset him. This is mentioned for a reason. Although the taxidermist sees many things, he can only record 'type', and type that the public expect to see. For example, the blackbird, wings down, tail up, on a post; even its silhouette can be recognised. But not one with its leg cocked over its wing, scratching its head. These are our boundaries, which we should try to enlarge; common behaviour, not the frog which is like something out of Wind-in-the-Willows, or would be if they produced it today. For wiring of the frog see the reptile section.

Edible frogs

European edible frogs differ from many other frogs, as the male is capable of 'puffing his cheeks', out when calling. It is possible to blow these up with either water or air. Both will be successful. The skin itself goes opaque, whereas in the live frog, one can see through it. I found the way to achieve a similar likeness was to use the acrylic plastic. Two firms in Leeds sell this product, Turner Research and Whetherby. They also sell primary colours to be added, and any shade can be made.

I make a cast from using a grape of suitable size, set it in a clear acrylic, then remove grape when set. I then wash out, and add a very fine layer of beeswax. The mould is then made. Mix the correct shade and pour in. Allow to set, then break away from outer shell. Trim end for check and fix with a suitable adhesive.

I used the same method in key rings for wine merchants. The short stalk is retained in the acrylic, and it is impossible to tell if they are real, if coloured correctly. Edibles need the green colour restored to the head by oil paint.

Frogs and toads just out of the tadpole stage can easily be freeze-dried. Frog-spawn and the like go very fragile and opaque, but when set into acrylic, return to their semi-transparency, and jelly-like appearance.

Natterjack Toads hold their colours quite well. **Frogs**, I find, have a dry appearance. I give them a coat of artist's varnish. This is thinner than the normal type, and is readily removed with petrol (see figure 8.22). This coat gives that damp look and brings the markings out better.

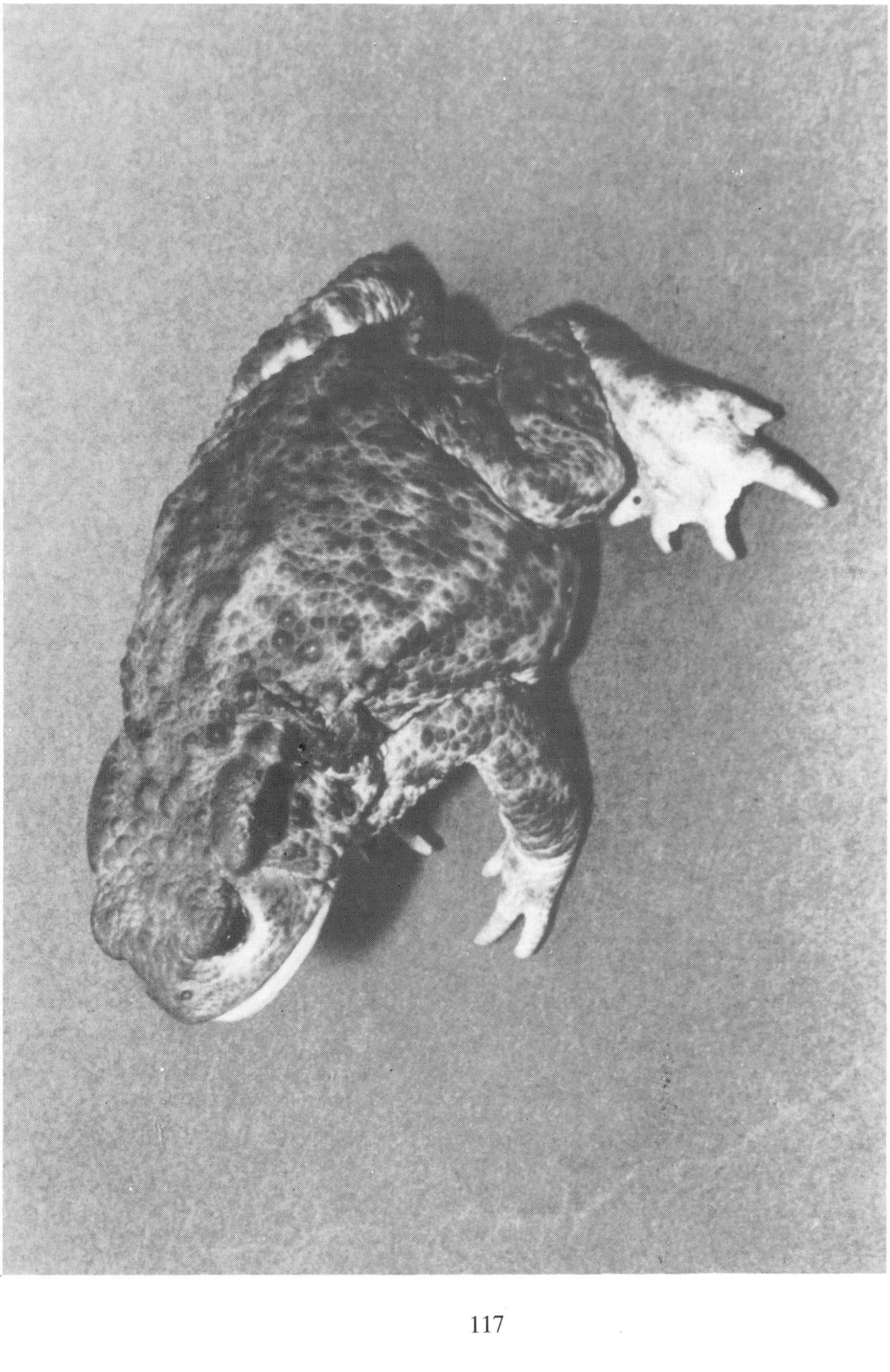

Figure 8.22 Common toad, female, freeze-dried

FREEZE-DRIED BATS

These specimens come in many shapes and sizes, but for the purposes of the freeze-dried approach, I reduce them to big eared and short eared types.

Short eared types present no more trouble than a mouse, and can be processed faster. It is only their sheer scarcity that makes me so meticulous with them. I have a soft spot for these maligned, gentle creatures, that has taken me many miles underground, on their behalf, and on behalf of their conservation. The eye size is 2 mm black, and is extremely difficult to insert.

Long eared varieties present more of a problem. The delicate ears can be approached in two ways. If the specimen is frozen up in the normal way, the removal of them to the EF2, even if only a few feet, can affect the ears. This is due to their surface area, in relation to their bulk, or cold retaining powers. If the ears have had no special treatment, then, when placed in the EF2, 24 hours should elapse before freeze-drying commences, and then only if the ear size and shape are satisfactory. Otherwise shrinkage and distortion takes place.

Another approach is to place a pin vertically in the ear, and fill it with plaster of Paris. The pin takes the weight and, as a unit, they are less prone to shrinkage, or damage. On completion, this protective layer is removed.

Flying specimens

I adopt the method used for flying birds, such as swifts and martins, for flying specimens of bats. Pins, however, should not be used, as they are too blunt, and will damage the delicate membrane of the wings. I use either needles or entomologist's pins for this purpose. The tail and legs also need pinning. The tail, spread, helps with identification for those inspecting the specimen.

If more ambitious specimens are required, then the methods for birds flying upstroke or downstroke can be used. In such flight patterns, the wings become baggy at times. Inserts of shaped balsa wood, between sections of the membrane, can achieve some amazing results.

Hibernating bats present no problem. The legs are anchored onto a twig, as previously explained. If the membrane is very prominent, such as the Horseshoe Bat, then a stitch of cotton to hold the wings together and stretch the membrane more convincingly, is a simple matter. I must stress at this point, that these creatures must be seen doing this, as a great deal of bad work exists, and 'mock-ups' by photographers. I mention this because I know this range fairly well, by keeping some species from furless 'pups', to establishing new successful colonies. **Observation is therefore essential to producing an accurate specimen.**

Figure 8.23 Wood mouse and young, freeze-dried; note the split ear caused by fighting other mice earlier in her life

	Number of days taken		
Species	Fully Freeze-dried	Freeze-dried but organs removed	Fully combined
SMALL BIRDS	32		
THRUSH SIZED	35		
NIGHTJAR	38*		
REDSHANK	50	27	
WATER RAIL	38	13	
GREEN WOODPECKER	40	25	
DIPPER	47		
GOLDEN PLOVER		37	
LAPWING		37	
WOODCOCK			12
SWIFT (FLYING)			
LITTLE GREBE			
TAWNY OWL			6
TERN CHICKS	30		
PHEASANT CHICKS	30		
DOVES NOT RING	42	27	10
MICE	35–40		
MOLE	76–108		
SHREWS	35–40		
STOAT		54–64	13
WEASEL		46	11
BLACK RAT		40	21
BROWN RAT	small 51	35–41	23
RABBIT			17
HARE			13
FAWN		53–68	
LION CUB		99	
HEDGEHOG		40	22
COYPU			28
BADGER CUB		62	
POLECAT		51	20
GREY SQUIRREL			11
RED SQUIRREL			11
DUBENTON'S BAT	33		
LONG EARED BAT	45		
NOCTULE BAT	38		
FOX CUB		84	21
PLATYPUS		30*	
LEVERET		24	

BLACK RAT SNAKE 7ft	72*		
CORNSNAKE 6ft	72*		
GOPER SNAKE	35		
DESERT IGUANA	58*		
CHAMELEON	28		
TORTOISE	106		
ADDER	32–34		
NEWTS	14–17		
EDIBLE FROGS	54–59		
COMMON FROGS	33–35		
COMMON TOAD	33–35		
NATTERJACK TOAD	33		
GIRDLED LIZARD	57*		
CATERPILLARS	8		
DEATH HEAD MOTHS	15		
SPIDERS LARGE BRITISH	8		

*** Indicates fewer than six examples processed.**

Figure 8.24 Tabulation of drying times

EF2 DRYING TIMES FOR COMMERCIAL USE OR CAPACITY LOADS

The Edwards Company quote times for various specimens using their appliance. These times are, of course, very accurate, but it should be noted that they apply only when there is a single specimen in the chamber. When one considers the cost of the machinery, labour, the ever rising cost of electricity, and wear and tear, these specimens done individually are expensive.

The EF2 is a tough model, and a good example of British reliability and engineering at its best. I have the longest running appliance in this range. It has only ever ceased operation for defrost, oil changes, and the occasional replacement components. One of mine is well over ten years old and has had no major replacement parts changed, other than the occasional motor. I mention this to show that heavy commercial loads are taken with ease by this workhorse.

My times are taken, as I have mentioned earlier, from more than five thousand specimens of various types. When one loads the chamber to capacity, it is natural to put the tougher specimens below. By tougher, I mean specimens which have no delicate parts, such as moles, stoats, water voles, and the like. As specimens lose weight they are progressively moved higher in the chamber; the higher up they are, the quicker is the drying process. I would think the very long mole times are mainly due to these items remaining low down in the chamber, and having a pelt that is reluctant to part with its moisture.

The specimen times are of specimens done in large quantities, and a few just for sheer curiosity value. The latter are marked with an asterisk if less than six have been so processed.

CHAPTER 9

COMBINED TAXIDERMY

Combined taxidermy is the mixture, in varying degrees, of old classical taxidermy and freeze-dried work. At one end of the scale, it consists of removing the body organs and introducing a full wiring structure, as used in classical work. At the other end of the scale, a large mammal, such as a hare, can have a full manikin (or false body), built-up head in the traditional manner, and ears reinforced by card, or a similar material. If anyone is puzzled as to why such lengths are needed, then I shall name the reasons as I see them today.

Reasons for combined taxidermy

A large creature, such as a hare, could occupy the EF2 chamber for the better part of a year if merely freeze-dried. The organs, being so large, would not allow for a natural appearance. That size of body needs a solid wiring structure. To do it this way reduces chamber time to approximately 13 days.

Why call it combined taxidermy, and not just taxidermy? Classical taxidermy has existed for many years, and has a completely different approach. The rules are the same, as I see them:

1. It must look natural when completed;

2. It must stay natural and not distort in any way.

The methods of classical work are directed to this end. They are as different as sailing ships are to our present day vessels. Combined taxidermy is another approach to creating preserved and mounted specimens. It is more expensive, but they have a better finish to them, and a longer life. Specimens that have defied the best efforts of taxidermists, now become more possible, and the taxidermist's range has multiplied many times.

Freeze-dried and combined taxidermy specimens, are best produced by the already existing taxidermist, whose background knowledge is essential to this work. Many taxidermists I know feel it may take the skill out of the profession and put their jobs at risk. Nothing is further from the truth; as the bakers say, it is as hard to produce a flawless loaf, as it is a wedding cake. The finest taxidermists I know seek to do the perfect specimen, in varying positions and postures. He does this, I believe, because he is an artist, naturalist (normally a conservationist too), and technician, rolled into one. He seeks to set up specimens that are 'ambassadors' for their species, not grotesque gargoyles.

COMBINED TAXIDERMY: BIRDS

As we have seen, many British birds can be covered fairly well by freeze-drying. If a bird suffers from fat, such as the wader family, this must be removed. It is fortunate that it exists

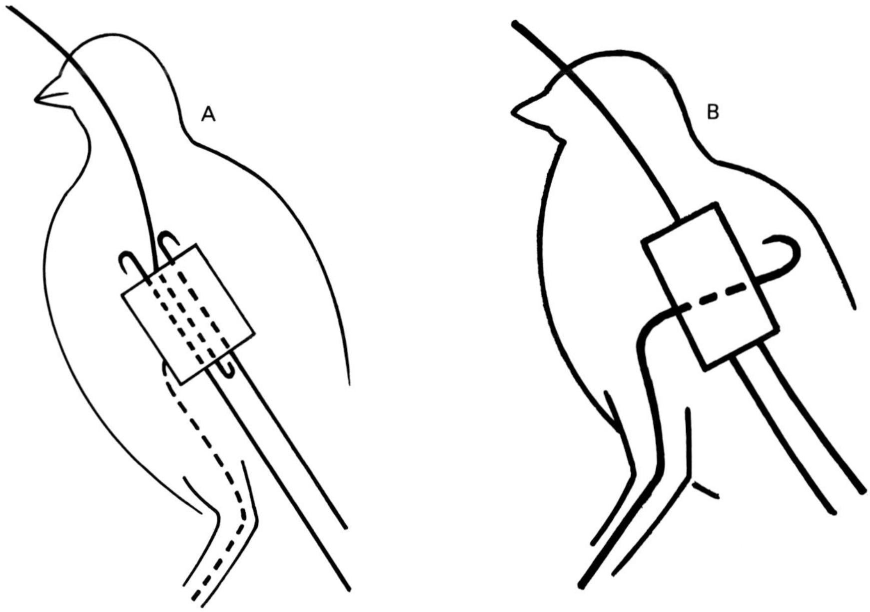

Figure 9.1 Anchoring wires in the body

mainly in the 'belly' region. The bird is laid on its back, after removing the eyes, as for freeze-drying birds. A cut is made from the rib-cage to the vent. The body organs are removed first. I find that small sections of newspaper, laid over the vent and tail feathers, make an ideal area to deposit them, until all are cleared. Scissors and blunt nosed forceps are used to remove them. Remove all moisture and fat from body cavity, using balls of absorbent paper, and protect feathers with a circle of cotton wool.

The head wire is driven in via the skull, as fully detailed in the bird freeze-drying method. The difference here is that a cork is attached and anchored to it, when it is through the body cavity as in figure 9.1. Two light tail wires follow, and the leg wires, again, are driven up the side of the foot and out into the cavity area. Care must be taken to see that the leg wires lie in the correct position for the final pose; then anchored off in the cork.

The cork can then be pulled deeper into the body cavity, by the head wire. The space left by organ removal is filled with cotton wool, and both abdominal wall and skin stitched up (see figures 9.2 and 9.3). The bird now has a good wiring system, essential for 'leggy' wader type birds, as the frame carries the weight, not the legs. Proceed in the normal manner described for freeze-dried birds. The times set in the chart (figure 8.24), show that freeze-drying periods are reduced approximately by half.

Dove-like birds

Every taxidermist knows the problem of producing doves. A delicate, tender skin, feathers coming away for no apparent reason, and the often 'tatty' results. If these birds are set up in the classic manner, and are treated for ten days in EF2, then the smart appearance of these birds is excellent.

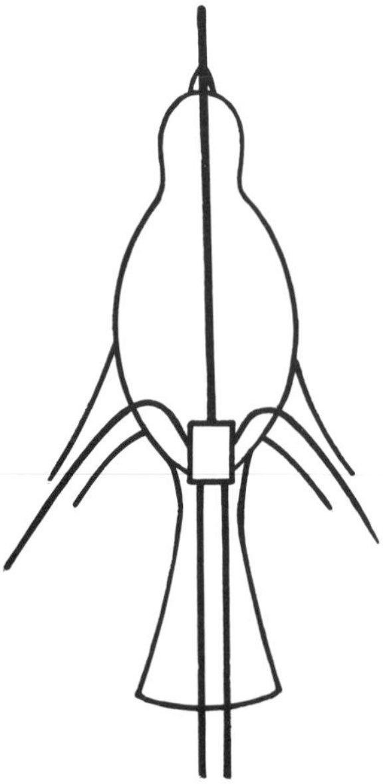

Figure 9.2 The cork may now be pulled towards the head using the head wire . . . .

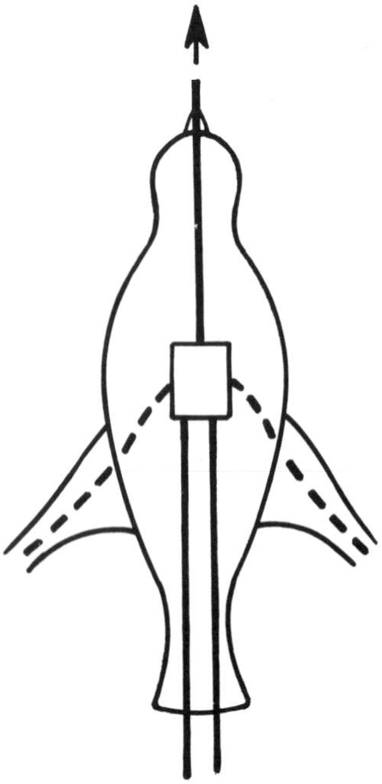

Figure 9.3 This results in the strong wiring system shown here

Heavy legged birds

A number of land type birds have really heavy fleshy legs. If one is considering doing a specimen, with a 'threshed skeleton', the legs are removed anyway. These legs can have their tendons drawn, and temporary wire inserted to keep their shape. The legs are then freeze-dried, and added to the manikin when done. With ostriches and large birds, the lower scaly leg would have to be cut, done in two halves, and repaired later. Museums with an EF6 could do them in one go. The finished specimen is well worth the trouble, as the size is truly recorded. Colour, as with classic birds, would have to be added.

Birds with combs

A number of these birds, such as jungle fowl, cockerels, and birds with fleshy warts or proboscises, like turkeys, are too large for the chamber, but otherwise are perfect subjects. My method of overcoming this is to skin down the bird in the classic manner, then cut the neck completely off. The rest of the skin should then be removed to cold storage. The head and neck are mounted on a wire and tow neck, and eyes added. This is frozen up and freeze-dried.

When completed, a normal manikin is made, including the now finished head and neck. The bird is now mounted in the traditional or classic way, and the neck is joined by stitching; colour is added to the comb and like parts. Two excellent examples of these are a pair of jungle fowl set up by myself, for the School Loan Service at Leeds City Museum.

Birds with overall head and neck measurements over 15½ inches (39.5 cm), can also be done. This is achieved by carefully picking a suitable resting posture, or by cutting higher up the neck. If this is done, it would be far more difficult to hide the stitch marks, and joining line. A useful tip here is that if this is to be tried, when frozen, and ready for the EF2, hold the edge of the neck skin in your fingers, until thawed. The item is then put into a running EF2 and vacuumed immediately. The unfrozen skin, and surrounding area, will not become freeze-dried.

This area needs to be preserved with borax, when completing the whole specimen. It will allow the join to lie better, and become less apparent. Needless to say, if the specimen is not going to be assembled immediately the head and part neck are removed from the drying chamber, it should be stored in a plastic sealed bag in deep freeze, where it should not be left for weeks, or breakdown can occur.

Bird tongues

Bird tongues can be removed and freeze-dried. These, added to normal classic work, would in fact change it to combined work. They are added by the use of beeswax to seal the throat, and make a bed for the tongue to be pressed into. It is simple, but can greatly enhance the finished product. Colour may or may not be added, depending mainly on the species concerned.

COMBINED TAXIDERMY – MAMMALS

Specimens below the size of a weasel are normally freeze-dried. If, however, they are pets or caged animals, then they will carry too much body fat. This must be removed, and dealt with as described below.

Removal of fat

The eyes are removed, plus the fatty tissue in the eye socket. The eye is filled with small cotton wool balls to fill eye socket, but leaving a depression for the eye. The mammal is laid on its back, and the fur carefully parted, from the sternum to the vent. Then the skin holding the fur is cut, and eased away from the body, as if one is starting a normal skin down. When this skin is loose, pack unworked areas with cotton wool. Cut abdominal wall, remove body organs and clean out, and moisten with absorbent paper. If fat exists, then most of it will have been removed with the organs. More will exist on the thighs of the hind legs, both at the front and back. This should also be removed.

Wiring

The main support wire can either be driven in from the front of the skull, into the lung cavity, or up through one of the nostrils. Then, via the base of the skull, into the lung cavity. Two corks fixed together as in figure 9.4 are linked to the main support wire and anchored, as in figure 9.5. These are to hold the leg wires.

The forelegs must be anchored first, and the wire frame pulled into the rib-cage. This allows the rear cork to be adjusted if necessary. Hind leg wires are pushed through the leg, and at the correct point of the abdominal wall, bearing in mind the final posture.

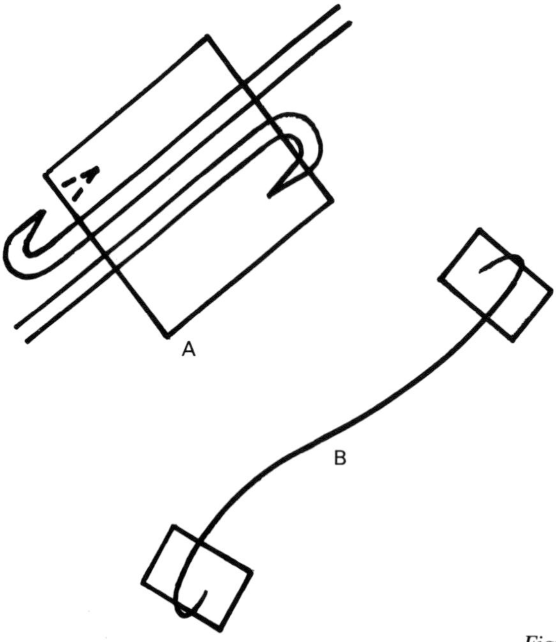

Figure 9.4 Fitting two corks together

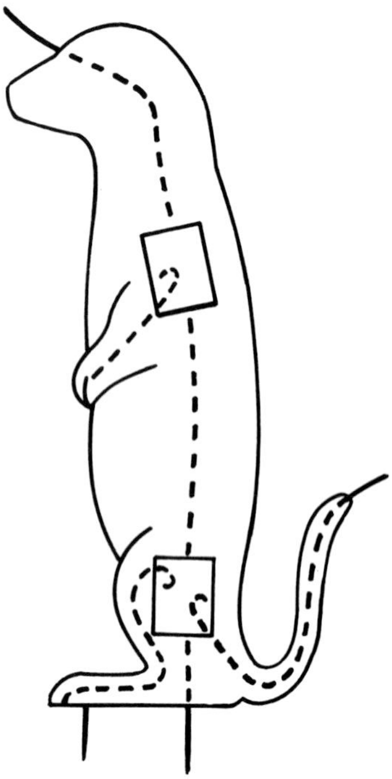

Figure 9.5 The corks linked to the main support wire

Cotton wool replaces organs and gives shape to the belly. Before stitching up the abdominal wall and skin, testicles made of cotton wool, if a male, can be put into place. A tail wire can be added to the rear cork, while the skin is open, if one wants a raised tail, or if this is considered desirable. This wire can be very light, as it supports very little weight. In rats I use only a short wire, an inch or two long, as it is almost impossible to drive a wire its full length.

The stance is corrected, and toes trapped into position by pins. The glass eyes are inserted and eyelids adjusted. The specimen is now frozen and processed through EF2. Any tips included in the freeze-drying section should be followed if appropriate.

Larger mammals

As we go on to larger sized creatures, such as squirrels, up to hare size, I prefer to use the method below. It has the advantage of freeze-drying the skin only, which makes for short chamber times, giving me all the freeze-dry advantages available, while allowing me to use my classic knowledge to the full. Any combination between the method already mentioned and the one about to be described, may be used. It is for the individual taxidermist considering an individual specimen, its condition, and so on, to decide.

Method

The specimen is skinned down in the normal way, and the skin parted from the body by finally cutting through the nostril cartilage. The skin is packed away in deep-freeze, along

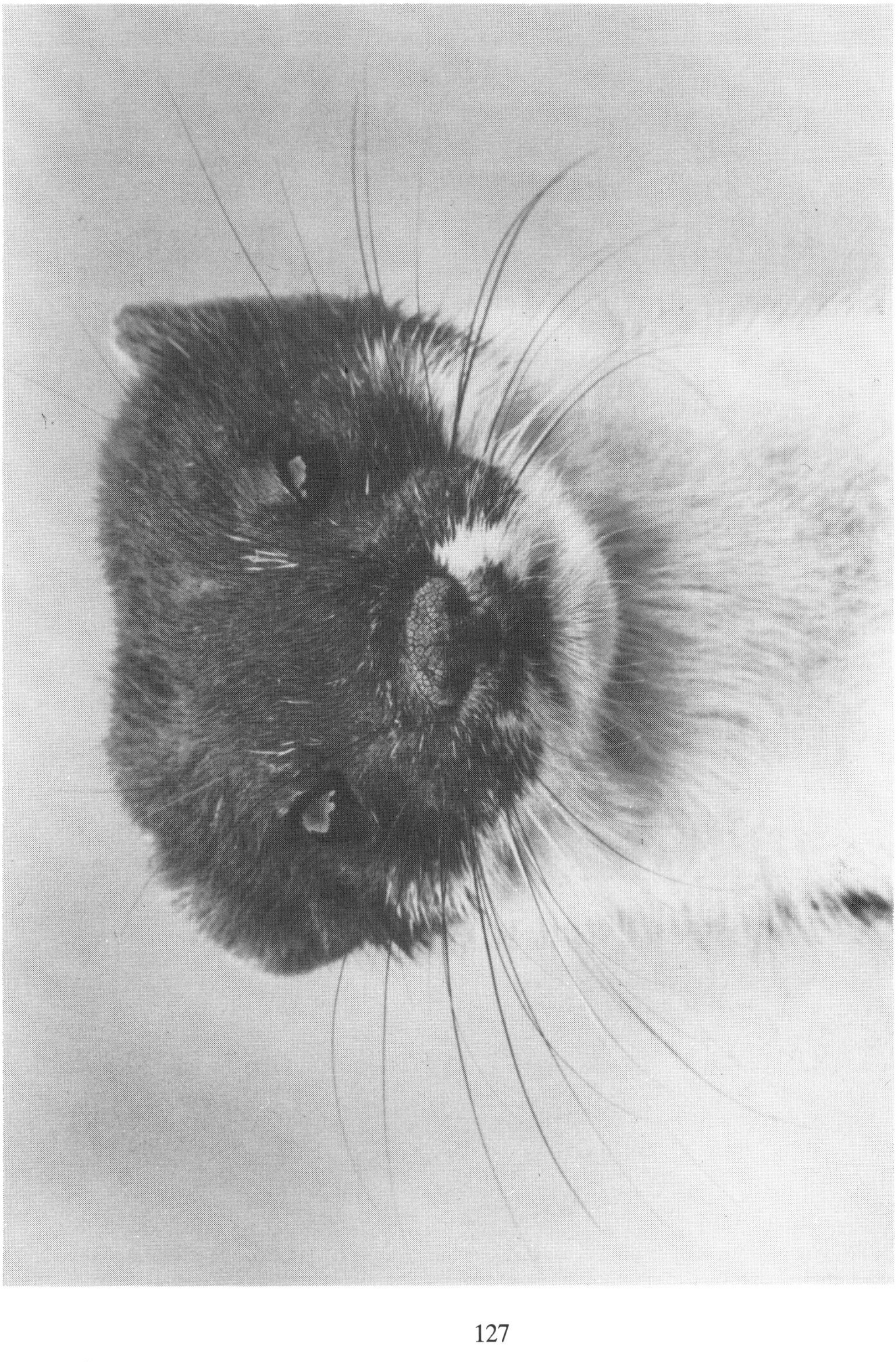

Figure 9.6 Stoat, a combined taxidermy specimen; note the quality of the muzzle

Figure 9.7 Muntjac fawns in combined taxidermy style

with any information relating to the skin and its condition. The head is now removed from the body, and either cooked to remove all flesh (in either saltwater or a borax solution), or it can be freeze-dried, as on its own it occupies very little chamber room.

A point in skinning down; I normally divide the legs at the junction of the knee, retaining this cleaned up bone with the skin. I know many taxidermists part the body at the ankle. I find a number of specimens I have seen failed to conceal this on assembly. Retaining this bone gives strength to the wire, and makes sure the lower leg length is correct. I personally think it makes for a more adjustable and stronger specimen, but again this is a personal choice.

The skin I trim, if possible, before freezing. This allows the skin to thaw more quickly and, if the specimen is long eared, like a hare and a rabbit, it allows the ears to be preserved chemically. This is done to protect that area of the skin while thawing, as the skin is very thin there.

This is done to the skull when freeze-dried, or in the case of the cooked one, when built up in a classic manner. It is ready to assemble the manikin or false body.

Manikin

The material for this is a personal choice. I use tow, or plumber's hemp for small bodies of squirrel or polecat size, and hay for rabbit or hare size. Photographs in this book show semi- and completed manikins. The legs are broader in width, than depth. These are built up with layers of tow or hay, and stitched into position (see figures 3.3 and 3.4). With larger manikins I used wire netting to reinforce them for overall strength.

Assembly

Assembly of the specimen is the same as classical taxidermy. The nose or snout of the creature has modelling clay packed inside and cotton wool on the outside, when set up, to retain shape. The ears have shaped cards inserted into them internally, if required, and modelling clay at their base to replace lost flesh in that area. The specimens are mounted on temporary cardboard stands for processing, with the eyelids pinned to prevent movement, and similar treatment to toes. Wire strengtheners can be added to the ears, externally. Then the specimen is frozen. The specimen, when frozen, must be checked to see that everything is in its desired position.

It is now ready for the appliance. I have included a series of detailed photographs of a coypu (figures 9.8 to 9.12), showing the tail, fore, and hind legs in close-up. The hind legs show scars received while living. The size, like that of the hare, was too large for the inner container of the chamber. Both were done by removing this completely, and continuing as normal. If the specimen lies against the metal coil, protect it by sandwiching cardboard between. I also reverse the specimen, halfway through the process, so the lower half also receives the advantage of the upper chamber. The best of this combined work easily surpasses the best of the classical form.

Part specimens

It is not necessary to do the whole specimen. Dovetailing with classic work can also be considered. Take, for instance, the tail of a coypu, done alone in the EF2 and mounted onto traditional work, as with the cockerel's head.

Figure 9.8 Combined taxidermy, using only the skin and tail of a coypu

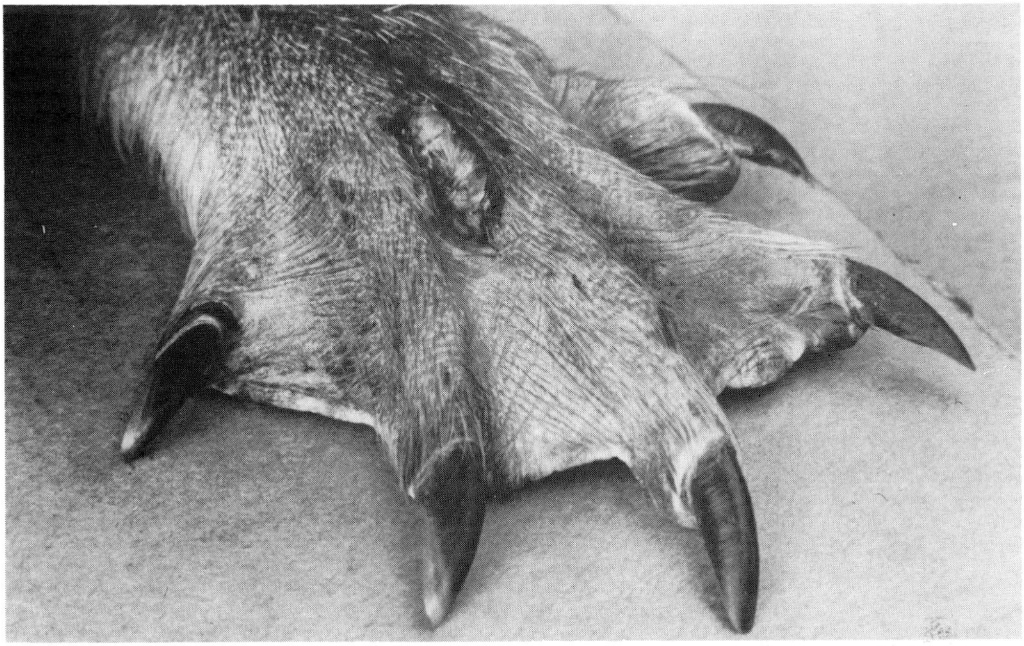

Figure 9.9 Hind leg of the coypu, showing no shrinkage or distortion; note the scar on the foot

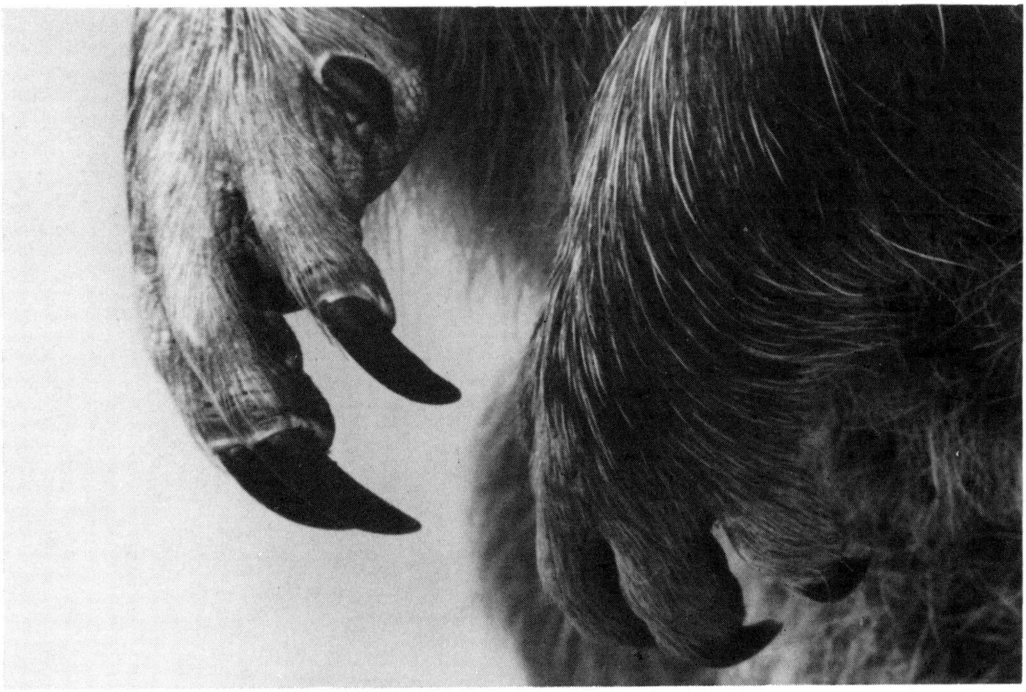

Figure 9.10 Forelegs of the coypu

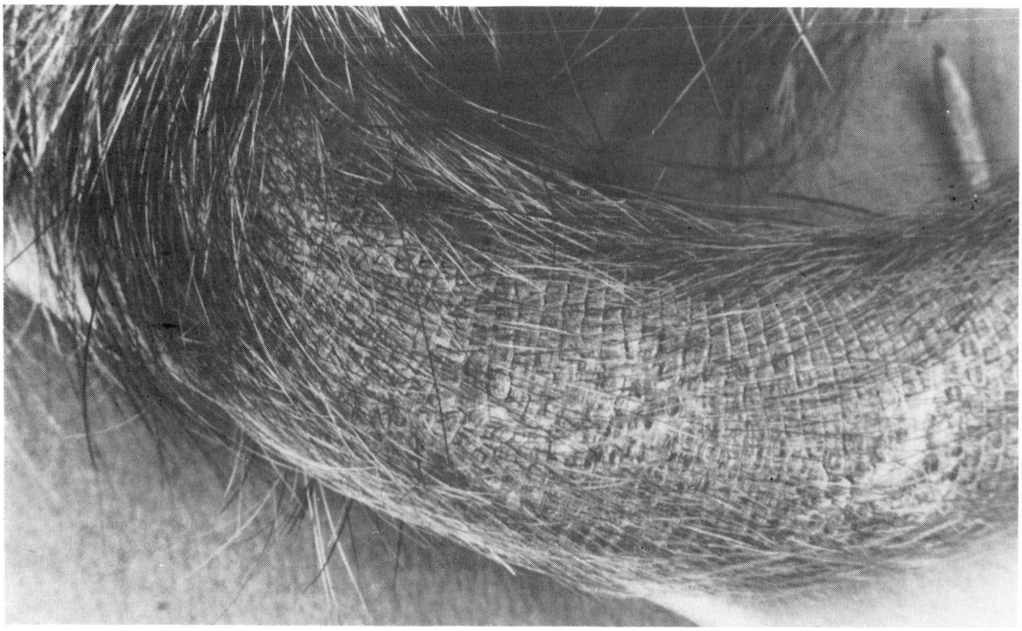

Figure 9.11 Tail, showing the perfection of freeze-drying techniques

Figure 9.12 Facial details of the coypu

Skulls can be done, allowing the detailed markings of the roof of the mouth to be seen. Tongues can also be done; shape when half frozen, then freeze and reshape to match jaw and finer finish. I have had some people say they are more prone to attack than chemically protected specimens. This is true to a point. There is no reason why the specimens dealt with above should not have their skins fully preserved, while they are skinned down.

During the auctions of the Great Britain Natural History Company, at Hampstead Town Hall, rats even gnawed the legs of rooks and crows of classical form. Against attacks like that, nothing is safe. I have no greater precaution for one type of specimen over another. A small piece of Vapona in a polythene bag with the specimen, and packed in boxes, should be enough. If in the open on display, regular checks should be made to all types of specimens.

EF2 TREATMENT OF PESTS

As we are mentioning pests, it would be as well to mention the freeze-drier as a great weapon against pests. If specimens are attacked, freeze them for 24 hours, then process for 24 to 48 hours. Nothing survives; even pests' eggs are freeze-dried. If the specimen was put immediately into the chamber without freezing, the beetle and larva would perish in the vacuum in an hour. This could be of use to a museum that may have limited freezer space, and a number of specimens affected. Once the larva and beetle were out of the way, then time has been made to destroy the eggs later. Vapona is an excellent guardian against unwanted pests, if tucked away in cases.

No museum should have insects or rodents running around the specimens. If they have, then they need experts in to deal with them. It is always possible to get a mouse into a building looking for winter quarters, or just being curious. I find a platform type mouse trap, set but unbaited, against a wall, will catch it. A few placed about a storage room is a must. One outbuilding I was asked to help out in ridding of mice, was overrun. I killed all of them in a month using only six traps, simply because wild mice do not like running across open spaces.

CHAPTER 10

GENERAL GUIDE TO TAXIDERMY LAW

The law changes from time to time. At the time of writing, it is going through a change in the British Isles. It is important that the taxidermist keeps up to date with the changing laws. Besides listing some addresses at the end of the chapter, where up-to-date information may be obtained, there are other local sources of information. Any gunshop, in any county, will supply a booklet on what can be shot, and when. It costs little. Police stations will also supply information, free of charge.

WILDLIFE AND COUNTRYSIDE ACT

The following points are intended as a guide to the *Wildlife and Countryside Act,* particularly as it relates to birds. If in any doubt, readers are advised to contact the Nature Conservancy, R.S.P.B. or R.S.P.C.A. for clarification. In essence, the *Act* provides a list of protected birds and animals which should not be killed, injured or interfered with in any way. There are also rules governing the movement of specimens between individuals.

Wild birds, eggs and nests

It is an offence to kill, injure, remove or damage wild birds, and their eggs, or their nests. This applies both to resident species and migrants.

Injured birds

Any injured bird can be taken only for the sole purpose of tending it and releasing it when recovered. This does not allow the bird to be kept permanently. It is an offence to have in one's possession or control any wild bird on the British list unless obtained under licence.

Traps

The killing or taking of any birds by the use of gin traps, hooks and lines, bird lime, poisonous baits, gas, maimed live decoys, etc., is strictly prohibited.

Animals

It is an offence to kill, injure, or take any of those on the protected list, unless special exception has been made. Similarly, it is an offence to damage, destroy or interfere in any way with an animal's place of shelter or breeding. Protected animals may not be sold, nor should cruel methods by employed to capture **any** wild animal.

Plants

It is an offence to pick or destroy any of the protected wild plants. The same applies to their flowers and seeds. No wild plant may be uprooted intentionally, unless it is on your own land or you have special permission.

Licences

The Nature Conservancy Council has power to grant licences for:
(a) Scientific or educational purposes;
(b) The purpose of ringing or marking or examining any ring or mark on wild birds;
(c) The purpose of conserving wild birds;
(d) The purpose of protecting any collection of wild birds;
(e) The purpose of falconry or aviculture;
(f) The purpose of any public exhibition or competition;
(g) The purpose of taxidermy;
(h) The purpose of photography;
(i) The purpose of preserving public health or safety;
(j) The purpose of preventing the spread of disease;
(k) The purpose of preventing serious damage to livestock, foodstuffs for livestock, crops, vegetables, fruit, growing timber or fisheries.

Enforcement

If a constable suspects with reasonable cause that any person is committing or has committed an offence under the *Act,* he may, without a warrant, stop and search that person, examine anything that person may have in his possession, arrest that person if he fails to give his name and address, seize and detain anything which may be evidence, and enter any land other than a dwelling house.

Individual rights

Even if there are reasonable grounds to suspect that the law is being broken, no one, other than a policeman, has any right to enter private premises unless the owner expressly gives his permission.

The representatives of the R.S.P.C.A., R.S.P.B., or any other protection society have no legal right to handle any birds or animals without the owner's permission. However, a constable does have the authority and must be allowed to handle the creatures if he wishes to do so.

Further details

The *Wildlife and Countryside Act 1981* covers many aspects related to the countryside and wildlife. Lists of protected birds and animals may be provided by the Nature Conservancy, the R.S.P.C.A., R.S.P.B., or various Government bodies. **Any person with any doubt as to his position in relation to the law is strongly advised to contact one of the above mentioned organizations.** It is the responsibility of the individual to ensure that he is conversant with the requirements of the law. The precise provisions of the *Act,* and the species protected, are liable to change, so the taxidermist should make himself familiar with the latest position.

Other points

As a word of advice to anyone seriously taking up taxidermy, I would suggest that **they obtain their specimens only from legal sources.** If they do not then, sooner or later, they will finish up in trouble.

The commercial taxidermist is particularly at risk. Parcels occasionally arrive without names and addresses included, with perfectly legal specimens, but one is not to know for certain. It is always possible that a trouble-maker could deliberately shoot and send an illegal specimen through the post under such conditions. If that happens, my advice is to dispose of it immediately, or if a Federation system is sorted out, telephone and have it booked into a log-book, to at least cover yourself. Such a system would have to have the approval and backing of the Department of the Environment, R.S.P.B., and other interested organizations. The facts would have to be reported to these bodies, but the identity of the person would be held only by the Federation in the initial stages, to ensure fair play.

All taxidermists should be involved in some sort of Natural History conservation work, and try to understand why they should be inconvenienced by changing laws. I am not saying that one should tolerate the occasional trouble-maker that all groups collect; just remember they are more of an embarrassment to the group they belong to. Remember, if a law enforcement officer visits you, he is there to see that you are behaving according to the law, and not there as a witch-hunter.

Dealing with protected specimens

If the specimen is on your premises, you need the person's name, home address, a note stating what species, sex, and date it was left with you. Also a cheque as part payment, to confirm his identity and involvement. If in doubt, telephone the Federation for advice. Remember, it will be up to yourself to prove that you did not obtain the specimen in question.

Do not pick up dead birds on roadsides. Do not assume how they died. If you do, get a witness; a stranger is ideal. Some years ago, a passing motorist called in to see me. He brought a tawny owl he had found dead at the roadside. He said it was too lovely to leave, but he did not want it himself. It was apparently a road casualty, so I accepted it. He left without leaving his name or address. It lay in the freezer for eight months, before I managed to set it up. It had died from shotgun wounds. I mention this as a warning. Had I had a visit from the R.S.P.B., they would have taken me to court over it; and who could blame them.

It is so easy to get into such a position, if you are not thinking clearly. Do not allow other members of your family to accept specimens, unless they are fully aware of the requirements needed by law.

Another danger is someone passing a specimen over under the wrong name. I have had a greenfinch handed in as a yellow hammer, a stock dove as a turtle dove, and a kestrel as a sparrowhawk, all in the last year. This could cause problems, as the species may be a protected one.

The R.S.P.B. are treated like bogey men, yet I have found they use their powers fairly, although it must be remembered that when an inspector calls, he will be representing a certain group, and will have that group as a priority in his mind. A number of groups exist, R.S.P.B. for the birds, A.S.R.A. for reptiles and amphibia, Forestry for the trees, R.S.P.C.A. and Mammal Society for animals, and for a long time their attitudes have been very narrow minded. Fortunately, the attitude is changing to a more adult one of looking at the Natural History picture as a whole, rather than a segment of it. One good reason for doing so is that many creatures' food-chains cross all these groups.

After certain television programmes, strangely enough mainly on rare birds, there are always the occasional telephone calls from people claiming to have various birds, normally mentioned in the programme, and wanting them set up. The best way to deal with them is to record their conversation, if you can, for possible use in a police action at a later date. If a parcel with a rare species does arrive, either with name and address or without, then it is a matter for the R.S.P.B. inspector, and you should be guided by him or the Federation, or for safety, by both. If you are not, then you become an accomplice to the crime.

If a rare bird comes in suffering from a 'road accident', and other illegal circumstances are seen, **stop working on it and report it to someone.** There have been more would-be 'I shot the specimen' collectors stopped by commercial taxidermists, as a group, without legal action, than most people would believe. That time and era must be at an end, although true recordings in the past, of bird plumage, and so on, were made by such people. So they had a role to play in world Natural History.

Today the world Natural History scene cannot take this battering, without many extinctions. Farming methods, industrial needs, and the commercial interests of man, will destroy many species, without the creators of these plans ever being aware they existed. Do not be small-minded and sneer at the hunter. He plays a vital role in conservation, by keeping large areas open for the creature he hunts. He pays 'keepers to raise stock that would be extinct or rare in a short time, and introduces new ones, and puts his hand in his pocket to do so.

To obtain legal specimens, write to or go and see the wardens of Bird Sanctuaries, local Natural History groups, patrolling policemen, museum Curators, and Education Officers, lighthouse keepers, and so on. Explain to them what you would like, and be prepared to pay for first class postage, or the person's petrol if he delivers them. You are allowed to pay for out of pocket expenses incurred, but you are not allowed to pay for any protected specimen; it is illegal. You can offer some of the mounted specimens back, for their work in Natural History, or perhaps help in some way towards the conservation of the area.

In conclusion, the Home Secretary told me some years ago that I could use any specimen that had died by **accidental violence, accidental electrocution, and accidental poisoning.** In that generous spirit, the law must be respected. It is a case of black and white, no greys.

Useful addresses

Law Enforcement Office, Fish and Wildlife Service, US Dept. of the Interior, C Street, between 18th and 19th Street North West, Washington DC 20240 U.S.A.

British Protection Acts; Her Majesty's Stationery Office, 49 High Holborn, London W.C.1.

Protection booklets; Royal Society for the Protection of Birds, The Lodge, Sandy, Bedfordshire, SG19 2DL.

Taxidermists' Federation of Great Britain and Ireland, 136 High Street, Leagrave, Luton, Bedfordshire, England. Tel. (0582) 53158.

Nature Conservancy, Natural Environment Research Council, 19 Belgrave Square, London S.W.1.

Department of the Environment, Wildlife Conservation Licensing Section, Room 311, Tollgate House, Houlton Street, Bristol, BS2 9DJ. Tel. (0272) 218176.

Mammal Society, Harvest House, 62 London Road, Reading RG1 5AS. Tel. (0734) 861345.

The Institute of Terrestrial Ecology, Monks Wood Experimental Station, Abbots Ripton, Huntingdon PE17 2LS. Tel. (048 73) 381.

Responsible for recording, practical help and protection, advice and conservation of all British Wildlife, including the Seas, and 'Air-strike'; bird and aircraft incidents.

Resident top naturalists include, Bob Stebbings, world authority on bats, and Henry R. Arnold.

A.S.R.A., (Association for the Study of Reptile and Amphibia), Cotswold Wildlife Park, Filkin, Nr. Bursford, Oxfordshire. Tel. (036 785) 3006.

CHAPTER 11

POSSIBLE FUTURE DEVELOPMENTS

MODERN TECHNIQUES

New methods in the art of taxidermy had slowed to a standstill after the Victorian era in most fields, and even started to go backwards, with many techniques becoming lost, especially in decor, until recently. In the 1950's, Moyer of New York brought macro-mammal techniques up to date, with present day materials, causing many taxidermists to look afresh at the new materials that were available to them, and advancement in industrial technology. Fish techniques have taken on a fresh lease of life, and fish taxidermy is a subject within itself. Sea fish, in the main, remain a problem to solve.

Reg Harris made a major breakthrough with freeze-drying techniques for many specimens, some of which had been impossible to consider beforehand, especially in the areas of vegetation, amphibia, reptile, micro-mammal and bird life, and really opened the future to many possibilities. Many taxidermists stick to the 'old rules' rather like a train on rails, because it is safer, and perhaps they fear change for various reasons, mainly I suspect, being personal.

Animal movement

At present I am doing research work into 'animal movement', such as light revolving and dappling to give a suggestion of movement to still animals, and on 'breathing' creatures, which do have movement. Small beginnings perhaps, but a start down this road, which needs coupling with other technologies, and eventually to robotics.

Looking at progress in other fields, one can give some predictions into the future of our own profession, and its importance to the animal kingdom. Recent sensational press reporting suggested that if the Russians found another mammoth frozen in Siberia, they could, with techniques available, 'clone' a living one from some of the creature's cells and tissues. Frankly, I think that with today's knowledge, this is rubbish. But with man's mind being directed to this subject, it would not be impossible in the future. Even if it takes man a thousand years to achieve this, then we should, in the next few years, work towards the future, and give our aid now.

Cloning

If cloning of deep frozen specimens can become a reality, then it should be possible later to clone freeze-dried specimens, especially if they have not been ruined by chemicals and preserves. The animal and vegetable kingdoms are under heavy pressure from man, and many species are due to become extinct in the foreseeable future. This will cause a chain reaction; more and more will follow.

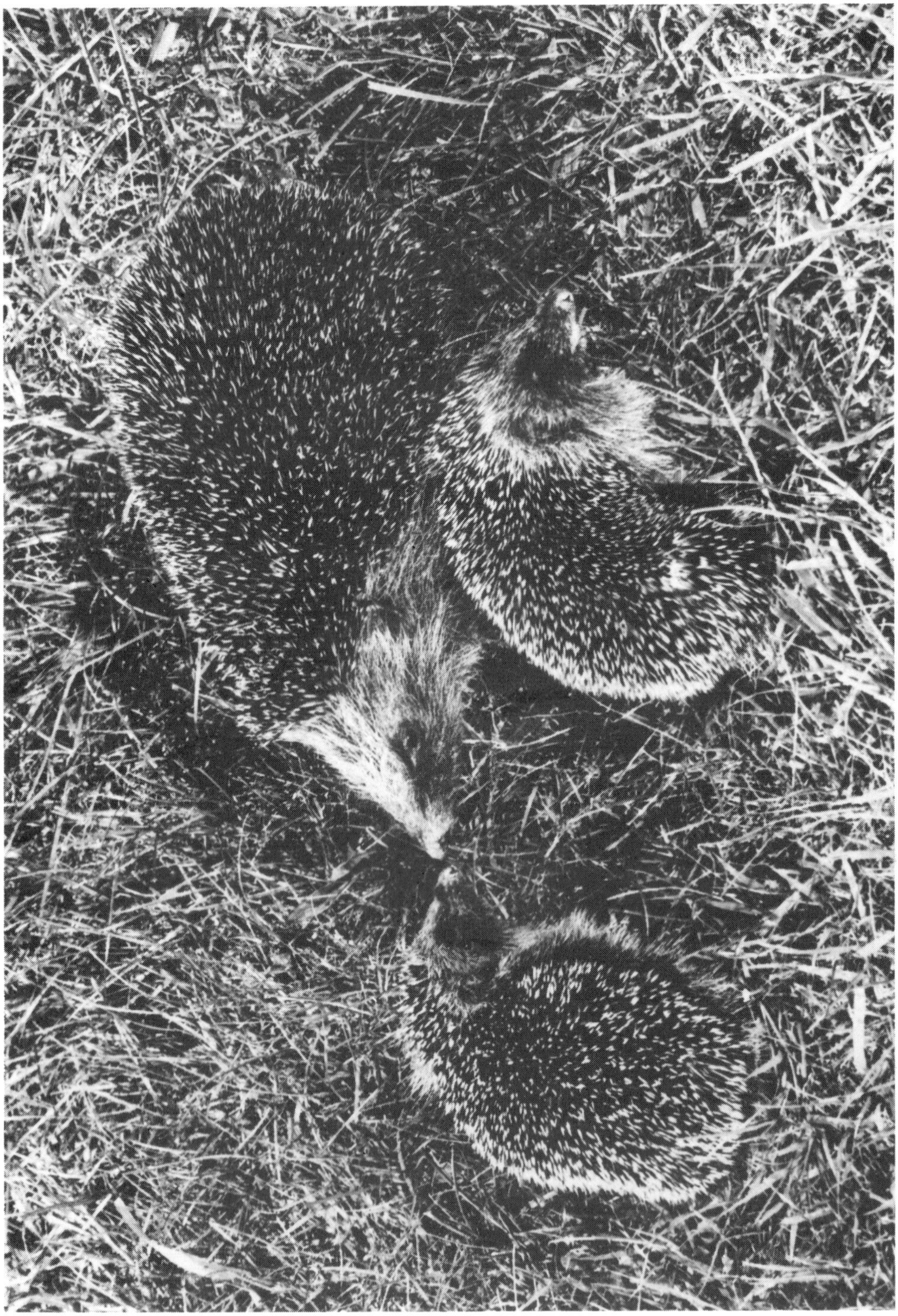

Figure 11.1 Adult female hedgehog, mounted by combined taxidermy; the two young being fully wired, glass eyed, freeze-dried specimens

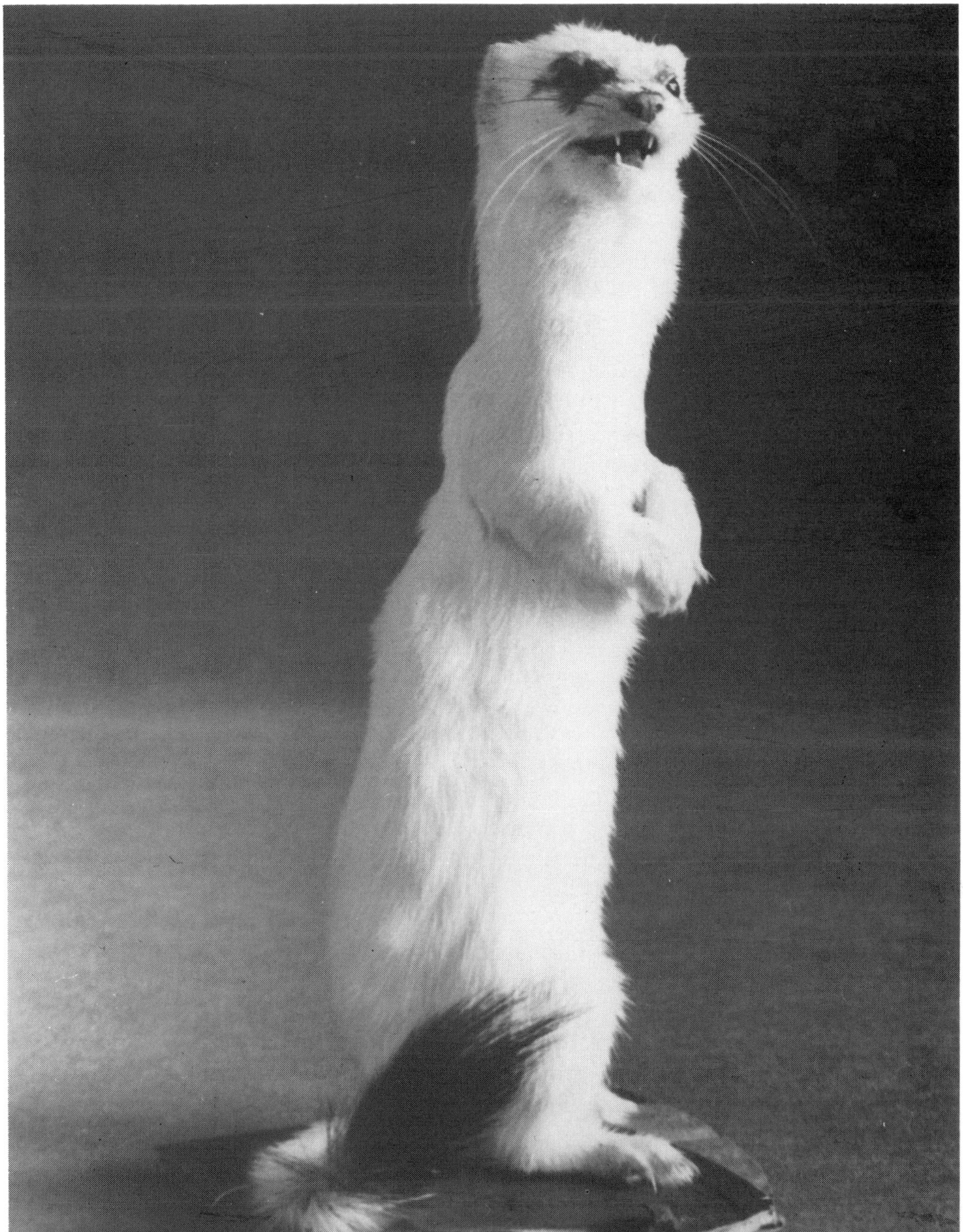

Figure 11.2 Ermine set up in classical style, on a temporary stand

Perhaps consideration should be given to preserving a selection of species in liquid nitrogen by new specialized national or world museums. Some existing museums are rich enough to start a department devoted to such a project.

World wildlife conservation organizations should be prepared to support such an enterprise, as a wise back-up to the efforts they are making. Humans hoping for another 'innings' are being preserved this way in America, so the equipment and know-how is available. Museums may take on a new role as store-houses not only of the past, but of life for the future; a real Noah's Ark.

Even with the advancement of science, and remembering that nine-tenths of all scientists who ever lived are alive today, some may suggest that such efforts are a waste of time. To these I would say that man genetically and chemically, will one day be able to produce the shapes and images of creatures, but without helpful groundwork, will not perhaps be able to produce creatures with inbred knowledge. This inbred knowledge is carried by all creatures, as they have no books, videos, or records, to refer to, and is carried in the genes.

A simplified facet to which I refer, is that the Tit family within my lifetime learnt from one Tit, how to remove the tinfoil from milk bottles. It was well recorded, because in the forties all milk bottles had cardboard caps. The chicks from eggs laid by this bird, and placed with foster parents, carried this capability, showing it was instinctive or inbred knowledge. The point is that the information was carried by the male sperm, and female ova, which are blueprints for construction of future adults, being consolidated in a fertile egg.

If this is accepted as sound sense, then it should also follow that any rare creature being mounted should have its sexual organs preserved in liquid nitrogen, or freeze-dried for future use, rather than thrown away. This applies to museum specimens especially, as they are more likely to survive the ravages of time more successfully.

These organs, if freeze-dried, could be built into the manikin, where it could easily be recovered, if required. A suggestion is that the organ is enclosed in a plastic bag, which is then inserted into a metal canister, in the belly region. This would protect these items from museum pests, and all data relating to the particular organ would be recorded with the specimen; age, sex, region, species or subspecies, and so on. A simple x-ray, or something less harmful to the contents, would readily locate it.

The additional expense incurred to do this would be fractional, and taxidermists without this equipment could have it done by the museum the specimen is for, or an agreement may be made with the nearest local museum to assist, or from our own Federation members.

At the time of writing, I am prepared to do this service free to any taxidermist or group that can see the importance, or potential, of such a minor effort. Embedding in acrylic could be useful long term storage.

Technology tomorrow may say we are wrong; next decade right. Right or wrong, we have the material that will not be available in the future, and we should make it secure, in various forms, for the future, as use may be made of it that we cannot visualise. It is our duty to preserve it and theirs to find the key to unlock this information. If we do not do this, then they cannot begin to start their job, and a vast natural wealth would be lost.

The only thing going for most of the failing world's creatures, is in captivity, vegetating in an alien environment, becoming zombies. Although National Parks will help some species, there are not enough of these. The true nomadic creature cannot be helped there, and has to compete with man. The more options and chances we can give these creatures, the greater the chances of success, because man will be the greatest loser if we fail.

This is why I urge every person, especially the newcomers, to think long and hard on this matter. To non taxidermists I would say, support the principle. To the taxidermists, your skill will improve over a period, and it is important that your inner spirit grows with it. With creatures this happens, but with man, at times, it is eroded by his own needs, environment and civilization. With the taxidermist there is no excuse; he is a privileged being knowing other creatures like very few people do, and is their unpaid, unheralded ambassador. And if any taxidermist honestly believes he is unpaid as an ambassador, then I feel a great sorrow for that man, because his work more than repays in kind.

APPENDIXES

The following details are vital to the work of the taxidermist. They have been compiled by the author over a long period. Copyright of the technical data is reserved by the author and should not be reproduced without written permission.

APPENDIX I

GALVANISED WIRE SIZES FOR BIRDS AND MAMMALS

Note: the size given is the diameter in millimetres. For unlisted specimens, look for similar type and size.

3 mm	Swans, eagles, heron, ibis, muntjac deer, wolf, wolverine, goat, and jackal.
2.5 mm	Vulture, goose, snowy owl, divers, buzzards, fox, badger, large coypu, otter, and wild cat.
2 mm	Grouse, coot, curlew, stone curlew, whimbrel, hooded and carrion crows, pheasant, large gulls (herring, greater and lesser black-backed), harriers, large and medium duck (such as mallard, eider, tufted, widgeon), goosander, mergansers, fulmar, great crested grebe, skuas, rook, rabbit, hare, sable, pine marten, fox cubs, coypu up to 9 lbs in weight, mongoose and large polecat.
1.60 mm	Sparrowhawk, kestrel, partridges, woodcock, barn owl, short eared owl, long eared owl, tawny owl, little owl, jay, magpie, jackdaw, stock and ring doves, teal and small ducks, moorhen, corncrake, plovers, petrels, mink, stoat, squirrels, hedgehog, ferret, medium polecat, brown rat, small gulls such as kittiwake and black headed, and all terns.
1.25 mm	Missel thrush, sandpipers, turtle and collared doves, rails, green and greater spotted woodpeckers, waxwing, nightjar, knot, dunlin, and other small plover and waders, cuckoo, black rat, weasel, water vole and hamster.
0.90 mm	Starlings, dipper, ring ousel, blackbird, song thrush, kingfisher, shrike, mole and edible dormouse.
0.60 to 0.50 mm	Flycatchers, wheatear, buntings, warblers, wagtails, larks, pipits, wren, goldcrest, wryneck, nuthatch, swallow, martins, tits, sparrows and most finches, mice, bats, shrew, and small voles and lemmings.

APPENDIX II

QUICK REFERENCE LIST OF FORMULAS

Carbolic-Acid solution

Carbolic-Acid or Phenol	: 1½ tablespoons (crystal or solution)
Water	: 1 gallon

Mix only as needed

B–S relaxer

Borax or Soda	: 1 oz
Water	: 1 gallon

Mix in warm water

Degreasing

Naphtha
Benzene

Degreasing solution

Benzene	: 4 parts
Commercial alcohol	: 1 part

White leather solution

Salt	: 2 lb
Alum	: 1 lb
Sal Ammoniac	: 1 oz
Water	: 2 gallons

Neats-foot oil solution

Water	: 1 part
Sulphonated Neats-Foot Oil	: 1 part

Used warm

Aluminium sulphate formula or combination solution

Salt	: 1 lb
Aluminium Sulphate (iron free)	: 1 lb
Gambier or Terra Japonica	: 3 oz
Soft Water	: 2 gallons

Beeswax modelling

Beeswax	: 3 parts
Resin	: 1 part

Lime water or dehairing solution

Lime	: 4 ozs
Water	: 1 gallon

Lye dehairing solution

Lye	: ¼ cup
Water	: 10 gallons

Boric-Acid solution

Boric-Acid	: 1 oz
Water	: 1 gallon

Snake skin solution

See under Chrome Tanning

Wickersheimer solution (for preserving moss, seaweed, etc.)

Alum	: 500 grains
Salt	: 125 grains
Saltpetre	: 60 grains
Potash	: 300 grains
White Arsenic	: 100 grains

Dissolve in 1 quart of boiling water. For every quart of filtered solution add 4 quarts of glycerine and 1 quart of alcohol. Submerge specimens for a minimum of 48 hours. Wash in warm water. Leaves moss, leaves and seaweed, plump and flexible. Solution good for holding needles on firs, hemlock, etc.

Wax for foliage casting (upper leaf)

Beeswax	: 1 lb
Paraffin Wax	: 4 lb

Blend together in a heated pan set in a water dish (water bath), and add 8 ozs of hot melted resin and mix (using sand bath).

Wax for impregnated cloth

Bleached pure beeswax	: 2 lb
Canada balsam gum (by measure)	: 3 ozs
Resin (by measure)	: 2 ozs
Boiled linseed oil (by measure)	: 2 ozs

Deodorizing solution

Bar Soap (chipped or grated)	:	4 lb
Soda	:	4 lb
Borax	:	3 – 4 ozs
Oil of Sassafras	:	1 – 2 ozs

Boil the soap and soda together and simmer until blended in. Then remove from heat, and while still hot add borax and Oil of Sassafras. Ready for use when cool.

Hubers solution

Petrol (colourless)	:	2 gallons
Alcohol (Industrial Methylated Spirit)	:	1 pint
Spirit of Turpentine	:	4 ozs

Substitute beeswax

Coata CX 1230 *See under* Colouring Beeswax, and address under Taxidermists' Suppliers.

APPENDIX III

INTRODUCTION TO THE EYE-LIST

The eye-list is intended as a general guide and not a gospel. When referring to the list, make sure you are looking under the correct country. What is a little owl in Britain could be a far different bird elsewhere.

In America, with a continental span of three thousand miles, some bird species manage to change the colour of their eyes within the same species. The boat-tailed grackle is one such bird. With mammals, local subspecies' eye colours can be different from the 'type' animal described.

The occasional eye size on a successful long-lived individual can make the list appear vastly incorrect. For instance, the average weight for a male raccoon is 8.6 kg (19 lbs), but the heaviest ever recorded weighed 28 kg (61 lbs 8 ozs) in Canada.

Bird eye colours can change with the breeding season. Juveniles, adults and old age can again cause dramatic change. Sexes can also have different colours. In birds of prey, many females are larger, and this includes their eye measurements. With big cats, like the mountain lion, leopard and tiger, the male has a greenish tinge added to the basic eye colour which the females do not have. Sometimes correct eye colours do not convey the correct impression. A jackdaw has a grey eye, but a white one is used, creating an optical illusion.

With the eye sizes given, these are the sizes that I would personally use. I would then adjust the eye-lid to perhaps make it smaller, or make the eye look 'weaker' as in the case of the hedgehog and badger. Bold eyes are made to protrude fractionally, weaker eyes are more countersunk and careful use of the eyelid completes the effect.

Most natural eyes, even black, are of a shade. If a creature has a very dark brown (VDB) eye, but looks black from a short distance away, then I suggest black, but put the correct colouring in brackets. Where only one colour is given for an adult, that colour applies to both sexes.

Construction

Eyes are normally made of glass, but they can be plastic or acrylic and can be made up in many forms. There is the straightforward ball type, normally black, and perhaps attached to a wire. These are excellent for many specimens. Another form exists rather like a ping-pong ball cut in half. These are called concave-convex. These can vary in quality but form part of the quality range. There is also the flat-backed and the flat-backed with white corners. A fairly new addition to the market is an almost flat-backed type, having a slight concave in the pupil area, which gives good results.

A 'special' can be any of these. It has been carefully put together for, at times, a single species, and it is well worth the extra money, as the eyes are an automatic focal point to a creature. A dealer should never send a poor quality or faulted eye out. He should change it without question. If he persists, as some do, change your dealer and tell everyone else to avoid him.

Supplies

In Britain many new dealers are springing up, many without an inkling as to taxidermists' requirements and without a naturalist background. It does not mean you will not get quality, but you may well receive the incorrect goods, however well meaning.

It pays to plan well ahead on eyes and carry stock that covers the greater range of species. Clear glass eyes, or 'flints' as the Americans refer to them, will allow you to make up your own in an emergency. It is no easy task to match a pair of eyes done by oneself to the professional standard that the quality eyes have, but it can be done with patience and time (which most of us do not have). If one tackles the eyes, do not do one pair only, but at least three pairs, because even drying can affect them.

Use of the list

The eye-lists are the first attempt to bring together practical information, generally used by many practising taxidermists, of all species in a given area. Specimens in the old days were sent back as skins, lacking eye detail of any form. The result of this is that creatures can be completely described, excluding their eyes. Modern books compound this fault by taking photographs of mounted specimens in natural surroundings. Artists then take their finer details from such photographs, and incorrectly coloured specimens add to the confusion. Even some of the old naturalists' artists have made gigantic blunders.

The lists will need adjustments here and there, but, in essence, the list is a strong foundation to which information can be added, i.e. local oddities, more juvenile and chick information.

All practising taxidermists will gain from the lists, and can add to them. Who can honestly look into an English jay's eyes and really settle for a pale blue 'special', or into the great clear depths of a cheetah's eye and replace it with a glass bauble? There is much to be done and here is the beginning, no more.

CHECK LIST OF EYE SIZES AND COLOURS OF BRITISH, SCANDINAVIAN AND EUROPEAN BIRDS

NB: The eye-lists which follow are the copyright of the author

Abbreviations: VDB=Very Dark Brown; DB=Dark Brown

Accentor, Alpine	4 mm Mid Brown
Accentor, Hedge	4 mm Dark Brown
Accentor, Siberian	4 mm Dark Brown
Albatross, Black-browed	Adult 15–16 mm (VDB) Black Juvenile 15–16 mm Dark Brown
Auk, Little	6 mm (VDB) Black
Avocet	8 mm Reddish Brown
Bee-eater	5 mm Mid Brown
Bee-eater, Blue Cheeked	5 mm Mid Brown
Bittern	Adult 12 mm Golden Yellow Juvenile 12 mm Pale Yellow
Bittern, Little	Adult male 7 mm Golden Yellow Adult female 7 mm Pale Yellow Juvenile 7 mm Greenish Yellow
Blackbird	7 mm (VDB)Black
Blackcap	4 mm (VDB) Black
Bluetail, Red Flanked	4 mm Brown
Bluethroat	4 mm Dark Brown
Brambling	4 mm (VDB) Black
Brant *see Brent Goose*	
Bullfinch	4 mm (VDB) Black
Bunting, Black Headed	4 mm (VDB) Black
Bunting, Cinereous	4 mm (VDB) Black
Bunting, Cirl	4mm Mid Brown
Bunting, Corn	5 mm (VDB) Black
Bunting, Cretzschmar's	4 mm (VDB) Black
Bunting, Lapland	4 mm (VDB) Black
Bunting, Little	3–4 mm (VDB) Black
Bunting, Ortolan	4 mm (VDB) Black
Bunting, Pine	4 mm (VDB) Black
Bunting, Red Headed	4 mm (VDB) Black
Bunting, Reed	4 mm (VDB) Black
Bunting, Rock	4 mm (VDB) Black
Bunting, Rustic	4 mm (VDB) Black
Bunting, Snow	4 mm (VDB) Black
Bunting, Yellow	4 mm (VDB) Black
Bunting, Yellow Breasted	4 mm (VDB) Black
Bustard, Great	Male 16 mm Greyish Brown (Special) Female 16 mm Brown to Yellow
Bustard, Houbara	Adult 12 mm Golden Mid Brown (Special) Juvenile 12 mm Brown (Special)
Bustard, Little	Male 9–10 mm Reddish Brown (Special) Female 9–10 mm Dark Brown
Bustard, MacQueen's *see Bustard, Houbara*	
Button-Quail	4 mm Brown
Buzzard	14 mm Dark Brown
Buzzard, Honey	Adult male 12 mm Golden Yellow Adult female 13 mm Yellow Juvenile 12 mm Brownish
Buzzard, Long-legged	14 mm Clayish Brown
Buzzard, Rough-legged	13–14 mm Clayish Brown

Canary	3 mm (VDB) Black
Cape pigeon	8 mm Dark Brown
Capercaillie	Male 12 mm Brown
	Female 10 mm Brown
Chaffinch	4 mm (VDB) Black
Chiffchaff	4 mm (VDB) Black
Chough	8 mm (VDB) Black
Chough, Alpine	8 mm (VDB) Black
Chough, Red-billed *see Chough*	
Chukar	8 mm Dark Brown
Coot	7–8 mm Mid Brown
Coot, Crested	7–8 mm Mid Brown
Cormorant	Adult 12 mm Dark Green
	Juvenile 12 mm Brown
Cormorant, Pygmy	Adult 9 mm Dark Green
	Juvenile, 9 mm Brown
Corncrake	Adult 6 mm Clayish Brown
	Juvenile 6 mm Brown
Courser, Cream-Coloured	7 mm (VDB) Black
Crake, Baillon's	Adult 4 mm Dark Red
	Juvenile 4 mm Light Brown
Crake, Little	Adult 4 mm Dark Red
	Juvenile 4 mm Light Brown
Crake, Spotted	Adult 5 mm Mid Brown
	Juvenile 5 mm Greyish Brown
Crane	13–14 mm Reddish Brown
Crane, Common *see Crane*	
Crane, Demoiselle	13 mm Reddish Brown
Crane, Siberian White	14 mm Golden Yellow
Crossbill	5 mm (VDB) Black
Crossbill, Parrot	4 mm (VDB) Black
Crossbill, Two-barred	4 mm Brown
Crossbill, White-winged *see Crossbill, Two-barred*	
Crow, Carrion	9 mm (VDB) Black
Crow, Hooded	9 mm (VDB) Black
Cuckoo	Adult male 7 mm Yellow
	Adult female 7 mm Clayish Yellow
Cuckoo, Black-billed	7 mm (VDB) Black
Cuckoo, Greater Spotted	8 mm Dark Brown
Cuckoo, Oriental	7 mm Yellow
Cuckoo, Yellow-billed	7 mm (VDB) Black
Curlew	10 mm (VDB) Black
Curlew, Slender-billed	9 mm (VDB) Black
Curlew, Stone	Adult 13 mm Pale Yellow
	Juvenile 13 mm Very Pale Yellow
Dabchick *see Grebe, Little*	
Dipper	5 mm Mid Brown
Diver, Black-throated	Adult 12 mm Red
	Juvenile 12 mm Brown
Diver, Great Northern	Adult 14 mm Red
	Juvenile 14 mm (VDB) Black
Diver, Red-throated	Adult 11 mm Red
	Juvenile 11 mm Brown
Diver, White-billed	Adult 14 mm Red
	Juvenile 14 mm (VDB) Black
Dotterel	8 mm (VDB) Black
Dove, Collared Turtle	Adult 6 mm Blackish Red. Use Black.
	Juvenile 6 mm Brown

Dove, Laughing *see Dove, Palm*	
Dove, Palm	6 mm Mid Brown
Dove, Ring	Adult 8 mm Pale Yellow
	Juvenile 8 mm Light Grey
Dove, Rock	Adult 8 mm Chestnut
	Juvenile 8 mm Yellowish Brown
Dove, Rufous Turtle	6 mm Mid Brown
Dove, Stock	Adult 8 mm (VDB) Black
	Juvenile 8 mm Grey-Brown
Dove, Turtle	Adult 6 mm Yellow
	Juvenile 6 mm Brown
Dowitcher, Long-billed	8 mm (VDB) Black
Dowitcher, Short-billed	8 mm (VDB) Black
Duck, Eider	Adult male 10 mm (VDB) Black
	Female adult 10 mm Yellowish Brown
	Juvenile 10 mm Grey-Brown
Duck, King Eider	Adult male 10 mm (VDB) Black
	Adult female 10 mm Dark Brown
Duck, Spectacled Eider	Adult male 9 mm (VDB) Black
	Adult female 9 mm Dark Brown
Duck, Steller's Eider	Adult male 8 mm Brown
	Adult female 8 mm (DB) Black
	Juvenile 8 mm Grey-Brown
Duck, Ferruginous	Adult male 6–7 mm White
	Adult female 6–7 mm Dark Brown
Duck, Gadwall	Adult 8 mm (VDB) Black
	Juvenile 8 mm Grey-Brown
Duck, Garganey	Adult 6 mm Mid Brown
	Juvenile 6 mm Grey-Brown
Duck, Goldeneye	Adult male 9 mm Pale Yellow
	Adult female 9 mm Dull Yellow
	Juvenile 9 mm Sex for colour
Duck, Barrow's Goldeneye	Adult male 9 mm Very Pale Yellow
	Adult female 9 mm Greenish Yellow
Duck, Goosander	Adult male 10 mm Reddish Brown
	Adult female 10 mm Clayish Mid Brown
	Juvenile 10 mm Grey-Brown
Duck, Harlequin	Adult male 9 mm Reddish Brown
	Adult female 9 mm Mid Brown
	Juvenile 9 mm Mid Brown
Duck, Long-tailed	Adult male 8 mm Reddish Yellow
	Adult female 8 mm Yellowish Brown
	Juvenile 8 mm Grey-Brown
Duck, Mallard	Adult male 8 mm (VDB) Black
	Adult female 8 mm Mid Brown
	Juvenile 8 mm Grey-Brown
Duck, Mandarin	8 mm Reddish Brown
Duck, Pintail	8 mm (DB) Black
Duck, Pochard	Adult male 8mm Bright Reddish Brown
	Adult female 8 mm Brown to Hazel
	Juvenile 8 mm (VDB) Black
	Adult male 8 mm Clayish-Brown, other than breeding season
Duck, Pochard Red Crested	Adult male 9 mm Orangy Red
	Adult female 9 mm Brownish Yellow
	Juvenile 9 mm Clayish Brown
Duck, Red Breasted Merganser	9 mm Clayish Brown to Yellow
Duck, Ring-necked	Adult male 8 mm Yellow
	Adult female 8 mm Clayish Yellow
Duck, Scaup	Adult male 8 mm Pale Yellow

	Adult female 8 mm Very Pale Yellow
	Juvenile 8 mm Greeny Brown
Duck, Scoter Black *see Duck, Scoter, Common*	
Duck, Scoter, Common	Male 8 mm (VDB) Black
	Female 8 mm Dark Brown
Duck, Scoter, Surf	Adult male 9 mm White
	Adult female 9 mm Dark Brown
	Juvenile 9 mm Grey-Brown
Duck, Scoter, Velvet	Adult male 9 mm White
	Adult female 9 mm Dark Brown
	Juvenile 9 mm Dark Brown
Duck, Shelduck	Adult male 9 mm (VDB) Black
	Adult female 9 mm Dark Brown
	Juvenile 9 mm Grey-Brown
Duck, Ruddy Shelduck	Adult male 9 mm (VDB) Black
	Adult female 9 mm Dark Brown
	Juvenile 9 mm Grey-Brown
Duck, Shoveller	Adult male 8 mm Pale Yellow
	Adult female 8 mm Mid Brown
	Juvenile 8 mm Greyish Yellow
	N.B. Pearl grey eyes in old mature males
Duck, Teal	Adult male 6 mm Dark Brown
	Adult female 6 mm Grey-Brown
Duck, Baikal Teal	Adult male 6 mm (VDB) Black
	Adult female 6 mm Dark Brown
Duck, Blue-winged Teal	Adult male 6 mm Dark Brown
	Adult female 6 mm Grey-Brown
Duck, Falcated Teal	Adult male 9 mm (VDB) Black
	Adult female 8 mm Dark Brown
Duck, Green-winged Teal	Adult male 6 mm Dark Brown or Black
	Adult female 6 mm Greysih Brown
Duck, Marbled Teal	Adult male 6 mm (VDB) Black
	Adult female 6 mm Grey Brown
Duck, Tufted	Adult male 8 mm Pale Yellow
	Adult female 8 mm Dull Yellow
Duck, White-headed	Adult male 8 mm (VDB) Black
	Adult female 8 mm Mid Brown
Duck, Widgeon	Adult 8 mm Mid Brown
Dunlin	5 mm (VDB) Black
Dunnock *see Accentor, Hedge*	

Eagles All eyes Special	
Eagle, Bonelli's	16 mm Clayish Brown
Eagle, Booted	Adult 14 mm Clayish Brown
	Juvenile 14 mm Dark Brown
Eagle, Golden	Adult male 18 mm Golden Yellow-Brown
	Adult female 19 mm Clayish Brown
	Juvenile 18 mm Brown
Eagle, Imperial	18–19mm Golden Yellow Brown
Eagle, Lesser Spotted	Adult 14 mm Dark Brown
	Juvenile 14 mm Clayish Brown
Eagle, Pallas Sea	13–14 mm Yellow to Mid Brown
Eagle, Short-toed	Male 16 mm Golden Yellow
	Female 17 mm Golden Yellow
	Juvenile 16 mm Yellow
Eagle, Spotted	Adult 13–14mm Mid Brown
	Juvenile 13–14 mm Clayish Brown
Eagle, Steppe	16–17 mm Greyish Brown

Eagle, Tawny *see Eagle, Steppe*	
Eagle, White-tailed	Adult male 17 mm Greyish Brown to Grey
	Adult female 18 mm Greyish Brown to Grey
	Juvenile 17 mm Dark Brown
Egret, Cattle	10 mm Pale Yellow
Egret, Great White	13 mm Pale Yellow
Egret, Little	9 mm Pale Yellow
Eiders *see Duck*	
Falcon, Eleanora's	10 mm (VDB) Black
Falcon, Gyr	Male 14 mm (VDB) Black
	Female 15 mm (VDB) Black
Falcon, Hobby	9 mm (VDB) Black
Falcon, Kestrel	9 mm (VDB) Black
Falcon, Lesser Kestrel	9 mm (VDB) Black
Falcon, Lanner	12 mm (VDB) Black
Falcon, Merlin	Male 7 mm (VDB) Black
	Female 8 mm (VDB) Black
Falcon, Peregrine	Male 11 mm (VDB) Black
	Female 12 mm (VDB) Black
Falcon, Red-footed	9 mm (VDB) Black
Falcon, Saker	Adult male 11 mm (VDB) Black
	Adult female 12 mm (VDB) Black
	Juvenile 11 mm Dark Brown
Fieldfare	7 mm (VDB) Black
Finch, Citril	4 mm (VDB) Black
Finch, Snow	4 mm (VDB) Black
Finch, Trumpeter	4 mm (VDB) Black
Firecrest	3 mm Dark Brown or Black
Flamingo	Adult 9 mm Pale Yellow
	Juvenile 9 mm Pale Grey
Flycatcher, Brown	4 mm (VDB) Black
Flycatcher, Collared	4 mm Dark Brown or Black
Flycatcher, Pied	4 mm Dark Brown or Black
Flycatcher, Red-breasted	4 mm (VDB) Black
Flycatcher, Semi-collared	4 mm (VDB) Black
Flycatcher, Spotted	5 mm (VDB) Black
Fulmer Petrel *see Petrels*	
Gadwall *see Ducks*	
Gallinule, Allen's	6 mm Red
Gallinule, Common *see Moorhen*	
Gallinule, Purple	8 mm Red
Gannet	13 mm Pale Cream
Garganey *see Ducks*	
Godwit, Bar-tailed	8 mm (VDB) Black
Godwit, Black-tailed	8 mm (VDB) Black
Goldcrest	3 mm (VDB) Black
Goldeneyes *see Ducks*	
Goldfinch	4 mm (VDB) Black
Goosander *see Ducks*	
Goose, Bar Head	11–12 mm (VDB) Black
Goose, Barnacle	10 mm (VDB) Black
Goose, Bean	11 mm (VDB) Black
Goose, Brent	9–10 mm (VDB) Black
Goose, Canada	12 mm Greyish Brown
Goose, Egyptian	10 mm Mid to Light Brown
Goose, Greylag	12 mm Dark Brown to Black

Goose, Lesser White-fronted	9–10 mm Black
Goose, Pink-footed	10 mm Dark Brown or Black
Goose, Red-breasted	9 mm (VDB) Black
Goose, Snow	10–11 mm (VDB) Black
Goose, White-fronted	11 mm (VDB) Black
Goshawk *see Hawks*	
Grebe, Black-necked	7 mm Orangy pink; silvery backing or Red (Special)
Grebe, Eared *see Grebe, Black-necked*	
Grebe, Great Crested	8 mm Red (Special)
Grebe, Horned *see Grebe, Slavonian*	
Grebe, Little	6 mm Reddish Brown
Grebe, Red-necked	8 mm Reddish Dark Brown
Grebe, Slavonian	7 mm Orangy pink; silvery backing or Red (Special)
Greenfinch	4 mm (VDB) Black
Greenshank	Adult 8 mm (VDB) Black Juvenile 8 mm Grey Brown
Grosbeak, Pine	5 mm (VDB) Black
Grosbeak, Scarlet	4 mm (VDB) Black
Grouse, Black	Adult male 9 mm (VDB) Black Adult female 9 mm Dark Brown
Grouse, Caucasian Black	Adult male 9 mm (VDB) Black Adult female 9 mm Dark Brown
Grouse, Hazel *see Hazelhen*	
Grouse, Red	Adult male 9 mm (VDB) Black Adult female 9 mm Dark Brown
Grouse, Willow	Adult male 9 mm (VDB) Black Adult female 9 mm Dark Brown
Guillemot	Adult 10 mm Dark Brown Juvenile 10 mm Greyish Brown
Guillemot, Black	Adult 7 mm Dark Brown Juvenile 7 mm Greyish Brown
Guillemot, Brunnich's	10 mm Dark Brown
Gull, Audouin's	10 mm (VDB) Black
Gull, Black-headed	Adult 8–9 mm Reddish Brown Juvenile 8–9 mm Mid Brown
Gull, Bonaparte's	8 mm Dark Brown
Gull, Common	9 mm (VDB) Black Juvenile 9 mm Greyish Brown
Gull, Glaucous	12 mm Bright Yellow
Gull, Great Black-backed	Adult 12 mm Pale Yellow Juvenile 12 mm Grey-Brown
Gull, Great Black-headed	12 mm Dark Brown
Gull, Herring	11 mm Pale Yellow
Gull, Iceland	Adult 11 mm Yellow Juvenile 11 mm Grey-Brown
Gull, Ivory	10 mm Dark Brown
Gull, Kittiwake	9 mm (VDB) Black
Gull, Lesser Black-backed	11 mm Very Pale Yellow
Gull, Little	7 mm (VDB) Black
Gull, Mediterranean	8 mm Dark Brown
Gull, Mew *see Gull, Common*	
Gull, Ross's	7 mm Dark Brown
Gull, Sabine's	7 mm Mid Brown
Gull, Slender-billed	9 mm Yellow
Gyrfalcon *see Falcons*	
Harlequin *see Ducks*	
Harrier, Hen	Adult male 9 mm Golden Yellow Adult female 10 mm Mid Brown

Harrier, Marsh	Adult male 10 mm Pale Yellow Adult female 11 mm Brownish Yellow	
Harrier, Montagu's	Adult male 9 mm Golden Yellow Adult female 10 mm Pale Yellow	
Harrier, Pallid	Adult male 9 mm Golden Yellow Adult female 10 mm Brownish Yellow	
Hawfinch	Adult male 5 mm Pale Rose or Pale Mauve Adult female 5 mm Grey-Brown	
Hawk, Fish *see Osprey*		
Hawk, Goshawk	Adult male 12 mm Golden Yellow Adult female 13–14 mm Orange tinted Yellow Juvenile 12 mm Clayish Brown	
Hawk, Osprey	Adult male 13 mm Pale Yellow Adult female 14 mm Pale Yellow Juvenile 13 mm Golden Yellow	
Hawk, Sparrowhawk	Adult male 8 mm Orangy-Yellow Adult female 9 mm Orangy-Yellow	} more orange with age
	Juvenile 8 mm Pale Grey-Green	
Hawk, Levant Sparrow	Male 8 mm Pale Yellow Female 9 mm Pale Yellow	
Hazelhen	Adult male 9 mm (VDB) Black Adult female 9 mm Dark Brown	
Heron *see Heron, Grey*		
Heron, Great White	Adult 13 mm Pale Yellow Juvenile 13 mm Cream	
Heron, Grey	Adult 13 mm Pale Yellow Juvenile 13 mm Cream	
Heron, Night	Adult 12 mm Red Juvenile 12 mm Golden Yellow	
Heron, Purple	Adult 12 mm Yellow Juvenile 12 mm Pale Yellow	
Heron, Squacco	Adult 7–8 mm Golden Yellow Juvenile 7–8 mm Pale Yellow	
Hobby *see Falcon*		
Hoopoe	5 mm Dark Brown	
Ibis, Glossy	8–9 mm Very Dark Brown or Black	
Ibis, Sacred	9–10 mm Very Dark Brown or Black	
Jackdaw	8 mm Light Grey – Use White (Special)	
Jay	8 mm Pale Blue (Special)	
Jay, Siberian	7 mm (VDB) Black	
Kestrel, *see Falcon*		
Kestrel, Lesser *see Falcon*		
Killdeer	9 mm (VDB) Black	
Kingfisher	6 mm (VDB) Black	
Kingfisher, Pied	8 mm Dark Brown	
Kite, Black	Adult 12 mm Grey-Brown Juvenile 12 mm (VDB) Black	
Kite, Black-shouldered	Adult 9 mm Reddish Brown	
Kite, Fork-tailed *see Kite, Red*		
Kite, Red	Adult 12–13 mm Very Pale Yellow Juvenile 12–13 mm Grey-White	
Kittiwake *see Gull*		
Knot	Adult 6 mm (VDB) Black Juvenile 6 mm Grey-Brown	

Lammergeier	Adult 18 mm Golden Yellow inner ring, Golden Brown outer, Red skin ring
	Juvenile 18 mm Pale Yellow
Lapwing	9 mm (VDB) Black
Lark, Black	5 mm (VDB) Black
Lark, Calandra	5 mm (VDB) Black
Lark, Crested	5 mm Mid Brown
Lark, Dupont's	4 mm Dark Brown
Lark, Horned *see Lark, Shore*	
Lark, Lesser Short-toed	4 mm Dark Brown
Lark, Shore	5 mm (VDB) Black
Lark, Short-toed	4 mm Dark Brown
Lark, Sky	4 mm Brown
Lark, Thekla	4 mm Dark Brown
Lark, White-winged	5 mm Dark Brown
Lark, Wood	4 mm Mid Brown
Linnet	4 mm (VDB) Black
Loon *see Divers*	
Magpie	9 mm (VDB) Black
Mallard *see Duck*	
Mandarin *see Duck*	
Martin, Crag	4 mm (VDB) Black
Martin, House	4 mm (VDB) Black
Martin, Sand	4 mm (VDB) Black
Merganser *see Duck*	
Merlin *see Falcon*	
Moorhen	Adult 6 mm (Brownish Red) Red (Special)
	Chick 3–4 mm Black
Nightingale	5 mm Dark Brown
Nightingale, Thrush	5 mm Dark Brown
Nightjar	9 mm (VDB) Black
Nightjar, Egyptian	9 mm (VDB) Black
Nightjar, Red-necked	9 mm (VDB) Black
Nutcracker	Adult 8 mm (VDB) Black
	Juvenile 8 mm Dark Brown
Nuthatch	4 mm Mid Brown
Nuthatch, Corsican	4 mm Mid Brown
Nuthatch, Kruper's	4 mm Mid Brown
Nuthatch, Neumayer's Rock	4 mm Mid Brown
Nuthatch, Rock, *see Nuthatch, Neumayer's Rock*	
Oriole, Golden	Adult male 6 mm Light Purple-Red
	Adult female 6 mm Brown
	Juvenile 6 mm Brown
Osprey *see Hawk*	
Ouzel, Ring	7 mm (VDB) Black
Owl, Barn	12 mm (VDB) Black
Owl, Eagle	24 mm Orangy Light Brown or Fire Orange
Owl, Great Grey	18 mm Yellow
Owl, Hawk	Adult 13 mm Pale Yellow
	Juvenile 13 mm Bluish Yellow
Owl, Little	Adult 12 mm Lime tinted Yellow
	Juvenile 12 mm Pale Yellow
Owl, Long-eared	Adult 12 mm Golden Orange
	Juvenile 12 mm Pale Yellow
Owl, Pygmy	8 mm Bright Yellow
Owl, Scops	Adult 9 mm Reddish Orange
	Juvenile 9 mm Yellow

Owl, Screech *see Owl, Barn*	
Owl, Short-eared	Adult 12 mm Pale Yellow
	Juvenile 12 mm Paler Yellow
Owl, Snowy	20 mm Straw Yellow
Owl, South African Marsh	11 mm Pale Yellow
Owl, Tawny	Adult 18 mm (VDB) Black
	Chick – Dark Grey
Owl, Tengmalm's	Adult 11 mm Pale Yellow
	Juvenile 11 mm Paler Yellow
Owl, Ural	18–20 mm (VDB) Black
Oystercatcher	Adult 9 mm Red
	Juvenile 9 mm Grey-Brown
Partridge	8 mm Brown
Partridge, Barbary	8 mm Reddish Brown
Partridge, Red-legged	Adult 8 mm Reddish Brown
	Juvenile 8 mm Brown
Partridge, Rock	8 mm Reddish Brown
Pelican, Dalmatian	13 mm Pale Yellow
Pelican, White	13 mm Dark Red
Peregrine *see Falcon*	
Petrel, Bulwer's	7 mm (VDB) Black
Petrel, Fulmar	11 mm (VDB) Black
Petrel, Leach's	5 mm (VDB) Black
Petrel, Storm	4 mm (VDB) Black
Petrel, Wilson's	5 mm (VDB) Black
Phalarope, Grey	5 mm (VDB) Black
Phalarope, Red-necked	4 mm (VDB) Black
Phalarope, Wilson's	5 mm (VDB) Black
Pheasant	Adult male 9–10 mm Yellow (Special)
	Adult female 9–10 mm Dark Brown
Pheasant, Caucasian Snow	Adult male 9–10 mm (VDB) Black
	Adult female 9–10 mm Dark Brown
Pheasant, Golden	Adult male 8 mm Pale Yellow
	Adult female 8 mm Brown
	Juvenile 8 mm Brown
Pheasant, Lady Amherst's	Male 8 mm Very Pale Yellow
	Female 8 mm Brown
Pheasant, Reeves'	Male 9 mm (VDB) Black
	Female 9 mm Brown
Pigeons *see Doves*	
Pintail *see Duck*	
Pipit, Indian Tree	4 mm (VDB) Black
Pipit, Meadow	4 mm (VDB) Black
Pipit, Pechora	4 mm (VDB) Black
Pipit, Red-throated	4 mm (VDB) Black
Pipit, Richard's	4 mm (VDB) Black
Pipit, Rock *see Pipit, Water*	
Pipit, Tawny	4 mm (VDB) Black
Pipit, Tree	4 mm (VDB) Black
Pipit, Water	4 mm (VDB) Black
Plover, Caspian	7 mm (VDB) Black
Plover, Golden	9 mm (VDB) Black
Plover, Greater Sand	7 mm (VDB) Black
Plover, Green or Lapwing	9 mm (VDB) Black
Plover, Grey	9 mm (VDB) Black
Plover, Kentish	6 mm (VDB) Black
Plover, Lesser Golden	8 mm (VDB) Black
Plover, Little Ringed	6 mm (VDB) Black

Plover, Ringed	6 mm (VDB) Black
Plover, Sociable	9 mm (VDB) Black
Plover, Spur-winged	9 mm (VDB) Black
Pochard *see Duck*	
Pratincole	8 mm (VDB) Black
Pratincole, Black-winged	8 mm (VDB) Black
Pratincole, Collared *see Pratincole*	
Ptarmigan	8 mm (VDB) Black
Puffin	7 mm Pearl-White to Orangy Brown (Breeding) Juvenile 7 mm Brown
Quail	Adult 5 mm Reddish Brown Juvenile 5 mm Mid Brown
Rail, Water	Adult male 6 mm Red Adult female 6 mm Reddish Brown Juvenile 6 mm Mid Brown
Raven	Adult 12 mm (VDB) Black Juvenile 12 mm Grey-Brown
Razorbill	10 mm (VDB) Black
Redpoll	3–4 mm (VDB) Black
Redpoll, Arctic	3–4 mm (VDB) Black
Redshank	Adult 7 mm (VDB) Black Juvenile 7 mm Grey-Brown
Redshank, Spotted	Adult 7 mm (VDB) Black Juvenile 7 mm Grey-Brown
Redstart	5 mm (VDB) Black
Redstart, Black	5 mm (VDB) Black
Redstart, Guldenstats	6 mm (VDB) Black
Redwing	6 mm (VDB) Black
Reedling *see Tit, Bearded*	
Robin	5 mm (VDB) Black
Robin, American	7 mm (VDB) Dark Brown or Black
Robin, Rufous Bush	5 mm (VDB) Black
Roller	5 mm Dark Brown
Rook	9 mm (VDB) Black
Rosefinch, Scarlet	4 mm (VDB) Black
Rubythroat, Siberian	5 mm (VDB) Black
Ruff	Adult male 7 mm (VDB) Black Adult female 6 mm (VDB) Black
Saker *see Falcon*	
Sanderling	Adult 5 mm (VDB) Black Juvenile 5 mm Grey-Brown
Sandgrouse, Black-bellied	Adult male 8 mm (VDB) Black Adult female 8 mm Dark Brown
Sandgrouse, Pintailed	Adult male 8 mm (VDB) Black Adult female 8 mm Dark Brown
Sandgrouse, Pallas'	Adult male 8 mm (VDB) Black Adult female 8mm Dark Brown
Sandpiper, Baird's	5 mm (VDB) Black
Sandpiper, Broad-billed	5 mm (VDB) Black
Sandpiper, Buff-breasted	6 mm (VDB) Black
Sandpiper, Common	6 mm (VDB) Black
Sandpiper, Curlew	5 mm (VDB) Black
Sandpiper, Green	5 mm (VDB) Black
Sandpiper, Least	6 mm (VDB) Black
Sandpiper, Marsh	5 mm (VDB) Black
Sandpiper, Pectoral	5 mm (VDB) Black

Sandpiper, Purple	6 mm (VDB) Black
Sandpiper, Semi-palmated	5 mm (VDB) Black
Sandpiper, Sharp-tailed	5 mm (VDB) Black
Sandpiper, Solitary	6 mm (VDB) Black
Sandpiper, Spotted	6 mm (VDB) Black
Sandpiper, Stilt	6 mm (VDB) Black
Sandpiper, Terek	6 mm (VDB) Black
Sandpiper, Upland	6 mm (VDB) Black
Sandpiper, White-rumped	5 mm (VDB) Black
Sandpiper, Wood	6 mm (VDB) Black
Scaup *see Duck*	
Scoters *see Duck*	
Serin	3 mm (VDB) Black
Serin, Gold-fronted	3 mm (VDB) Black
Shag	Adult 10 mm Dark Green (Special) Juvenile 10 mm Grey-Brown
Shearwater, Cory's	10 mm (VDB) Black
Shearwater, Great	10 mm (VDB) Black
Shearwater, Little	7 mm (VDB) Black
Shearwater, Manx	8 mm (VDB) Black
Shearwater, Sooty	9 mm (VDB) Black
Shelducks *see Duck*	
Shoveller *see Duck*	
Shrike, Great Grey	7 mm (VDB) Black
Shrike, Lesser Grey	6 mm (VDB) Black
Shrike, Masked	6 mm (VDB) Black
Shrike, Red-backed	5–6 mm Brown
Shrike, Woodchat	5–6 mm Mid Brown
Siskin	3 mm (VDB) Black
Skua, Arctic	8 mm (VDB) Black
Skua, Great	10 mm (VDB) Black
Skua, Long-tailed	8 mm (VDB) Black
Skua, Pomarine	9 mm (DB) Black or Dark Brown
Skylark *see Lark*	
Smew *see Duck*	
Snipe, Common	6 mm (VDB) Black
Snipe, Great	6 mm (VDB) Black
Snipe, Jack	5 mm (VDB) Black
Sparrow, Hedge *see Accentor, Hedge*	
Sparrow, House	4 mm (DB) Black
Sparrow, Italian	4 mm (DB) Black
Sparrow, Rock	4 mm (DB) Black
Sparrow, Spanish	4 mm (DB) Black
Sparrow, Tree	3–4 mm Mid Brown
Sparrowhawks *see Hawk*	
Spoonbill	Adult 10 mm Reddish Brown to Red Juvenile 10 mm Rust Brown
Starling	5 mm (DB) Black
Starling, Rose-coloured	5 mm (VDB) Black
Starling, Spotless	5 mm (VDB) Black
Stilt, Black-winged	7 mm Reddish-Brown
Stint, Little	4 mm (VDB) Black
Stint, Temminck's	4 mm (VDB) Black
Stonechat	4 mm (DB) Black
Stork, Black	12–13 mm Brown
Stork, White	12–13 mm Brown
Swallow	4 mm (VDB) Black
Swallow, Red-rumped	4 mm (VDB) Black
Swan, Bewick's	Adult male 10 mm Brown

	Adult female 11 mm Brownish Yellow
	Juvenile 10 mm Mid Brown
Swan, Mute	Adult male 12 mm (VDB) Black
	Adult female 11 mm (VDB) Black
Swan, Whistling *see Swan, Bewick's*	
Swan, Whooper	Adult male 12 mm (VDB) Black
	Adult female 11 mm (VDB) Black
Swift	6 mm (VDB) Black
Swift, Alpine	7 mm (VDB) Black
Swift, Pallid	6 mm (VDB) Black
Swift, White-rumped	5 mm (VDB) Black
Teal *see Duck*	
Tern, Arctic	7 mm (VDB) Black
Tern, Black	5 mm (VDB) Black
Tern, Caspian	10 mm (VDB) Black
Tern, Common	7 mm (VDB) Black
Tern, Gull-billed	8 mm (VDB) Black
Tern, Little	5 mm (VDB) Black
Tern, Roseate	6 mm (VDB) Black
Tern, Sandwich	8 mm (VDB) Black
Tern, Sooty	7 mm Dark Reddish Brown
Tern, Whiskered	5 mm (VDB) Black
Tern, White-winged Black	5 mm (VDB) Black
Thrush, Black-throated	6 mm (DB) Black
Thrush, Blue Rock	6 mm (DB) Black
Thrush, Dusky	6 mm (DB) Black
Thrush, Eye-browed	5 mm (DB) Black
Thrush, Grey-cheeked	5 mm (DB) Black
Thrush, Hermit	5 mm (DB) Black
Thrush, Mistle *also Missel*	7 mm (DB) Black
Thrush, Naumann's	6 mm (DB) Black
Thrush, Olive-backed	5 mm (DB) Black
Thrush, Rock	6 mm (DB) Black
Thrush, Siberian	6 mm (DB) Black
Thrush, Song	6 mm (DB) Black
Thrush, White's	7 mm (DB) Black
Tit, Azure	4 mm (VDB) Black
Tit, Bearded	Adult male 4 mm Pale Yellow
	Adult female 4 mm Clayish Yellow
	Juvenile 4 mm Very Pale Yellow
Tit, Blue	3 mm (VDB) Black
Tit, Coal	3 mm (VDB) Black
Tit, Crested	3 mm Reddish Brown
Tit, Great	4 mm (VDB) Black
Tit, Long-tailed	3 mm (DB) Black
Tit, Marsh	4 mm (DB) Black
Tit, Penduline	3 mm (DB) Black
Tit, Siberian	4 mm (DB) Black
Tit, Sombre	4 mm (DB) Black
Tit, Tom *see Tit, Blue*	
Tit, Willow	4 mm (DB) Black
Treecreeper	3 mm (DB) Black
Treecreeper, Short-toed	3 mm (DB) Black
Turnstone	Adult 7 mm (VDB) Black
	Juvenile 7 mm Grey-Brown
Twite	4 mm (DB) Black

Vulture, Bearded *see Lammergeter*	
Vulture, Black	13–14 mm (VDB) Black
Vulture, Egyptian	Adult 9 mm Brown Juvenile 9 mm Brown
Vulture, Griffon	12 mm (VDB) Black
Wagtail, Ashy Headed	4 mm (VDB) Black
Wagtail, Black Headed	4 mm (VDB) Black
Wagtail, Blue Headed	4 mm Black
Wagtail, Citrine	4 mm (VDB) Black
Wagtail, Grey	4 mm (VDB) Black
Wagtail, Grey Headed	4 mm (VDB) Black
Wagtail, Kirghiz Steppes	4 mm (VDB) Black
Wagtail, Pied	4 mm (VDB) Black
Wagtail, Spanish	4 mm (VDB) Black
Wagtail, Sykes	4 mm (VDB) Black
Wagtail, Water *see Wagtail, Pied*	
Wagtail, White	4 mm (VDB) Black
Wagtail, Yellow	4 mm (VDB) Black
Wallcreeper	4 mm (VDB) Black
Warbler, Aquatic	5 mm Brown
Warbler, Arctic	4 mm (DB) Black
Warbler, Barred	Adult male 5 mm Bright Yellow Adult female 5 mm Pale Yellow Juvenile 5 mm Greyish White
Warbler, Blyth's Reed	4 mm Brown
Warbler, Bonelli's	4 mm (VDB) Black
Warbler, Booted	4 mm (VDB) Black
Warbler, Cetti's	4 mm (VDB) Dark Brown or Black
Warbler, Dartford	4 mm Reddish Orange to Reddish Brown
Warbler, Desert	4 mm Very Pale Yellow
Warbler, Dusky	4 mm (VDB) Black
Warbler, Fan-tailed	3 mm Dark Brown
Warbler, Garden	5 mm Dark Brown or Black
Warbler, Grasshopper	4 mm Brown
Warbler, Great Reed	5 mm Brown
Warbler, Green	4 mm (DB) Black
Warbler, Greenish	4 mm (DB) Black
Warbler, Icterine	4 mm (DB) Black or Dark Brown
Warbler, Lanceolated	4 mm Dark Brown
Warbler, Marmora's	4 mm Brown
Warbler, Marsh	4 mm Dark Brown or Black
Warbler, Melodious	4 mm Dark Brown
Warbler, Menetries	4 mm Dark Red
Warbler, Moustached	4 mm (DB) Black
Warbler, Olivaceous	4 mm (VDB) Black
Warbler, Olive Tree	5 mm (VDB) Black
Warbler, Orphean	5 mm Very Pale Yellow
Warbler, Paddy Field	4 mm Dark Brown
Warbler, Pallas's	3 mm Dark Brown
Warbler, Pallas's Grasshopper	4 mm Dark Brown
Warbler, Radde's Willow	4 mm (VDB) Black
Warbler, Reed	4 mm Brown
Warbler, River	4 mm Dark Brown
Warbler, Rufous	5 mm Brown
Warbler, Ruppell's	4 mm Red or Reddish Brown
Warbler, Sardinian	4 mm Brown
Warbler, Savi's	4 mm Dark Brown
Warbler, Sedge	4 mm (VDB) Black

Warbler, Spectacled	4 mm Dark Brown
Warbler, Subalpine	4 mm Reddish Brown
Warbler, Willow	4 mm (VDB) Black
Warbler, Wood	4 mm (VDB) Black
Warbler, Yellow-browed	3 mm (DB) Black
Waterhen *see Moorhen*	
Waxwing	Adult 6 mm Reddish Brown Juvenile 6 mm Brown
Wheatear	Adult 5 mm Dark Brown or Black Juvenile 5 mm Grey-Brown
Wheatear, Black	5 mm (VDB) Black
Wheatear, Black-eared	5 mm (DB) Black
Wheatear, Desert	5 mm (VDB) Black
Wheatear, Isabelline	5 mm (DB) Black
Wheatear, Pied	5 mm (DB) Black
Whimbrel	9 mm (VDB) Black
Whinchat	4 mm Dark Reddish Brown
Whitethroat	4 mm Mid Brown
Whitethroat, Lesser	4 mm Light Brown
Widgeon *see Duck*	
Woodcock	10 mm (VDB) Black
Woodlark *see Lark*	
Woodpecker, Black	10 mm Yellow
Woodpecker, Great Spotted	Adult 6 mm Red Juvenile 6 mm Brown
Woodpecker, Green	Adult male 8 mm Yellow Adult female 8 mm Very Pale Yellow Juvenile 8 mm Greyish White
Woodpecker, Grey-headed	Adult male 7 mm Yellow Adult female 7 mm Very Pale Yellow Juvenile (VDB) Black
Woodpecker, Lesser Spotted	4 mm Red
Woodpecker, Middle Spotted	6 mm Red
Woodpecker, Syrian	6 mm Red
Woodpecker, Three-toed	6 mm (VDB) Black
Woodpecker, White-backed	6 mm Reddish Brown
Woodpigeon *see Dove, Ring*	
Wren	3 mm (DB) Black
Wryneck	Adult 5 mm Mid Brown Juvenile 5 mm Grey-Brown
Yellowhammer *see Bunting, Yellow*	
Yellowlegs	8 mm (VDB) Black
Yellowlegs, Lesser	7 mm (VDB) Black

CHECK LIST OF EYE SIZES AND COLOURS OF BRITISH, SCANDINAVIAN AND EUROPEAN MAMMALS

Badger	10 mm (VDB) Black
*Bat, Barbastelle	2 mm* Black
Bat, Bechstein's	2 mm Black
Bat, Blasius Horseshoe	2 mm Black
Bat, Daubenton's	2 mm Black
Bat, Egyptian Hollow-faced	2 mm Black
Bat, European Free-tailed	3 mm Black
Bat, Geoffroy's	2 mm Black
Bat, Greater Horseshoe	3 mm Black
Bat, Grey Long Eared	2 mm Black
Bat, Hoary	3 mm Black
Bat, Ikonnikov's	2 mm Black
Bat, Kuhl's Pipistrelle	2 mm Black
Bat, Large Mouse-Eared	3 mm Black
Bat, Leisler's	3 mm Black
Bat, Lesser Horseshoe	2 mm Black
Bat, Lesser Mouse-Eared	3 mm Black
Bat, Long Eared	2 mm Black
Bat, Long Fingered	2 mm Black
Bat, Mediterranean Horseshoe	3 mm Black
Bat, Mehely's Horseshoe	3 mm Black
Bat, Nathusius's Pipistrelle	2 mm Black
Bat, Natterer's	2 mm Black
Bat, Noctule	3 mm Black
Bat, Northern	2 mm Black
Bat, Parti-coloured	3 mm Black
Bat, Pipistrelle	2 mm Black
Bat, Pond	3 mm Black
Bat, Savi's Pipistrelle	2 mm Black
Bat, Schreiber's	3 mm Black
Bat, Serotine	3 mm Black
Bat, Whiskered	2 mm Black
Bear, Brown, Small	13–14 mm Brown (Special)
Bear, Brown, Medium	15–16 mm Brown (Special)
Bear, Brown, Large	16–18 mm Brown (Special)
Bear, Polar	17–20 mm Brown (Special)
Beaver,	12 mm Dark Brown
Bison, European	30–33 mm Dark Brown Slot (Special)
Boar	18–20 mm Dark Brown (Special)
Buffalo	31–36 mm Dark Brown Slot pupil (Special)
Cat, Wild	16 mm Green tinted Yellow Slit or oval pupil (Special)
Chamois,	20–22 mm Dark Brown Slot pupil (Special)
Coypu, Medium (9 lbs)	8 mm (VDB) Black
Coypu, Large (18 lbs)	10 mm (VDB) Black
Deer, Chinese Muntjac	20 mm Dark Brown
Deer, Chinese Water	16–18 mm (VDB) Black
Deer, Fallow	28–32 mm Dark Brown Slot pupil (Special)
Deer, Red	28–34 mm Dark Brown Slot pupil (Special)
Deer, Reeves Muntjac *see Chinese Muntjac*	
Deer, Rein	26–28 mm Dark Brown Slot pupil (Special)
Deer, Roe	20–22 mm Dark Brown Slot pupil (Special)
Deer, Sika	26–28 mm Dark Brown Slot pupil (Special)

***N.B. for Bats: sizes are for eyes used. Each should be reduced by 1 mm, by eye-lids, to convey smaller eye impression.**

Deer, White Tailed	28–32 mm Dark Brown Slot pupil (Special)
Desman, Pyrenean and Russian *see Shrews*	
Dormouse, Common	4 mm (VDB) Black
Dormouse, Edible	6 mm (VDB) Black
Dormouse, Fat *see Edible*	
Dormouse, Forest	5 mm (VDB) Black
Dormouse, Garden	5 mm (VDB) Black
Dormouse, Hazel *see Common*	
Dormouse, Oak *see Garden*	
Dormouse, Ognev's	4 mm (VDB) Black
Dormouse, Squirrel-tailed *see Edible*	
Elk	34–36 mm Dark Brown & Dark Golden mix Slot pupil (Special)
Ermine, *see Stoat*	
Fox, Arctic	16 mm Golden Yellow Slit pupil (Special)
Fox, Red	18 mm Brown Slit pupil (Special)
Genet	14–16 mm Golden-Brown (Special)
Goat, Wild	21–23 mm Dark Brown to Golden Yellow Slot pupil (Special)
Hamster, Common	8 mm (VDB) Black
Hamster, Golden	6 mm (VDB) Black
Hamster, Grey	4 mm (VDB) Black
Hamster, Migratory *see Grey*	
Hare, Blue	15-16 mm Clayish Mid Brown
Hare, Brown	16 mm Clayish Mid Brown
Hare, Cape *see Brown*	
Hare, Irish	15–16 mm Clayish Mid Brown
Hare, Mountain *see Blue*	
Hare, Varying *see Blue*	
Hedgehog	6 mm (Blackish Grey) Black
Hedgehog, Vagrant	6 mm (Blackish Grey) Black
Horses, Wild	26–30 mm Dark Brown Oval pupil (Special)
Ibex	22–26 mm Dark Golden Brown Slot pupil (Special)
Jackal, Golden	18 mm Brown (Special)
Jackal, Indian *see Golden*	
Lemming, Arctic	3–4 mm (VDB) Black
Lemming, Norway	3–4 mm (VDB) Black
Lemming, Wood	3 mm (VDB) Black
Lynx, European	18–20 mm Yellow to Golden Brown Slit pupil (Special)
Lynx, Northern *see European*	
Lynx, Pardel	18–20 mm Yellow to Golden Brown Slit pupil (Special)
Lynx, Spanish *see Pardel*	
Marmot	10–12 mm (VDB) Black
Marmot, Alpine *see Marmot*	
Marmot, Bobak	10–12 mm (DB) Brown
Martin, Beech	9–10 mm (DB) Brown
Martin, Stone *see Beech*	
Mink, American	8–9 mm (VDB) Black
Mink, European	8–9 mm (VDB) Black
Mole, Blind	2 mm Black
Mole, Common	2 mm Black

Mole, Mediterranean *see Blind*	
Mole, Roman	2 mm Black
Mole Rat, Greater	4 mm Black
Mole Rat, Lesser	3 mm Black
Mole Rat, Russian *see Greater*	
Mongoose, Egyptian	9 mm Dark Brown
Mongoose, Ichneumon *see Egyptian*	
Moose *see Elk*	
Mouflon	22–24 mm Olive Dark Brown to Dark Brown. Can vary to Mid Brown with local species. Slot pupil (Special)
Mouse, Dormouse, *see Dormouse*	
Mouse, Cairo Spiney *see Spiney*	
Mouse, Field, Broad-toothed	4–5 mm (VDB) Black
Mouse, Field, Common *see Mouse, Long-tailed*	
Mouse, Field, Long-tailed	4 mm (VDB) Black
Mouse, Field, Striped	4 mm (VDB) Black
Mouse, Field, Yellow-necked	4 mm (VDB) Black
Mouse, Harvest	2–3 mm (VDB) Black
Mouse, House	3 mm (VDB) Black
Mouse, Northern Birch	3 mm (VDB) Black
Mouse, Rock *see Mouse, Field, Broad-toothed*	
Mouse, St Kilda *see Mouse, House*	
Mouse, Southern Birch	3 mm (VDB) Black
Mouse, Spiney	4 mm (VDB) Black
Mouse, Wood *see Mouse, Field, Long-toothed*	
Muntjac *see Deer*	
Musk Ox	28–33 mm Dark Brown Slot pupil (Special)
Muskrat	8 mm (VDB) Black
Otter	9–10 mm (VDB) Black
Polecat, European	Adult male 9 mm (VDB) Black Adult female 8 mm (VDB) Black
Polecat, Marbled	8–9 mm (VDB) Black
Polecat, Steppe	8–9 mm (VDB) Black
Porcupine, Crested	12 mm Dark Brown
Rabbit, Wild	16 mm Dark Brown
Raccoon	14 mm Dark Brown (Special)
Raccoon, Dog	14 mm Dark Brown (Special)
Rat, Black	6–7 mm (VDB) Black
Rat, Brown	6–7 mm (VDB) Black
Rat, Common *see Rat, Brown*	
Rat, Greater Mole *see Molerat*	
Rat, Lesser Mole *see Molerat*	
Rat, Ship *see Rat, Black*	
Reindeer *see Deer*	
Sable	Adult male 8 mm (VDB) Black Adult female 7 mm (VDB) Black
Saiga	20–22 mm Dark Brown Slit pupil (Special)
Seal,* Atlantic *see Seal, Grey*	
Seal, Bearded	26–30 mm Dark Brown (Special)
Seal, Common	Adult male 24–26 mm Dark Brown (Special) Adult female 23–25 mm Dark Brown (Special)
Seal, Grey	Adult male 26–28 mm Dark Brown (Special) Adult female 24–26 mm Dark Brown (Special)

***Sea-lions and Seals all have special eyes. The surface of the eye is flattened for underwater vision.**

Seal, Harbour *see Seal, Common*	
Seal, Harp	22–24 mm Dark Brown (Special)
Seal, Hooded	24–26 mm Dark Brown (Special)
Seal, Monk	25–28 mm Dark Brown (Special)
Seal, Ringed	21–23 mm Dark Brown (Special)
Sheep, Wild, Soay	21–23 mm Dark Brown to Golden Yellow Slit pupil (Special)
Sheep, Wild *see Mouflon*	
Shrew, Alpine	2 mm (VDB) Black
Shrew, Bicoloured white toothed	2 mm (VDB) Black
Shrew, Common	2 mm (VDB) Black
Shrew, Desman, Pyrenean	3 mm (VDB) Black
Shrew, Desman, Russian	4 mm (VDB) Black
Shrew, Etruscan *see Savi's Pygmy*	
Shrew, European, Common White toothed	2 mm (VDB) Black
Shrew, European, Water *see Water*	
Shrew, Laxanns *see Masked*	
Shrew, Least	1 mm (VDB) Black
Shrew, Lesser, White toothed	2 mm (VDB) Black
Shrew, Masked	1 mm (VDB) Black
Shrew, Mediterranean *see Miller's Water*	
Shrew, Miller's Water	2 mm (VDB) Black
Shrew, Pygmy	1 mm (VDB) Black
Shrew, Savi's Pygmy	1 mm (VDB) Black
Shrew, Scilly *see Lesser*	
Shrew, Water	2–3 mm (VDB) Black
Shrew, White toothed *see European Common White toothed*	
Squirrel, Flying	6 mm (VDB) Black
Squirrel, Grey	9 mm (VDB) Black
Squirrel, Red	8 mm (VDB) Black
Squirrel, Red, Spanish (Sub species)	9 mm (VDB) Black
Squirrel, Russian, Flying *see Flying*	
Stoat	Adult male 8 mm (VDB) Black Adult female 7 mm (VDB) Black
Suslik, European	8 mm Dark Brown
Suslik, Spotted	8 mm Dark Brown
Tarpan, *see Horses, Wild*	
Vole, Alpine *see Snow*	
Vole, Bank	3 mm (VDB) Black
Vole, Cabrera's	3 mm (VDB) Black
Vole, Common	3 mm (VDB) Black
Vole, Common, Red backed *see Bank*	
Vole, Eigg Subspecies of Short tailed	
Vole, European, Pine *see Pine*	
Vole, Fatio's Pine *see Root*	
Vole, Field *see Short tailed*	
Vole, Guernsey, Subspecies of Common	3 mm (VDB) Black
Vole, Ground	4 mm (VDB) Black
Vole, Grey sided	3 mm (VDB) Black
Vole, Guenthers	3 mm (VDB) Black
Vole, Hebridean	3 mm (VDB) Black
Vole, Iberian, Root *see Mediterranean*	
Vole, Large Toothed Red backed *see Grey sided*	
Vole, Mediterranean *see Guenthers*	

Vole, Mediterranean, Pine	3 mm (VDB) Black
Vole, Mediterranean, Root *see Savi's Pine*	
Vole, Nehrings Snow	3 mm (VDB) Black
Vole, Northern Red backed *see Ruddy*	
Vole, Orkney, Subspecies of Common	4 mm (VDB) Black
Vole, Pine	3 mm (VDB) Black
Vole, Root	3 mm (VDB) Black
Vole, Ronaldsay, Subspecies of Common	4 mm (VDB) Black
Vole, Rousay, Subspecies of Common	4 mm (VDB) Black
Vole, Ruddy	3 mm (VDB) Black
Vole, Sanday, Subspecies of Common	4 mm (VDB) Black
Vole, Savi's Pine	3 mm (VDB) Black
Vole, Short tailed	3 mm (VDB) Black
Vole, Snow	3 mm (VDB) Black
Vole, Water	5 mm (VDB) Black
Vole, Westray, Subspecies of Common	4 mm (VDB) Black
Wallaby, Red-necked	18-20 mm Greyish Brown
Walrus	Adult male 28–32 mm Dark Brown (Special) Adult female 25–28 mm Dark Brown (Special)
Weasel	Adult male 6 mm (VDB) Black Adult female 4–5 mm (VDB) Black
Wildcat *see Cat, Wild*	
Wild Goat *see Goat, Wild*	
Wolf	18–20 mm Brown (Special)
Wolverine	13–15 (DB) Black

APPENDIX III

CHECK LIST OF EYE SIZES AND COLOURS OF NORTH AMERICAN BIRDS

Albatross, Black-footed	13–14 mm (VDB) Black
Albatross, Laysan	13 mm (VDB) Black
Anhinga	Adult 12 mm Brown
	Chick (VDB) Black
Ani, Groove-billed	8 mm (VDB) Black
Ani, Smooth-billed	8 mm (VDB) Black
Ani chicks	(VDB) Black
Auklet, Cassin's	Adult 1st year 6 mm Dark Brown, lightening with age
	Adult Breeding 6 mm White
Auklet, Crested	Adult 7 mm White
	Juvenile 7 mm Dark Brown at 1 Year
Auklet, Least	Adult 5 mm White
	Juvenile 5 mm Dark Brown at 1 Year
Auklet, Parakeet	Adult 7 mm White
	Juvenile 7 mm Dark Brown at 1 Year
Auklet, Rhinoceros	Adult 8 mm White
	Juvenile 8 mm Dark Brown at 1 Year
Auklet, Whiskered	Adult 5 mm White
	Juvenile 5 mm Dark Brown at 1 Year
Auklet Chicks	(VDB) Black
Avocet, American	8 mm Reddish Dark Brown
Baldpate *see Widgeon, American*	
Becard, Rose-throated	4 mm (VDB) Black
Bittern, American	12 mm Yellow
Bittern, Least	Adult male 7 mm Golden Yellow
	Adult female 7 mm Yellow
Blackbird, Brewer's	Adult male 7 mm Yellow
	Adult female 7 mm Brown
Blackbird, Red-winged	6 mm (VDB) Black
Blackbird, Rusty	Adult male 6 mm Yellow-White
	Adult female 6 mm Yellow
Blackbird, Tri-coloured	6 mm (VDB) Black
Blackbird, Yellow-headed	7 mm (VDB) Black
Bluebird, Eastern	6 mm (VDB) Black
Bluebird, Mexican *see Bluebird, Western*	
Bluebird, Mountain	6 mm (VDB) Black
Bluebird, Western	6 mm (VDB) Black
Bluethroat	4 mm (VDB) Black
Bobolink	4 mm (VDB) Black
Bobwhite Quail	7 mm (DB) Black
Booby, Blue-faced	12 mm Pale Yellow
Booby, Blue-footed	13 mm Pale Yellow
Booby, Brown	12 mm Pale Yellow
Booby, Masked *see Booby, Blue-faced*	
Booby, Red-footed	12 mm Pale Yellow
Booby, White-bellied *see Booby, Brown*	
Brant *see Goose*	
Bufflehead *see Duck*	
Bulbul, Red-whiskered	5 mm (VDB) Black
Bunting, Bay-winged *see Sparrow, Vesper*	
Bunting, Indigo	4 mm (VDB) Black
Bunting, Lark	4–5 mm (VDB) Black
Bunting, Lazuli	4 mm (VDB) Black
Bunting, McKay's	4–5 mm (VDB) Black
Bunting, Painted	4 mm (VDB) Black

Bunting, Snow	4–5 mm (VDB) Black
Bunting, Varied	3–4 mm (VDB) Black
Bushtit	Adult male 3 mm (VDB) Black Adult female 3 mm Pale Yellow
Bushtit, Black-eared *see Bushtit*	
Bushtit, Common	Adult male 3 mm (VDB) Black Adult female 3 mm Pale Yellow
Bushtit, Lloyd's *see Bushtit*	
Butcher Bird *see Shrike, Loggerhead*	
Butterball *see Duck, Bufflehead*	
Butterbill *see Duck, Scoter, Black*	
Buzzard, Black *see Vulture, Black*	
Buzzard, Turkey *see Vulture, Turkey*	
Camp Robber *see Jay, Grey*	
Canary, Wild *see Goldfinch, American*	
Canvasback *see Duck*	
Caracara	Adult 12–13 mm Dark Brown Chick Reddish Brown
Cardinal	Male 5 mm (VDB) Black Female 5 mm (DB) Dark Brown or Black
Catbird *see Catbird, Grey*	
Catbird, Grey	5 mm (VDB) Black
Chachalaca	8 mm Dark Brown
Chat, Yellow-breasted	5 mm (VDB) Black
Chickadee, Black-capped	4 mm (VDB) Black
Chickadee, Boreal	4 mm (VDB) Black
Chickadee, Carolina	3 mm (VDB) Black
Chickadee, Chestnut-backed	3 mm (VDB) Black
Chickadee, Grey-headed	4 mm (VDB) Black
Chickadee, Mexican	4 mm (VDB) Black
Chickadee, Mountain	4 mm (VDB) Black
Chuck-Will's Widow	10 mm (VDB) Black
Chukar	8 mm Dark Brown
Condor, Californian	18–20 mm Dark Brown
Coot, American	Adult 8 mm Reddish Tinged Mid Brown Juvenile 8 mm Mid Brown Chick (VDB) Black
Cormorant, Brandt's	Adult 12 mm Dark Green Juvenile 12 mm Brown
Cormorant, Double Crested	Adult 12 mm Dark Green Juvenile 12 mm Brown
Cormorant, Great	Adult 13 mm Dark Green Juvenile 13 mm Brown
Cormorant, Neotropical	Adult 9 mm Dark Green Juvenile 9 mm Brown
Cormorant, Olivaceous *see Cormorant, Neotropical*	
Cormorant, Pelagic	Adult 10 mm Dark Green Juvenile 10 mm Brown
Cormorant, Red-faced	Adult 10 mm Dark Green Juvenile 10 mm Brown
Cormorant, All Cormorant Chicks	(VDB) Black
Cowbird, Bronzed	6 mm Reddish Dark Brown
Cowbird, Brown-headed	5 mm (VDB) Black
Cowbird, Common *see Cowbird, Brown-headed*	
Cowbird, Red-eyed *see Cowbird, Bronzed*	
Crane, Little Brown *see Crane, Sandhill*	
Crane, Sandhill	13–14 mm Reddish Dark Brown Chick Dark Brown

Crane, Whooping	14 mm Golden Yellow Chick Dark Grey-Brown
Creeper, Brown	3 mm (DB) Black
Crossbill, Red	4 mm (DB) Black
Crossbill, White-winged	4 mm (DB) Black
Crow, American	9–10 mm (VDB) Black
Crow, Common *see Crow, American*	
Crow, Fish	9 mm (VDB) Black
Crow, Mexican	8–9 mm (VDB) Black
Crow, North Western	9 mm (VDB) Black
Cuckoo, Black-billed	7 mm (VDB) Black
Cuckoo, Mangrove	7 mm (DB) Black
Cuckoo, Yellow-billed	7 mm (DB) Black
Curlew, Bristle-thighed	9 mm (VDB) Black
Curlew, Eskimo	8 mm (VDB) Black
Curlew, Hudsonian *see Whimbrel*	
Curlew, Long-billed	10 mm (VDB) Black
Darters *see Anhinga*	
Dickcissel	4 mm (DB) Black
Dipper	5 mm (DB) Dark Brown or Black
Dove, Barbary	6 mm Brown
Dove, Ground	4 mm (VDB) Black
Dove, Inca	5 mm (VDB) Black
Dove, Mourning	6 mm (VDB) Black
Dove, Ringed Turtle	6 mm Blackish Red. Use Black
Dove, Rock	Adult 8 mm Chestnut Juvenile 8 mm Yellowish Brown
Dove, Spotted	6 mm Olive Brown
Dove, White-fronted	6 mm Pale Clay-Brown
Dove, White-winged	6 mm Reddish Brown
Dovekie	5 mm (VDB) Black
Dowitcher, Eastern *see Dowitcher, Short-billed*	
Dowitcher, Long-billed	7 mm (VDB) Black
Dowitcher, Short-billed	7 mm (VDB) Black
Duck, Black	Male 9 mm (VDB) Black Female 9 mm Dark Brown
Duck, Black-bellied Tree	Adult male 8 mm (VDB) Black Adult female 8 mm (VDB) Black Duckling (VDB) Black
Duck, Black-bellied Whistling *see Duck, Black-bellied Tree*	
Duck, Black Mallard *see Duck, Black*	
Duck, Bufflehead	Adult male 6 mm (VDB) Black Adult female 6 mm (VDB) Black
Duck, Canvasback	Adult male 9 mm Reddish Brown Adult female 9 mm (VDB) Black
Duck, Carolina *see Duck, Wood*	
Duck, Dusky *see Duck, Mottled*	
Duck, Eider, Common	Adult male 10 mm (VDB) Black Adult female 10 mm Yellowish Brown Juvenile 10 mm Grey-Brown
Duck, Eider, King	Adult male 10 mm (VDB) Black Adult female 10 mm Dark Brown
Duck, Eider, Spectacled	Adult male 9 mm (VDB) Black Adult female 9 mm Dark Brown
Duck, Eider, Steller's	Adult male 8 mm (VDB) Black Adult female 8 mm Dark Brown Juvenile Grey-Brown
Duck, Eider: Ducklings	(VDB) Black

Duck, Fulvous, Tree	Adult male 8 mm (VDB) Black
	Adult female 8 mm (VDB) Black
	Duckling (VDB) Black
Duck, Fulvous, Whistling *see Duck, Fulvous, Tree*	
Duck, Gadwall	Adult 8 mm (VDB) Black
	Juvenile 8 mm Grey-Brown
Duck, Garganey	Adult 6 mm Mid Brown
	Juvenile 6 mm Grey-Brown
Duck, Goldeneye, Barrow's	Adult male 9 mm Very Pale Yellow
	Adult female 9 mm Greenish Yellow
Duck, Goldeneye, Common	Adult male 9 mm Pale Yellow
	Adult female 9 mm Dull Yellow
	Juvenile 9 mm Sex for Colour
Duck, Goldeneye: Ducklings	(VDB) Black
Duck, Harlequin	Adult male 9 mm Reddish Brown
	Adult female 9 mm Dark Brown
	Juvenile 9 mm Brown
	Duckling (VDB) Black
Duck, Long-tailed *see Duck, Oldsquaw*	
Duck, Mallard	Adult male 8 mm (VDB) Black
	Adult female 8 mm Dark Brown
	Juvenile 8 mm Grey-Brown
	Duckling (VDB) Black
Duck, Mandarin	8 mm Reddish Dark Brown or Black
Duck, Masked	Adult male 6 mm (VDB) Black
	Adult female 6 mm Dark Brown
Duck, Merganser, Common	Adult male 9 mm Reddish Dark Brown
	Adult female 9 mm Dark Brown
Duck, Merganser, Hooded	Adult male 8 mm Golden Yellow
	Adult female 8 mm Reddish Brown
Duck, Merganser, Red-breasted	Adult male 9 mm Reddish Brown
	Adult female 9 mm Reddish Brown
Duck, Merganser: Duckling	Grey
Duck, Mexican	Adult male 8 mm (VDB) Black
	Adult female 8 mm Dark Brown
Duck, Mexican Squealer *see Duck, Fulvous, Tree*	
Duck, Mottled	Adult male 8 mm (VDB) Black
	Adult female 8 mm Dark Brown
Duck, Muscovy	Adult male 10 mm Mid Golden-Brown
	Adult female 10 mm Dark Brown
Duck, New Mexican *see Duck, Mexican*	
Duck, Oldsquaw	Adult male 8 mm Reddish Yellow
	Adult female 8 mm Dark Brown
	Juvenile 8 mm Grey-Brown
	Duckling (VDB) Black
Duck, Pintail	Adult male 8 mm (VDB) Black
	Adult female 8 mm Dark Brown
	Duckling (VDB) Black
Duck, Pochard, Common	Adult male 9 mm Winter: Reddish Yellow
	Summer: Bright Red-Brown
	Adult female 9 mm Winter: Reddish Yellow
	Summer: Reddish Hazel-Brown
	Juvenile 9 mm Dark Brown
Duck, Redhead	Adult male 8 mm Orangy Mid Brown
	Adult female 8 mm (VDB) Black
	Duckling (VDB) Black
Duck, Ring-billed *see Duck, Ring-necked*	
Duck, Ring-necked	Adult male 8 mm Golden Yellow
	Adult female 8 mm (VDB) Black

Duck, Ruddy	Adult male 7 mm (VDB) Black Adult female 7 mm Dark Brown Duckling (VDB) Black
Duck, Scaup, Greater	Adult male 8 mm Yellow Adult female 8 mm Reddish Brown
Duck, Scaup, Lesser	Adult male 8 mm Yellow Adult female 8 mm Dull Yellow Duckling (VDB) Black
Duck, Scoter, Black	Adult male 8 mm (VDB) Black Adult female 8 mm Dark Brown
Duck, Scoter, Common *see Duck, Scoter, Black*	
Duck, Scoter, Surf	Adult male 9 mm White Adult female 9 mm Dark Brown Juvenile 9 mm Greyish Brown
Duck, Scoter, White-winged	Adult male 9 mm White Adult female 9 mm Dark Brown Juvenile 9 mm Brown
Duck, Scoter: All Ducklings	(VDB) Black
Duck, Shoveler, Northern	Adult male 8 mm Golden Yellow Adult female 8 mm Dark Brown Juvenile 8 mm Greyish Yellow Ducklings (VDB) Black
Duck, Summer *see Duck, Wood*	
Duck, Teal, Blue-winged	Adult male 6 mm (VDB) Black Adult female 6 mm Dark Brown
Duck, Teal, Common *see Duck, Teal, Green-winged*	
Duck, Teal, Cinnamon	Adult male 6 mm Reddish Brown Adult female 6 mm Dark Brown
Duck, Teal, Green-winged	Adult male 6 mm Dark Brown Adult female 6 mm Dark Brown Juvenile 6 mm Greyish Brown
Duck, Teal: Ducklings	(VDB) Black
Duck, Tree *see Duck, Black-bellied or Fulvous*	
Duck, Tufted	Adult male 8 mm Yellow Adult female 8 mm Dull Yellow Juvenile 8 mm (VDB) Black
Duck, Widgeon, American	Adult male 8 mm (DB) Black Adult female 8 mm Dark Brown
Duck, Widgeon, European	Adult male 8 mm (DB) Black Adult female 8 mm Dark Brown
Duck, Widgeon: Ducklings	(VDB) Black
Duck, Wood	Adult male 8 mm Brownish Red Adult female 8 mm (VDB) Black Ducklings (VDB) Black
Dunlin	5 mm (VDB) Black
Eagle, Bald	Male 18 mm Pale Yellow Female 19 mm Pale Yellow Juvenile 18 mm Yellow-Brown Chick Brown
Eagle, Fish *see Osprey*	
Eagle, Grey Sea *see Eagle, White-tailed Sea*	
Eagle, Golden	Adult male 18 mm Golden Yellow-Brown Adult female 19 mm Clayish Brown Juvenile 18 mm Brown Chick Brown
Eagle, Mexican *see Caracara*	

Eagle, White-tailed Sea	Adult male 17 mm Greyish Brown Adult female 18 mm Greyish Brown Juvenile 17 mm Dark Brown
Egret, American *see Egret, Great*	
Egret, Cattle	10 mm Pale Yellow
Egret, Common *see Egret, Great*	
Egret, Great	13–14 mm Pale Yellow
Egret, Reddish	12 mm Pale Yellow
Egret, Snowy	11 mm Pale Yellow
Egret, White *see Egret, Great*	
Egret: All Egret Chicks	Pale Yellow
Eiders *see Duck*	
Falcon, Aplomado	Adult male 10 mm (VDB) Black Adult female 11 mm (VDB) Black
Falcon, Kestrel, American *see Kestrel, American*	
Falcon, Merlin *see Merlin*	
Falcon, Peregrine	Adult male 11 mm (VDB) Black Adult female 12 mm (VDB) Black
Falcon, Prairie	Adult male 11 mm (VDB) Black Adult female 12 mm (VDB) Black
Fieldfare	7 mm (VDB) Black
Finch, Black Rosy	4 mm (VDB) Black
Finch, Brown-Capped Rosy	4 mm (VDB) Black
Finch, Cassin's	4 mm (VDB) Black
Finch, Cassin's Purple *see Finch, Cassin's*	
Finch, Grey Crowned Rosy	4 mm (VDB) Black
Finch, House	4 mm (VDB) Black
Finch, Purple	4 mm (VDB) Black
Finch: All Finch Chicks	Black
Flicker, Common	8 mm (VDB) Black
Flicker, Gilded *see Flicker, Common. Colour variant*	
Flicker, Red-Shafted *see Flicker, Common. Colour variant*	
Flicker, Yellow-Shafted *see Flicker, Common. Colour variant*	
Flycatcher, Acadian	5 mm (VDB) Black
Flycatcher, Alder	5 mm (VDB) Black
Flycatcher, Ash-throated	6 mm (VDB) Black
Flycatcher, Beardless	4 mm (VDB) Black
Flycatcher, Brown-crested *see Flycatcher, Wied's Crested*	
Flycatcher, Buff-breasted	4 mm (VDB) Black
Flycatcher, Coue's	5 mm (VDB) Black
Flycatcher, Crested *see Flycatcher, Great Crested*	
Flycatcher, Derby *see Flycatcher, Kiskadee*	
Flycatcher, Dusky	5 mm (VDB) Black
Flycatcher, Fork-tailed	5 mm (VDB) Black
Flycatcher, Grey	4 mm (VDB) Black
Flycatcher, Great Crested	6 mm (VDB) Black
Flycatcher, Hammond's	4 mm (VDB) Black
Flycatcher, Kiskadee	7 mm (DB) Black
Flycatcher, Least	4 mm (VDB) Black
Flycatcher, Mexican *see Flycatcher, Wied's Crested*	
Flycatcher, Mexican Crested *see Flycatcher, Wied's Crested*	
Flycatcher, Olivaceous	5 mm (VDB) Black
Flycatcher, Olive-sided	6 mm (VDB) Black
Flycatcher, Scissor-tailed	5 mm (VDB) Black
Flycatcher, Silky *see Flycatcher, Yellow-bellied*	
Flycatcher, Sulphur-bellied	6 mm (VDB) Black
Flycatcher, Traill's *see both Flycatcher, Alder and Flycatcher, Willow*	
Flycatcher, Tyrant *see both Flycatcher, Alder and Flycatcher, Willow*	

Flycatcher, Vermilion	5 mm (VDB) Black
Flycatcher, Western	5 mm (VDB) Black
Flycatcher, Wied's Crested	6 mm (VDB) Black
Flycatcher, Willow	5 mm (VDB) Black
Flycatcher, Wright's *see Flycatcher, Dusky*	
Flycatcher, Yellow-bellied	4 mm (VDB) Black
Frigatebird, Magnificent	12 mm (VDB) Black
Fulmar, Northern	11 mm (VDB) Black
Gadwall, *see Duck*	
Gallinule, Common (Moorhen)	6 mm Reddish Brown or Red
Gallinule, Purple	6 mm Reddish Brown or Red
Gallinule: All Gallinule Chicks	Black
Gannet *see Booby*	
Gnatcatcher, Black-capped	4 mm (VDB) Black
Gnatcatcher, Black-tailed	4 mm (VDB) Black
Gnatcatcher, Blue-Grey	4 mm (VDB) Black
Gnatcatcher, Plumbeous *see Gnatcatcher, Black-tailed*	
Goatsucker *see Nightjar*	
Godwit, Bar-tailed	8 mm (VDB) Black
Godwit, Black-tailed	8 mm (VDB) Black
Godwit, Hudsonian	8 mm (VDB) Black
Godwit, Marbled	9 mm (VDB) Black
Goldeneye, Barrow's *see Duck*	
Goldeneye, Common *see Duck*	
Goldfinch, American	4 mm (VDB) Black
Goldfinch, Arkansas *see Goldfinch, Lesser*	
Goldfinch, Common *see Goldfinch, American*	
Goldfinch, Dark-backed *see Goldfinch, Lesser*	
Goldfinch, Lawrence's	3 mm (VDB) Black
Goldfinch, Lesser	3 mm (VDB) Black
Gooney Bird *see Albatross*	
Goose, Barnacle	10 mm (VDB) Black
Goose, Blue	10–11 mm (VDB) Black
Goose, Brant	9–10 mm (VDB) Black
Goose, Brant, Black *see Goose, Brant*	
Goose, Brant, Blue *see Goose, Blue*	
Goose, Brant, White *see Goose, Snow*	
Goose, Canada	12 mm Greyish Brown
Goose, Emperor	10 mm (VDB) Black
Goose, Interior Canada *see Goose, Canada*	
Goose, Lesser Canada *see Goose, Canada*	
Goose, Pink-footed	10 mm (DB) Black
Goose, Richardson's Canada *see Goose, Canada*	
Goose, Ross's	9–10 mm (VDB) Black
Goose, Snow	10–11 mm (VDB) Black
Goose, Tule, *see Goose, White-fronted*	
Goose, Western Canada *see Goose, Canada*	
Goose, White-fronted	11 mm (VDB) Black
Goose: All Goslings	Black
Goshawk	Adult male 12 mm Golden Yellow
	Adult female 13–14 mm Orange tinted Yellow
	Juvenile 12 mm Clayish Brown
Grackle, Boat-tailed	Male 5–6 mm Often Brown or Yellow
	Female 5 mm Dark Brown
	N.B. Louisiana & Texas: Species always yellow-eyed
Grackle, Common, Bronzed	5 mm Yellow (always)
Grackle, Common, Purple	5 mm Bright Yellow (always)
Grackle, Great Tailed	5–6 mm Yellow (always)

Grebe, Eared	7 mm Orangy-Pink; Silvery backing or Red (Special)
Grebe, Holboell's *see Grebe, Red-necked*	
Grebe, Horned	7 mm Brownish Red
Grebe, Least	6 mm Red-tinted Clay or Mid Brown
Grebe, Mexican *see Grebe, Least*	
Grebe, Pied Billed	7–8 mm Dark Brown
Grebe, Red-necked	Adult 7–8 mm Reddish Dark Brown Juvenile 7–8 mm Yellow
Grebe, Western	9 mm Red
Greenshank	Adult 8 mm (VDB) Black Juvenile 8 mm Greyish Brown
Grosbeak, Black-headed	6 mm (VDB) Black
Grosbeak, Blue	5 mm (VDB) Black
Grosbeak, Evening	6 mm (VDB) Black
Grosbeak, Pine	6–7 mm (VDB) Black
Grosbeak, Rose-breasted	6 mm (VDB) Black
Groundchat	4 mm (VDB) Black
Grouse, Blue	9 mm Dark Brown
Grouse, Pinnated *see Prairie Chicken, Greater*	
Grouse, Ruffled	9 mm Dark Brown
Grouse, Sage	11 mm Dark Brown
Grouse, Sharp-tailed	9 mm Dark Brown
Grouse, Spruce	Adult male 9 mm (VDB) Black Adult female 9 mm Dark Brown
Grouse: All Grouse Chicks	(DB) Dark Brown or Black
Guillemot, Black	7 mm (VDB) Black
Guillemot, Pigeon	7 mm (VDB) Black
Guillemot: All Chicks	(VDB) Black
Gull, Boneparte's	8 mm Dark Brown
Gull, California	Adult 11 mm Yellow Juvenile First Year 11 mm (VDB) Black
Gull, Common *see Gull, Mew*	
Gull, Franklin's	8–9 mm (VDB) Black
Gull, Glaucous	12 mm Bright Yellow Juvenile (VDB) Black
Gull, Glaucous-winged	Adult 12 mm (DB) Black Juvenile (up to 2 years) 12 mm (VDB) Black
Gull, Greater Black-backed	Adult 12 mm Pale Yellow Juvenile 12 mm Grey-Brown
Gull, Heermann's	Adult 9 mm (DB) Black Juvenile 1st Year 9 mm (VDB) Black
Gull, Herring	Adult 11 mm Pale Yellow Juvenile 11 mm (VDB) Black
Gull, Iceland	Adult 11 mm Yellow Juvenile 11 mm Grey-Brown
Gull, Ivory	10 mm Dark Brown
Gull, Kittiwake, Black-legged	9 mm (VDB) Black
Gull, Kittiwake, Red-legged	8 mm (VDB) Black
Gull, Laughing	9 mm Black or Dark Red
Gull, Lesser Black-backed	Adult 11 mm Very Pale Yellow Juvenile 11 mm (VDB) Black
Gull, Little	8 mm (VDB) Black
Gull, Mew	9 mm (VDB) Black Juvenile 9 mm Greyish-Brown
Gull, Ring-billed	9 mm Yellow
Gull, Sabine's	7 mm (DB) Dark Brown or Black
Gull, Sea *see Gull, Herring*	
Gull, Thayer's	12 mm (DB) Dark Brown or Black
Gull, Western	Adult 12 mm Yellow

	Juvenile 12 mm (VDB) Black
Gull, Yellow-footed *see Gull, Western*	
Gyrfalcon	Adult male 14 mm (VDB) Black
	Adult female 15 mm (VDB) Black
	Chicks (VDB) Black
Hawk, Black	Male 13 mm Dark Brown
	Female 14 mm Dark Brown
Hawk, Broad-winged	Male 9 mm Yellow
	Female 10 mm Yellow
Hawk, Cooper's	Adult male 10 mm Reddish Brown
	Adult female 11 mm Reddish Brown
Hawk, Duck *see Falcon, Peregrine*	
Hawk, Ferruginous	Adult male 13 mm Brown
	Adult female 14 mm Brown
Hawk, Ferruginous, Rough-legged *see Hawk, Ferruginous*	
Hawk, Fish *see Osprey*	
Hawk, Grey	Adult male 10 mm Dark Brown
	Adult female 11 mm Dark Brown
Hawk, Harlan's *see Hawk, Red-tailed*	
Hawk, Harris'	Adult male 12 mm Dark Brown
	Adult female 13 mm Dark Brown
Hawk, Krider's Red-tailed	Male 13 mm Yellow
	Female 14 mm Yellow
Hawk, Marsh	Adult male 12 mm Yellow
	Adult female 13 mm Pale Yellow
Hawk, Mexican Black *see Hawk, Black*	
Hawk, Pigeon *see Merlin*	
Hawk, Red-shouldered	Adult male 12 mm Dark Brown
	Adult female 13 mm Dark Brown
	Juvenile Greyish Brown
Hawk, Red-tailed	Adult male 13 mm Dark Brown
	Adult female 14 mm Dark Brown
	Juvenile 13 mm Greyish Brown
Hawk, Rough-legged	Adult male 13 mm Pale Yellow to Clayish Brown
	Adult female 14 mm Pale Yellow to Clayish Brown
Hawk, Sennett's White-tailed *see Hawk, White-tailed*	
Hawk, Sharp-shinned	Adult male 7 mm Reddish Brown
	Adult female 8 mm Reddish Brown
	Juvenile 7 mm Pale Yellow
Hawk, Short-tailed	Adult male 8 mm Dark Brown
	Adult female 9 mm Dark Brown
Hawk, Sparrow *see Kestrel, American*	
Hawk, Swainson's	Adult male 12 mm Dark Brown
	Adult female 13 mm Dark Brown
Hawk, White-tailed	Adult male 13 mm Dark Brown
	Adult female 14 mm Dark Brown
Hawk, Zone-tailed	Adult male 13 mm Dark Brown
	Adult female 14 mm Dark Brown
Heron, Black-crowned Night	Adult 12 mm Reddish Brown
	Juvenile 12 mm Reddish Clay-Brown
	Chick Pale Yellow
Heron, Great Blue	Adult 13 mm Pale Yellow
	Juvenile 13 mm Pale Cream
	Chick Yellow
Heron, Great White *see Heron, Great Blue*	
Heron, Green	Adult 8 mm Yellow
	Juvenile 8 mm Clayish Brown

Heron, Little Blue	Adult 12 mm Yellow Juvenile 12 mm Pale Yellow
Heron, Louisiana *see Heron, Tri-coloured*	
Heron, Tri-coloured	Adult 12 mm Reddish Brown Chick Very Pale Yellow
Heron, Yellow-crowned Night	Adult 12 mm Reddish Brown Juvenile 12 mm Clayish Brown
Hummingbird, Allen's	2 mm (VDB) Black
Hummingbird, Anna's	3 mm (VDB) Black
Hummingbird, Black-chinned	2 mm (VDB) Black
Hummingbird, Blue-throated	3 mm (VDB) Black
Hummingbird, Broad-billed	2 mm (VDB) Black
Hummingbird, Broad-tailed	3 mm (VDB) Black
Hummingbird, Buff-bellied	3 mm (VDB) Black
Hummingbird, Calliope	2 mm (VDB) Black
Hummingbird, Costa's	2 mm (VDB) Black
Hummingbird, Lucifer	2 mm (VDB) Black
Hummingbird, Rieffer's	2 mm (VDB) Black
Hummingbird, Rivoli's	3 mm (VDB) Black
Hummingbird, Ruby-throated	2 mm (VDB) Black
Hummingbird, Rufous	2 mm (VDB) Black
Hummingbird, Violet-crowned	3 mm (VDB) Black
Hummingbird, White-eared	2 mm (VDB) Black
Hummingbird: All Nestlings	Black
Ibis, Glossy	8–9 mm Very Dark Brown or Black Chick Dark Brown
Ibis, White	Adult 9 mm Yellow Juvenile 9 mm Dark Brown
Ibis, White-faced	9 mm Brown
Ibis, White-faced Glossy *see Ibis, White-faced*	
Ibis, Wood *see Stork, Wood*	
Jacana	5 mm (VDB) Black
Jaeger, Long-tailed	8 mm (VDB) Black
Jaeger, Parasitic	8 mm (VDB) Black
Jaeger, Pomarine	9 mm (DB) Black or Dark Brown
Jay, Arizona *see Jay, Mexican*	
Jay, Blue	8 mm (VDB) Black
Jay, California *see Jay, Scrub*	
Jay, Canada *see Jay, Grey*	
Jay, Grey	7 mm (VDB) Black
Jay, Green	8 mm (VDB) Black
Jay, Mexican	8 mm (VDB) Black
Jay, Pinyon	7 mm (VDB) Black
Jay, Scrub	8 mm (VDB) Black
Jay, Steller's	8 mm (VDB) Black
Jay, Texas *see Jay, Scrub*	
Junco, Dark-eyed	4 mm (VDB) Black
Junco, Grey-headed	4 mm (VDB) Black
Junco, Oregon *see Junco, Dark-eyed*	
Junco, Slate-coloured *see Junco, Dark-eyed*	
Junco, White-winged *see Junco, Dark-eyed*	
Junco, Yellow-eyed	5 mm Yellow-Orange
Kestrel, American	9 mm (VDB) Black
Killdeer	8 mm (VDB) Black
Kingbird, Arkansas *see Kingbird, Western*	

Kingbird, Cassin's	5 mm (VDB) Black
Kingbird, Couch's *see Kingbird, Tropical*	
Kingbird, Eastern	5 mm (VDB) Black
Kingbird, Grey	5 mm (VDB) Black
Kingbird, Olive-backed *see Kingbird, Tropical*	
Kingbird, Tropical	5 mm (VDB) Black
Kingbird, Western	5 mm (VDB) Black
Kingfisher, Belted	9 mm (VDB) Black
Kingfisher, Green	7 mm (VDB) Black
Kingfisher, Ringed	9 mm (VDB) Black
Kinglet, Golden-crowned	3 mm (VDB) Black
Kinglet, Ruby-crowned	3 mm (VDB) Black
Kite, Everglade	Adult male 9 mm Reddish Mid Brown Adult female 10 mm Reddish Mid Brown
Kite, Mississippi	Adult male 8 mm Reddish Mid Brown Adult female 9 mm Reddish Mid Brown
Kite, Snail *see Kite, Everglade*	
Kite, Swallow-tailed	Adult male 9 mm Reddish Mid Brown Adult female 10 mm Reddish Mid Brown
Kite, White-tailed	Adult male 9 mm Reddish Mid Brown Adult female 10 mm Reddish Mid Brown
Kite: All Kite Chicks	Dark Brown
Kittiwake, Black-legged *see Gull, Kittiwake, Black-legged*	
Kittiwake, Red-legged *see Gull, Kittiwake, Red-legged*	
Kittiwake: Chicks	(VDB) Black
Knot	Adult 6 mm (VDB) Black Juvenile 6 mm Grey-Brown
Knot, Red *see Knot*	

Lark, Horned	5 mm (VDB) Black
Lark, Sky	4 mm Brown
Limpkin	11 mm Reddish Brown
Longspur, Chestnut-collared	4 mm (VDB) Black
Longspur, Lapland	4 mm (VDB) Black
Longspur, McCown's	4 mm (VDB) Black
Longspur, Smith's	4 mm (VDB) Black
Loon, Arctic	Adult 12 mm Red Juvenile 12 mm Brown
Loon, Common	Adult 14 mm Red Juvenile 14 mm (VDB) Black
Loon, Pacific *see Loon, Arctic*	
Loon, Red-throated	Adult 11 mm Red Juvenile 11 mm Brown
Loon, Yellow-billed	Adult 14 mm Red Juvenile 14 mm (VDB) Black

Magpie, Black-billed	8–9 mm (VDB) Black
Magpie, Yellow-billed	8 mm (VDB) Black
Mallard, *see Ducks*	
Man-o'-War Bird *see Frigatebird, Magnificent*	
Marsh Hen, Saltwater *see Rail, Clapper*	
Martin, Grey-breasted	4 mm (VDB) Black
Martin, Purple	4 mm (VDB) Black
Meadowlark, Eastern	6 mm (VDB) Black
Meadowlark, Western	6 mm (VDB) Black
Merganser, American *see Duck, Merganser, Common*	
Mergansers *see Duck*	

Merlin	Male 7 mm (VDB) Black
	Female 8 mm (VDB) Black
Mockingbird	5 mm Grey-Brown
Moorhens *see Gallinule*	
Murre, Common	10 mm (VDB) Black
Murre, Thick-billed	10 mm (VDB) Black
Murre: Chicks	(VDB) Black
Murrelet, Ancient	7 mm (VDB) Black
Murrelet, Craveri's	6–7 mm (VDB) Black
Murrelet, Kittlitz's	6 mm (VDB) Black
Murrelet, Marbled	7 mm (VDB) Black
Murrelet, Xantus'	7 mm (VDB) Black
Murrelet: Chicks	(VDB) Black
Mutton Bird *see Shearwater, Short-tailed*	
Myna, Crested	7 mm Yellow
Nighthawk, Common	9 mm (VDB) Black
Nighthawk, Lesser	8 mm (VDB) Black
Nighthawk, Texas *see Nighthawk, Lesser*	
Nighthawk, Trilling *see Nighthawk, Lesser*	
Noddies *see Terns*	
Nutcracker, Clark's	8 mm (VDB) Black
Nuthatch, Brown-headed	3 mm (DB) Black
Nuthatch, Pygmy	3 mm (DB) Black
Nuthatch, Red-breasted	3 mm (DB) Black
Nuthatch, White-breasted	4 mm (DB) Black
Oldsquaw *see Ducks*	
Oriole, Alta Mira *see Oriole, Lichtenstein's*	
Oriole, Audubon's *see Oriole, Black-headed*	
Oriole, Baltimore *see Oriole, Northern*	
Oriole, Black-headed	6 mm (VDB) Black
Oriole, Bullock's *see Oriole, Northern*	
Oriole, Hooded	5 mm (VDB) Black
Oriole, Lichtenstein's	6 mm (VDB) Black
Oriole, Northern	5 mm (VDB) Black
Oriole, Orchard	5 mm (VDB) Black
Oriole, Scott's	5 mm (VDB) Black
Oriole, Spotted-breasted	5 mm (VDB) Black
Osprey	Adult male 13 mm Pale Yellow
	Adult female 14 mm Pale Yellow
	Juvenile 13 mm Golden Yellow
Ovenbird	4 mm (VDB) Black
Owl, Barn	12 mm (VDB) Black
Owl, Barred	18 mm (VDB) Black
Owl, Boreal	Adult 11 mm Yellow
	Juvenile 11 mm Pale Yellow
Owl, Burrowing	10 mm Orangy Yellow
Owl, Cat *see Owl, Great Horned*	
Owl, Elf	8 mm Golden Yellow
Owl, Ferruginous	9 mm Golden Yellow
Owl, Flammulated	9 mm (VDB) Black
Owl, Flammulated Screech *see Owl, Flammulated*	
Owl, Great Grey	18 mm Yellow
Owl, Great Horned	20 mm Golden Yellow
Owl, Hawk	Adult 13 mm Pale Yellow
	Juvenile 13 mm Bluish Yellow
Owl, Long-eared	Adult 12 mm Golden Orange
	Juvenile 12 mm Pale Yellow

Owl, Pygmy	9 mm Pale Yellow
Owl, Richardson's *see Owl, Boreal*	
Owl, Saw-Whet	9 mm Golden Yellow
Owl, Screech	10 mm Yellow. Red Phase 10 mm Yellow. Grey Phase
Owl, Short-eared	Adult 12 mm Pale Yellow Juvenile 12 mm Paler Yellow
Owl, Snowy	20 mm Straw Yellow
Owl, Spotted	18 mm (VDB) Black
Owl, Whiskered	9 mm Yellow
Oystercatcher, American	9 mm Yellow
Oystercatcher, Black	9 mm Clayish Yellow
Partridge, Grey	8 mm Brown
Partridge, Hungarian *see Partridge, Grey*	
Parula, Northern *see Warbler, Parula, Northern*	
Parula, Tropical *see Warbler, Parula, Tropical*	
Pauraque	10 mm (VDB) Black
Pelican, Brown	12 mm Very Pale Blue
Pelican, White	13 mm Dark Red
Petrel, Ashy	5 mm (VDB) Black
Petrel, Black	5 mm (VDB) Black
Petrel, Fork-tailed	5 mm (VDB) Black
Petrel, Fulmar *see Fulmar, Northern*	
Petrel, Harcourt's	5 mm (VDB) Black
Petrel, Leach's	5 mm (VDB) Black
Petrel, Least	4 mm (VDB) Black
Petrel, Madeira *see Petrel, Harcourt's*	
Petrel, White-faced	5 mm (VDB) Black
Petrel, Wilson's	5 mm (VDB) Black
Pewee, Eastern Wood	5 mm (VDB) Black
Pewee, Western Wood	5 mm (VDB) Black
Phainopepla	5 mm (VDB) Black
Phalarope, Northern	4 mm (VDB) Black
Phalarope, Red	4 mm (VDB) Black
Phalarope, Red-necked *see Phalarope, Northern*	
Phalarope, Wilson's	5 mm (VDB) Black
Pheasant, Ring-necked	Adult male 9–10 mm Yellow (Special) Adult female 9 mm Dark Brown
Phoebe, Black	5 mm (VDB) Black
Phoebe, Eastern	5 mm (VDB) Black
Phoebe, Say's	5 mm (VDB) Black
Pigeon, Band-tailed	8 mm Pale Yellow
Pigeon, Domestic *see Dove, Rock*	
Pigeon, Hawk *see Merlin*	
Pigeon, Red-billed	8 mm Pale Yellow
Pigeon, Sea *see Guillemot, Black*	
Pigeon, White-crowned	8 mm Pale Beige
Pigeon, White-fronted *see Dove, White-fronted*	
Pigeon, White-winged *see Dove, White-winged*	
Pintail *see Duck*	
Pipit, American *see Pipit, Water*	
Pipit, Meadow	4 mm (VDB) Black
Pipit, Red-throated	4 mm (VDB) Black
Pipit, Rock *see Pipit, Water*	
Pipit, Sprague's	4 mm (VDB) Black
Pipit, Water	4 mm (VDB) Black
Pipit: All Pipit Nestlings	(VDB) Black
Plover, American Golden	8 mm (VDB) Black

Plover, Black-bellied	9 mm (VDB) Black
Plover, Grass *see Sandpiper, Upland*	
Plover, Kentish *see Plover, Snowy*	
Plover, Lesser Golden *see Plover, American Golden*	
Plover, Mountain	7 mm (VDB) Black
Plover, Piping	6 mm (VDB) Black
Plover, Ringed *see Plover, Semipalmated*	
Plover, Ring-necked *see Plover, Semipalmated*	
Plover, Semipalmated	6 mm (VDB) Black
Plover, Snowy	6 mm (VDB) Black
Plover, Thick-billed *see Plover, Wilson's*	
Plover, Upland *see Sandpiper, Upland*	
Plover, Wilson's	6 mm (VDB) Black
Plover: All Plover Chicks	(VDB) Black
Poor-will	8 mm (VDB) Black
Prairie Chicken, Attwater's *see Prairie Chicken, Greater*	
Prairie Chicken, Greater	9 mm Dark Brown
Prairie Chicken, Lesser	9 mm Dark Brown
Prairie Chicken: All Chicks	(DB) Dark Brown or Black
Prairie Dove *see Gull, Franklin's*	
Ptarmigan, Rock	8 mm (VDB) Black
Ptarmigan, White-tailed	8 mm (VDB) Black
Ptarmigan, Willow	8 mm (VDB) Black
Ptarmigan: All Ptarmigan Chicks	(DB) Dark Brown or Black
Puffin, Atlantic *see Puffin, Common*	
Puffin, Common	7 mm Pearl-White to Orangy-Brown (Breeding)
Puffin, Horned	8 mm Pearl-White to Orangy-Brown (Breeding)
Puffin, Tufted	8 mm Pearl-White to Orangy-Brown (Breeding)
Puffin: All Puffin Chicks	(VDB) Black
	Juvenile Brown
Pyrrhuloxia	5 mm (VDB) Black

Quail, Blue *see Quail, Scaled*	
Quail, Bobwhite	4–5 mm (DB) Black
Quail, California	4–5 mm (DB) Black
Quail, Gambel's	5–6 mm (VDB) Black
Quail, Harlequin *see Quail, Montezuma*	
Quail, Mearn's *see Quail, Montezuma*	
Quail, Montezuma	4–5 mm (VDB) Black
Quail, Mountain	4–5 mm (VDB) Black
Quail, Scaled	5–6 mm (VDB) Black
Quail, Valley *see Quail, Mountain*	

Rail, Black	5 mm Dark Reddish Black
Rail, Clapper	8 mm Brown
Rail, King	8 mm Reddish Brown
Rail, Sora	5 mm Reddish Dark Brown
Rail, Virginia	6 mm Reddish Brown
Rail, Yellow	4 mm Reddish Dark Brown
Rail: All Rail Chicks	(VDB) Black
Raven, Northern	11–12 mm (VDB) Black
Raven, White-necked	10 mm (VDB) Black
Razorbill	10 mm (VDB) Black
Redhead *see Duck, Redhead*	
Redpoll, Common	3–4 mm (VDB) Black
Redpoll, Hoary	3–4 mm (VDB) Black
Redstart, American	4 mm (VDB) Black

Redstart, Painted	4 mm (VDB) Black
Roadrunner	9 mm Bright Yellow at Close Range, Greyish Yellow at Distance.
Robin, American	7 mm (VDB) Black
Salt-water Marsh Hen *see Rail, Clapper*	
Sanderling	Adult 5 mm (VDB) Black
	Juvenile 5 mm Greyish Brown
Sandpiper, Baird's	5 mm (VDB) Black
Sandpiper, Buff-breasted	5 mm (VDB) Black
Sandpiper, Curlew	5 mm (VDB) Black
Sandpiper, Least	4 mm (VDB) Black
Sandpiper, Pectoral	6 mm (VDB) Black
Sandpiper, Purple	6 mm (VDB) Black
Sandpiper, Red-backed *see Dunlin*	
Sandpiper, Rock	6 mm (VDB) Black
Sandpiper, Rufous-necked	4 mm (VDB) Black
Sandpiper, Semipalmated	4–5 mm (VDB) Black
Sandpiper, Sharp-tailed	5 mm (VDB) Black
Sandpiper, Solitary	6 mm (VDB) Black
Sandpiper, Spotted	6 mm (VDB) Black
Sandpiper, Stilt	6 mm (VDB) Black
Sandpiper, Upland	6 mm (VDB) Black
Sandpiper, Western	5 mm (VDB) Black
Sandpiper, White-rumped	5 mm (VDB) Black
Sapsucker, Red-breasted *see Sapsucker, Yellow-bellied*	
Sapsucker, Red-naped *see Sapsucker, Yellow-bellied*	
Sapsucker, Williamson's	6 mm (Dark Reddish Black) Black
Sapsucker, Yellow-bellied	6 mm (Dark Reddish Black) Black
Sawbill, *see Duck, Merganser, Common*	
Sawbill, Hooded *see Duck, Merganser, Hooded*	
Scaup, Greater *see Duck, Scaup, Greater*	
Scaup, Lesser *see Duck, Scaup, Lesser*	
Scoters *see Duck*	
Seagull *see Gull, Herring*	
Seedeater, Morrelet *see Seedeater, White-collared*	
Seedeater, Sharpes *see Seedeater, White-collared*	
Seedeater, White-collared	3 mm (VDB) Black
Shearwater, Audubon's	7 mm (VDB) Black
Shearwater, Black-vented *see Shearwater, Manx*	
Shearwater, Cory's	10 mm (VDB) Black
Shearwater, Flesh-footed	9 mm (VDB) Black
Shearwater, Greater	10 mm (VDB) Black
Shearwater, Little	7 mm (VDB) Black
Shearwater, Manx	8 mm (VDB) Black
Shearwater, New Zealand	9 mm (VDB) Black
Shearwater, Pale-footed *see Shearwater, Flesh-footed*	
Shearwater, Pink-footed	10 mm (VDB) Black
Shearwater, Short-tailed	8 mm (VDB) Black
Shearwater, Slender-billed *see Shearwater, Short-tailed*	
Shearwater, Sooty	9 mm (VDB) Black
Sheldrake *see Duck, Merganser, Common*	
Sheldrake, Salt-water *see Duck, Merganser, Red-breasted*	
Sheldrake, Swamp *see Duck, Merganser, Hooded*	
Shoveler *see Duck*	
Shoveler, Northern *see Duck, Shoveler, Northern*	
Shrike, Loggerhead	7 mm (VDB) Black
Shrike, Northern	7 mm (VDB) Black
Shrike, Northwestern *see Shrike, Northern*	
Sicklebill *see Curlew, Long-billed*	

Siskin, Pine	3–4 mm (VDB) Black
Skimmer, Black	8 mm (VDB) Black
Skua	10 mm (VDB) Black
Skylark	4 mm Brown
Snakebird *see Anhinga*	
Snipe, Common	6 mm (VDB) Black
Solitaire, Townsend's	6 mm (VDB) Black
Sora	5 mm Reddish Dark Brown
Sparrow, Bachman's	4 mm (VDB) Black
Sparrow, Baird's	4 mm (DB) Black
Sparrow, Black-chinned	4 mm (DB) Black
Sparrow, Black-throated	3–4 mm (VDB) Black
Sparrow, Botteri's	4 mm (DB) Black
Sparrow, Brewer's	4 mm (VDB) Black
Sparrow, Cape Sable *see Sparrow, Seaside*	
Sparrow, Cassin's	4 mm (DB) Black
Sparrow, Chipping	4 mm (DB) Black
Sparrow, Clay-coloured	4 mm (DB) Black
Sparrow, Desert *see Sparrow, Black-throated*	
Sparrow, Dusky Seaside *see Sparrow, Seaside*	
Sparrow, English *see Sparrow, House*	
Sparrow, Eurasian Tree	4 mm (DB) Dark Brown or Black
Sparrow, Field	4 mm (VDB) Black
Sparrow, Fox	4 mm (VDB) Black
Sparrow, Gambel's *see Sparrow, White-crowned*	
Sparrow, Golden-crowned	4 mm (DB) Black
Sparrow, Grasshopper	3–4 mm (DB) Black
Sparrow, Harris'	4–5 mm (VDB) Black
Sparrow, Henslow's	4 mm (VDB) Black
Sparrow, House	4 mm (DB) Black
Sparrow, Ipswich *see Sparrow, Savannah*	
Sparrow, Lark	4 mm (DB) Black
Sparrow, Le Conte's	4 mm (VDB) Black
Sparrow, Lincoln's	4 mm (VDB) Black
Sparrow, Olive	4 mm Dark Brown
Sparrow, Pine-woods *see Sparrow, Bachman's*	
Sparrow, Rufous-crowned	4 mm (DB) Black
Sparrow, Rufous-winged	4 mm (DB) Black
Sparrow, Sage	4 mm (VDB) Black
Sparrow, Savannah	3–4 mm (VDB) Black
Sparrow, Seaside	4 mm (VDB) Black
Sparrow, Sharp-tailed	4 mm (VDB) Black
Sparrow, Song	4 mm (VDB) Black
Sparrow, Swamp	3–4 mm (VDB) Black
Sparrow, Texas *see Sparrow, Olive*	
Sparrow, Tree	4 mm (DB) Black
Sparrow, Vesper	4 mm (VDB) Black
Sparrow, White-crowned	4 mm (DB) Black
Sparrow, White-throated	4 mm (DB) Black
Spoonbill, Roseate	Adult 10 mm Red Juvenile 10 mm Rust-Brown
Sprig *see Duck, Pintail*	
Starling	5 mm (DB) Black
Stilt, Black-necked	7 mm Reddish Dark Brown
Stork, Wood	13 mm (VDB) Black
Storm Petrels (also known as Petrels) *see under Petrels*	
Surfbird	6 mm (VDB) Black
Swallow, Bank	3–4 mm (VDB) Black
Swallow, Barn	4 mm (VDB) Black

Swallow, Cave	4 mm (VDB) Black
Swallow, Cliff	4 mm (VDB) Black
Swallow, Coahuila Cliff *see Swallow, Cave*	
Swallow, Rough-winged	4 mm (VDB) Black
Swallow, Tree	4 mm (VDB) Black
Swallow, Violet-Green	4 mm (VDB) Black
Swan, Mute	Adult male 12 mm (VDB) Black
	Adult female 11 mm (VDB) Black
Swan, Trumpeter	Adult male 13 mm (VDB) Black
	Adult female 12 mm (VDB) Black
Swan, Whistling	Adult male 11 mm (VDB) Black
	Adult female 10 mm (VDB) Black
Swift, Black	6 mm (VDB) Black
Swift, Chimney	5 mm (VDB) Black
Swift, Vaux	4 mm (VDB) Black
Swift, White-throated	6 mm (VDB) Black
Tanager, Blue-Grey	5 mm (VDB) Black
Tanager, Cooper's *see Tanager, Summer*	
Tanager, Hepatic	5 mm (VDB) Black
Tanager, Scarlet	5 mm (VDB) Black
Tanager, Summer	5 mm (VDB) Black
Tanager, Western	5 mm (VDB) Black
Tattler, Wandering	7 mm (VDB) Black
Teal, Blue-winged	Adult male 6 mm Dark Brown
	Adult female 6 mm Dark Brown
Teal, Cinnamon	Adult male 6 mm Red
	Adult female 6 mm Dark Brown
Teal, Green-winged	Adult male 6 mm Dark Brown
	Adult female 6 mm Grey-Brown
Tern, Aleutian	7 mm (VDB) Black
Tern, Arctic	7 mm (VDB) Black
Tern, Black	5 mm (VDB) Black
Tern, Black Noddy	7 mm (VDB) Black
Tern, Brown Noddy	8 mm (VDB) Black
Tern, Cabot's *see Tern, Sandwich*	
Tern, Caspian	10 mm (VDB) Black
Tern, Common	7 mm (VDB) Black
Tern, Elegant	8 mm (VDB) Black
Tern, Forster's	7 mm (VDB) Black
Tern, Gull-billed	8 mm (VDB) Black
Tern, Least	5 mm (VDB) Black
Tern, Noddy *see Tern, Brown Noddy*	
Tern, Noddy, White-capped *see Tern, Noddy, Black*	
Tern, Roseate	6 mm (VDB) Black
Tern, Royal	9 mm (VDB) Black
Tern, Sandwich	8 mm (VDB) Black
Tern, Sooty	7 mm (VDB) Black
Thrasher, Bendire's	6 mm Yellow
Thrasher, Brown	6 mm Yellow
Thrasher, California	6 mm Dark Brown
Thrasher, Crissal	Adult 6 mm Very Dark Yellowish Brown
	Juvenile 6 mm Whitish Yellow
Thrasher, Curve-billed	6 mm Pale Red-Orange
Thrasher, Le Conte's	6 mm Dark Brown
Thrasher, Long-billed	6 mm Yellow
Thrasher, Sage	6 mm Pale Yellow
Thrush, Grey-cheeked	5 mm (VDB) Black
Thrush, Hermit	5 mm (VDB) Black

Thrush, Olive-backed *see Thrush, Swainson's*	
Thrush, Russet-backed *see Thrush, Swainson's*	
Thrush, Swainson's	5 mm (VDB) Black
Thrush, Varied	6 mm (VDB) Black
Thrush, Veery	5 mm (VDB) Black
Thrush, Wood	6 mm (VDB) Black
Titmouse, Black-crested	4 mm (VDB) Black
Titmouse, Bridled	4 mm (VDB) Black
Titmouse, Plain	4 mm (VDB) Black
Titmouse, Tufted	4 mm (VDB) Black
Towhee, Albert's	5 mm Dark Brown
Towhee, Brown	5 mm Brown
Towhee, Eastern *see Towhee, Rufous-sided*	
Towhee, Green-tailed	5 mm Dark Brown
Towhee, Red-eyed *see Towhee, Rufous-sided*	
Towhee, Rufous-sided	Male 5 mm Red
	Female 5 mm Reddish Brown
Towhee, Spotted *see Towhee, Rufous-sided*	
Trogon, Coppery-tailed	5 mm (VDB) Black
Tropicbird, Red-tailed	9 mm (DB) Black
Tropicbird, White-tailed	9 mm (DB) Black
Tropicbird, Yellow-billed *see Tropicbird, White-tailed*	
Turkey	12 mm Dark Brown or Black
Turnstone, Black	5 mm (VDB) Black
Turnstone, Ruddy	5 mm (VDB) Black
Tyrant-flycatchers *see Flycatchers*	
Veery *see Thrush, Veery*	
Verdin	3 mm (VDB) Black
Vireo, Bell's	5 mm (VDB) Black
Vireo, Black-capped	4–5 mm Brown
Vireo, Black-whiskered	5 mm (VDB) Black
Vireo, Blue-headed *see Vireo, Solitary*	
Vireo, Grey	5 mm (VDB) Black
Vireo, Hutton's	4–5 mm (VDB) Black
Vireo, Philadelphia	5 mm (VDB) Black
Vireo, Red-eyed	5 mm Red
Vireo, Solitary	5 mm (VDB) Black
Vireo, Warbling	5 mm (VDB) Black
Vireo, White-eyed	Adult 5 mm White
	Juvenile 5 mm (VDB) Black
Vireo, Yellow-Green	5 mm Red
Vireo, Yellow-throated	5 mm (VDB) Black
Vulture, Black	Adult 10 mm Brown
	Chick (VDB) Black
Vulture, Turkey	Adult 12 mm (VDB) Black
	Chick Dark Brown
Wagtail, White	4 mm (VDB) Black
Wagtail, Yellow	4 mm (VDB) Black
Warbler, Arctic	4 mm (VDB) Black
Warbler, Audubon's *see Warbler, Yellow-rumped*	
Warbler, Bachman's	3–4 mm (VDB) Black
Warbler, Bay-breasted	5 mm (VDB) Black
Warbler, Black & White	4 mm (VDB) Black
Warbler, Black & Yellow *see Warbler, Magnolia*	
Warbler, Blackburnian	4 mm (VDB) Black
Warbler, Blackpoll	4 mm (VDB) Black

Warbler, Black-throated, Blue	4 mm (VDB) Black
Warbler, Black-throated, Grey	4 mm (VDB) Black
Warbler, Black-throated, Green	4 mm (VDB) Black
Warbler, Blue-winged	4 mm (VDB) Black
Warbler, Brasher's *see Warbler, Golden-crowned*	
Warbler, Brewster's *see Warbler, Golden-winged*	
Warbler, Calavera's *see Warbler, Nashville*	
Warbler, Canada	4 mm (VDB) Black
Warbler, Cape May	4 mm (VDB) Black
Warbler, Cerulean	4 mm (VDB) Black
Warbler, Chestnut-sided	4 mm (VDB) Black
Warbler, Colima	4 mm (VDB) Black
Warbler, Connecticut	5 mm (VDB) Black
Warbler, Golden-cheeked	4 mm (VDB) Black
Warbler, Golden-crowned	4 mm (VDB) Black
Warbler, Golden-winged	4 mm (VDB) Black
Warbler, Grace's	4 mm (VDB) Black
Warbler, Hermit	4 mm (VDB) Black
Warbler, Hooded	5 mm (VDB) Black
Warbler, Kentucky	5 mm (VDB) Black
Warbler, Kirtland's	5 mm (VDB) Black
Warbler, Lawrence's *see Warbler, Golden-winged*	
Warbler, Lucy's	4 mm (VDB) Black
Warbler, McGillivray's	4–5 mm (VDB) Black
Warbler, Magnolia	4 mm (VDB) Black
Warbler, Mourning	5 mm (VDB) Black
Warbler, Myrtle *see Warbler, Yellow-rumped*	
Warbler, Nashville	4 mm (VDB) Black
Warbler, Northern Parula	4 mm (VDB) Black
Warbler, Olive	4 mm (VDB) Black
Warbler, Olive-backed *see Warbler, Tropical Parula*	
Warbler, Orange-crowned	4 mm (VDB) Black
Warbler, Palm	5 mm (VDB) Black
Warbler, Parula *see Warbler, Northern Parula*	
Warbler, Pileolated *see Warbler, Wilson's*	
Warbler, Pine	5 mm (VDB) Black
Warbler, Pitiayumi *see Warbler, Olive-backed*	
Warbler, Prairie	4 mm (VDB) Black
Warbler, Prothonotary	5 mm (VDB) Black
Warbler, Red-faced	4–5 mm (VDB) Black
Warbler, Sennett's *see Warbler, Olive-backed*	
Warbler, Swainson's	4 mm (VDB) Black
Warbler, Tennessee	4 mm (VDB) Black
Warbler, Townsend's	4 mm (VDB) Black
Warbler, Tropical Parula	4 mm (VDB) Black
Warbler, Virginia's	4 mm (VDB) Black
Warbler, Wilson's	4 mm (VDB) Black
Warbler, Worm-eating	5 mm (VDB) Black
Warbler, Yellow	4 mm (VDB) Black
Warbler, Yellow-rumped	4–5 mm (VDB) Black
Warbler, Yellow-throated	4 mm (VDB) Black
Water Turkey *see Anhinga*	
Waterthrush, Louisiana	5 mm (VDB) Black
Waterthrush, Northern	5 mm (VDB) Black
Waxwing, Bohemian	5 mm (VDB) Black
Waxwing, Cedar	5 mm (VDB) Black
Wheatear	Adult 5 mm Dark Brown or Black Juvenile 5 mm Grey-Brown
Whimbrel	9 mm (VDB) Black

Whip-poor-will	9 mm (VDB) Black
Whiskey Jack *see Jay, Grey*	
Whistler *see Duck, Goldeneye*	
Whistling Ducks *see Ducks, Black-bellied and Fulvous*	
Widgeon, American *see Duck, Widgeon, American*	
Willet	9 mm (VDB) Black
Woodcock, American	9 mm (VDB) Black
Woodpecker, Acorn	6 mm Light Yellow
Woodpecker, Arctic	6 mm (VDB) Black
Woodpecker, Arizona	5 mm (VDB) Black
Woodpecker, Black-backed Three-toed *see Woodpecker, Arctic*	
Woodpecker, California *see Woodpecker, Acorn*	
Woodpecker, Downy	4 mm (VDB) Black
Woodpecker, Gila	6 mm (VDB) Black
Woodpecker, Golden-fronted	6 mm (DB) Black
Woodpecker, Hairy	6 mm (VDB) Black
Woodpecker, Ivory-billed	10 mm Yellow
Woodpecker, Ladder-backed	4–5 mm (VDB) Black
Woodpecker, Lewis'	7 mm (DB) Black
Woodpecker, Mexican *see Woodpecker, Ladder-backed*	
Woodpecker, Northern Three-toed	6 mm (VDB) Black
Woodpecker, Nuttall's	5 mm (VDB) Black
Woodpecker, Pileated	10 mm Yellow
Woodpecker, Red-bellied	6 mm (VDB) Black
Woodpecker, Red-cockaded	6 mm (VDB) Black
Woodpecker, Red-headed	6 mm (VDB) Black
Woodpecker, White-headed	6 mm (VDB) Black
Wood Pewee *see Pewee*	
Wren, Bewick's	3 mm Dark Brown or Black
Wren, Cactus	4 mm Dark Brown
Wren, Canyon	3 mm Dark Brown or Black
Wren, Carolina	3 mm Dark Brown or Black
Wren, House	3 mm Dark Brown or Black
Wren, Long-billed Marsh	3 mm Dark Brown or Black
Wren, Rock	3 mm Dark Brown or Black
Wren, Short-billed Marsh	3 mm Dark Brown or Black
Wren, Winter	3 mm Dark Brown or Black
Wrentit	4 mm White
Yellowlegs, Greater	8 mm (VDB) Black
Yellowlegs, Lesser	6 mm (VDB) Black
Yellowthroat *see Yellowthroat, Common*	
Yellowthroat, Common	4 mm (VDB) Black
Yellowthroat, Grey-crowned	4 mm (VDB) Black
Yellowthroat, Rio Grande *see Groundchat*	

APPENDIX III

CHECK LIST OF EYE SIZES AND COLOURS OF NORTH AMERICAN MAMMALS

American Bison *see Buffalo and Buffalo, Wood*	
Antelope *see Pronghorn*	
Badger	Adult male 11–13 mm Brown Adult female 10–12 mm Brown
Bat, Big Brown	3 mm (VDB) Black
Bat, Big Free-tailed	3 mm (VDB) Black
Bat, California	2 mm (VDB) Black
Bat, Eastern Pipistrelle	2 mm (VDB) Black
Bat, Evening	2 mm (VDB) Black
Bat, Fringed	2 mm (VDB) Black
Bat, Hoary	3 mm (VDB) Black
Bat, Keen's	2 mm (VDB) Black
Bat, Little Brown	2 mm (VDB) Black
Bat, Long-eared	2 mm (VDB) Black
Bat, Long-legged	2 mm (VDB) Black
Bat, Pallid	3 mm (VDB) Black
Bat, Pipistrelle *see Bat, Eastern Pipistrelle*	
Bat, Red	2 mm (VDB) Black
Bat, Silver-haired	2 mm (VDB) Black
Bat, Small-footed	2 mm (VDB) Black
Bat, Townsend's Big-eared	2 mm (VDB) Black
Bat, Yuma	2 mm (VDB) Black
Bear, American Black	Adult 15–17 mm Brown (Special) Cub 12–15 mm Brown (Special)
Bear, Brown *see Bear, Grizzly*	
Bear, Glacial *see Bear, American Black*	
Bear, Grizzly	16–18 mm (Normally, but can go to 20 mm on massive specimens) Brown (Special)
Bear, Kodiak (Kodiak Island Grizzly)	17–20 mm Brown (Special)
Bear, Polar	Adult 17–18 mm Brown (Special) Cub 12–15 mm Brown (Special)
Bear, White *see Bear, American Black*	
Beaver, American	12–13 mm Dark Brown
Beaver, Mountain	9 mm (VDB) Black or Dark Brown
Bighorn Sheep *see Sheep, Bighorn*	
Bison *see Buffalo and Buffalo, Wood*	
Black-tailed Prairie Dog	9 mm (VDB) Black
Bobcat	16–18 mm Colour range from Yellow, Yellowish tinged Brown to Brown (Special)
Bog Lemming, Northern *see Lemming, Northern Bog*	
Bog Lemming, Southern *see Lemming, Southern Bog*	
Buffalo	31–35 mm Dark Brown Horizontal Oval pupil (Special)
Buffalo, Wood	31–36 mm Dark Brown Horizontal Oval pupil (Special)
Bushy-tailed Wood Rat	6 mm (VDB) Black
Caribou, Barren-Ground	26–28 mm Dark Brown Horizontal Slot (Special)
Caribou, Woodland	26–28 mm Dark Brown Horizontal Slot (Special)
Cascade Deer Mouse	4 mm (VDB) Black
Chipmunk, Big *see Ground Squirrel, Golden-mantled*	
Chipmunk, Eastern	6 mm (VDB) Black
Chipmunk, Least	5 mm (VDB) Black
Chipmunk, Red-tailed	5 mm (VDB) Black
Chipmunk, Townsend's	5 mm (VDB) Black
Chipmunk, Western *see Chipmunk, Least*	
Chipmunk, Yellow Pine	5 mm (VDB) Black

Civet Cat *see Skunk, Western Spotted*	
Cottontail, Eastern	16 mm Dark Brown
Cottontail, Nuttall's	16 mm Dark Brown
Cougar	Male 24–25 mm Green tinged Clayish Brown (Special) Female 22–23 mm Clayish Brown (Special)
Coyote	16–18 mm Greyish Brown
Coypu	9 lbs: 8 mm (VDB) Black 18 lbs: 10 mm (VDB) Black
Cross Fox *see Fox, Red*	
Deer, Black-tailed	Adult male 28–29 mm Dark Brown Slot pupil (Special) Adult female 26–27 mm Dark Brown Slot pupil (Special)
Deer, Fallow	28–32 mm Dark Brown Horizontal Slot pupil (Special)
Deer, Mule	Adult male 28–30 mm Dark Brown Slot pupil (Special) Adult female 26–27 mm Dark Brown Slot pupil (Special)
Deer, Red *see Elk*	
Deer, Rein	26–28 mm Dark Brown Slot pupil (Special)
Deer, Sitka	26–28 mm Dark Brown Slot pupil (Special)
Deer, Virginia *see Deer, White-tailed*	
Deer, White-tailed	24–28 mm Dark Brown Slot pupil (Special)
Deer Mouse	4 mm (VDB) Black
Elk	Adult male 31–34 mm Brown Slot pupil (Special) Adult female 28–32 mm Brown Slot pupil (Special)
Ermine	Adult male 8 mm (VDB) Black Adult female 7 mm (VDB) Black
Ferret, Black-footed	Adult male 9 mm (VDB) Black Adult female 8 mm (VDB) Black
Fisher	Adult male 10 mm (VDB) Black Adult female 9 mm (VDB) Black
Flying Squirrel, Northern	6 mm (VDB) Black
Flying Squirrel, Southern	5–6 mm (VDB) Black
Fox, Arctic	16 mm Golden Yellow Oval-slit (Special)
Fox, Cross *as for Red Fox*	
Fox, Grey	14–16 mm Brown Oval-slit (Special)
Fox, Kit	13 mm Brown Oval or Slit (Special)
Fox, Red	16–18 mm Brown Oval or Slit (Special)
Fox, Silver (Type of Red Fox)	16–18 mm Brown Oval or Slit (Special)
Fox, Squirrel	11 mm Dark Brown
Fox, Swift	13–14 mm Brown Oval or Slit (Special)
Fox, White *see Fox, Arctic*	
Goat, Mountain	22–25 mm Yellow (Dark Brown Pupil) Horizontal Oval pupil (Special)
Gopher *also known as Richardson's Ground Squirrel*	9 mm (VDB) Black
Gopher, Grey *see Gopher and Pocket Gophers*	
Groundhog *see Woodchuck*	
Ground Squirrel, Arctic	8–9 mm (VDB) Black
Ground Squirrel, Columbian	8–9 mm (VDB) Black
Ground Squirrel, Franklin's	8–9 mm (VDB) Black
Ground Squirrel, Golden-mantled	8–9 mm (VDB) Black
Ground Squirrel, Richardson's *see Gopher*	
Ground Squirrel, Thirteen-lined	5–6 mm (VDB) Black
Hare, Arctic	15–16 mm Oval shaped iris which can be Brown or Yellowish-Brown
Hare, European	16 mm Clayish Mid Brown
Hare, Snowshoe	16 mm Dark Brown

Hydrophobia Cat *see Skunk, Western Spotted*

Jack Rabbit, White-tailed	16 mm Clayish Yellow (Special)
Jerboas *see Jumping Mouse*	
Jumping Mouse, Meadow	4 mm (VDB) Black
Jumping Mouse, Pacific	4 mm (VDB) Black
Jumping Mouse, Western	4 mm (VDB) Black
Jumping Mouse, Woodland	4 mm (VDB) Black
Kangaroo Rat	4–5 mm (VDB) Black
Kangaroo Rat, Ord's *see Kangaroo Rat*	
Lemming, Brown	3 mm (VDB) Black
Lemming, Collared	3 mm (VDB) Black
Lemming, Northern Bog	3 mm (VDB) Black
Lemming, Southern Bog	3 mm (VDB) Black
Lemming, Ungava	3 mm (VDB) Black
Lynx	18–20 mm Yellowish Brown to Golden Brown Slit pupil (Special)
Marmot, Hoary	13–15 mm Dark Brown
Marmot, Vancouver Island	10–11 mm Dark Brown
Marmot, Yellow-bellied	10–11 mm Dark Brown
Marten	Adult male 10 mm (VDB) Black Adult female 9 mm (VDB) Black
Mink	8–9 mm (VDB) Black
Mole, Eastern	2 mm (VDB) Black
Mole, Hairy-tailed	2 mm (VDB) Black
Mole, Pacific Coast	2 mm (VDB) Black
Mole, Shrew *see Shrew, Mole*	
Mole, Star-nosed	2 mm (VDB) Black
Mole, Townsend	2 mm (VDB) Black
Moose	32–36 mm Very Dark Brown Slot pupil (Special)
Mountain Goat *see Goat, Mountain*	
Mountain Lion *see Cougar*	
Mouse, Bean *see Vole, Meadow*	
Mouse, Cascade Deer	4 mm (VDB) Black
Mouse, Field *see Vole, Meadow*	
Mouse, House	3 mm (VDB) Black
Mouse, Northern Grasshopper	4 mm (VDB) Black
Mouse, Sitka	4 mm (VDB) Black
Mouse, Western Harvest	2–3 mm (VDB) Black
Mouse, White-footed	4 mm (VDB) Black
See also: *Jumping Mice, Pocket Mice and Deer Mice*	
Muskox	28–33 mm Dark Brown Slot pupil (Special)
Muskrat	8 mm (VDB) Black
Nutria *see Coypu*	
Opossum	10–12 mm (VDB) Black
Opossum, Virginia *see Opossum*	
Otter, River	9 mm (VDB) Black
Otter, Sea	12 mm (VDB) Black
Pika	8 mm (VDB) Black
Pocket Gopher, Northern	6–7 mm (VDB) Black
Pocket Gopher, Plains	7–8 mm (VDB) Black
Pocket Mouse, Great Basin	4 mm (VDB) Black
Pocket Mouse, Olive-backed	3–4 mm (VDB) Black
Polecat *see Skunk, Western Spotted*	

Porcupine	10 mm Dark Brown or Black
Prairie Dog	9–10 mm (VDB) Black
Pronghorn	Adult male 28–30 mm Very Dark Brown Slot pupil-horizontal (Special)
	Adult female 27–28 mm Very Dark Brown Slot pupil-horizontal (Special)
Puma *see Cougar*	
Rabbit, White-tailed Jack *see Jack Rabbit*	
Rabbit, Snowshoe *see Hare Snowshoe*	
Raccoon	10–12 mm Very Dark Brown (occasional specimen larger) (Special)
Rat, Alexandrian Roof *name given to brown colour phase of Black Rat*	
Rat, Black	6–7 mm (VDB) Black
Rat, Bushy-tailed Wood	8 mm (VDB) Black
Rat, Norway	6–7 mm (VDB) Black
Rat, Pack *see Rat, Bushy-tailed Wood*	
Rat, Roof *see Black rat*	
Reindeer *see Deer, Rein*	
Sea-lion,* California	24–26 mm Very Dark Brown (Special)
Sea-lion, Northern	Adult male 26–30 mm Very Dark Brown (Special)
	Adult female 24–26 mm Very Dark Brown (Special)
Sea-lion, Steller's *see Sea-lion, Northern*	
Sea Mink. *Extinct in New England 1860-70. Last mounted specimen taken at Campobello Island, New Brunswick 1894.*	
	Adult male 11–12 mm (VDB) Black
	Adult female 10 mm (VDB) Black
Seal, Bearded	26–30 mm Dark Brown (Special)
Seal, Eared *see Sea-lions*	
Seal, Elephant *see Seal, Northern Elephant*	
Seal, Fur *see Seal, Northern Fur*	
Seal, Greenland *see Seal, Harp*	
Seal, Grey	Adult male 26–28 mm Dark Brown (Special)
	Adult female 24–26 mm Dark Brown (Special)
Seal, Harbour	Adult male 24–26 mm Dark Brown
	Adult female 23–25 mm Dark Brown
Seal, Harp	22–24 mm Dark Brown (Special)
Seal, Hooded	24–26 mm Dark Brown (Special)
Seal, Netsik *see Seal, Ringed*	
Seal, Northern Elephant	26–32 mm Very Dark Brown (Special)
Seal, Northern Fur	Adult 21–24 mm Dark Brown (Special)
	Pup 14 mm Dark Brown
Seal, Ringed	21–23 mm Dark Brown (Special)
Seal, Square-flipper *see Seal, Bearded*	
Sheep, Bighorn	26–29 mm Usually Golden-Brown Horizontal Oval pupil (Special)
Sheep, Dall's	26–28 mm Golden Bronze Horizontal Oval pupil (Special)
Sheep, Fanin's *see Sheep, Stone's*	
Sheep, Mountain *all Sheep listed are Mountain*	
Sheep, Saddle-backed *see Sheep, Stone's*	
Sheep, Stone's	26–28 mm Golden-Bronze Horizontal Oval pupil (Special)
Sheep, White	26–27 mm Golden-Bronze Horizontal Oval pupil (Special)
Shrew,† American Water *see Shrew, Water*	
Shrew, Arctic	2 mm (VDB) Black
Shrew, Bendire's	2–3 mm (VDB) Black
Shrew, Dusky	2 mm (VDB) Black

***Sea-lions and Seals all have special eyes. The surface of the eye is flattened for underwater vision.**

†All Shrews: sizes are for eyes used. Each to be reduced by up to 1 mm using eyelid to convey smaller eye impression.

Shrew, Gaspé	1–2 mm (VDB) Black
Shrew, Least	1–2 mm (VDB) Black
Shrew, Masked	2 mm (VDB) Black
Shrew, Pygmy	1–2 mm (VDB) Black
Shrew, Short-tailed	2–3 mm (VDB) Black
Shrew, Smoky	2 mm (VDB) Black
Shrew, Thompson's Pygmy	1–2 mm (VDB) Black
Shrew, Trowbridge's	2 mm (VDB) Black
Shrew, Vagrant	2–3 mm (VDB) Black
Shrew, Water	2–3 mm (VDB) Black
Shrew-mole	2 mm (VDB) Black
Sik Sik *see Ground Squirrel, Arctic*	
Skunk, Western Spotted	8–9 mm (VDB) Black
Skunk, Striped	9–10 mm (VDB) Black
Snowshoe Hare *see Hare, Snowshoe*	
Snowshoe Rabbit *see Hare, Snowshoe*	
Squirrel, American Red	8–9 mm (VDB) Black
Squirrel, Black *see Squirrel, Grey*	
Squirrel, Douglas'	8–9 mm (VDB) Black
Squirrel, Fox *see Fox, Squirrel*	
Squirrel, Grey	9–10 mm (VDB) Black
Squirrel, Northern Flying *see Flying Squirrel, Northern*	
Squirrel, Red *see Squirrel, American Red*	
Squirrel, Southern Flying *see Flying Squirrel, Southern*	
See also Ground Squirrels	
Stoat *see Ermine*	
Vole, Chestnut-cheeked	3 mm (VDB) Black
Vole, Creeping	3 mm (VDB) Black
Vole, Field *see Vole, Meadow*	
Vole, Gapper's Red-backed	3 mm (VDB) Black
Vole, Heather	3 mm (VDB) Black
Vole, Long-tailed	3 mm (VDB) Black
Vole, Meadow	3 mm (VDB) Black
Vole, Montane	3 mm (VDB) Black
Vole, Northern Red-backed	3 mm (VDB) Black
Vole, Prairie	3 mm (VDB) Black
Vole, Richardson's Water	5 mm (VDB) Black
Vole, Rock	3 mm (VDB) Black
Vole, Sagebrush	3 mm (VDB) Black
Vole, Singing	3 mm (VDB) Black
Vole, Townsend's	3 mm (VDB) Black
Vole, Tundra	3 mm (VDB) Black
Vole, Western Red-backed	3 mm (VDB) Black
Vole, Woodland	3 mm (VDB) Black
Walrus*	Males 28–32 mm Dark Brown (Special) Females 25–28 mm Dark Brown (Special)
Wapiti *see Elk*	
Weasel	Adult male 6 mm (VDB) Black Adult female 4–5 mm (VDB) Black
Weasel, Long-tailed	Adult male 8–9 mm (VDB) Black Adult female 7–8 mm (VDB) Black
Weasel, Short-tailed *see Ermine*	
Whistler *see Marmot, Hoary*	
Wolf	18–20 mm Yellowish Brown (Special)
Wolverine	13–14 mm (VDB) Black
Woodchuck	11–12 mm Dark Brown

***N.B.: Pacific Walrus much longer than Atlantic species.**

APPENDIX IV

BIBLIOGRAPHY

Anderson, R.M., 'Methods of Collecting and Preserving Vertebrate Animals', *Bulletin No. 69, Biological Series No. 18,* National Museum of Canada, 1965.

Baldwin, S.P., Oberholser, H.C., and Worley, L.G., *Measurements of Birds,* vol. 2, Cleveland Museum of Natural History, 1931.

Beddard, Frank E., *The Structure and Classification of Birds,* London, 1889.

Boswell, Peter, *Art of Taxidermy,* W.R. McPhun, Glasgow, 1834.

Brown, Capt. Thomas, *Taxidermist's Manual,* Archibald Fullarton & Co., Glasgow, 1833.

Brown, Capt. Thomas, *Taxidermist's Manual,* Thomas C. Jack, London, 1885.

Browne, Montagu, *Practical Taxidermy,* London. L. Upcott Gill, 1884.

Browne, Montagu, *Artistic and Scientific Taxidermy and Modelling,* Adam and Charles Black, London, 1896.

Corbet, G.B., *The Identification of British Mammals,* British Natural History Museum, London, 1969.

Cornwallis and Smith, *The Bird in the Hand,* London, 1960.

Davie, Oliver, *Methods in the Art of Taxidermy,* Philadelphia, 1900.

Ellenberger, W., Dityrich, H., and Baun, H., *An Atlas of Animal Anatomy for Artists,* Ed. Louis F. Brown, New York, 1956.

Frankowiak, Bob., *Fun With Fish,* Milwaukee Public Museum, 800, West Wells Street, Milwaukee. WI 53223. U.S.A.

Frost, Christopher, *Victorian Taxidermy,* Enchanted Averies, Long Melford, Suffolk, 1981.

Grantz, Gerald J., *Home Book of Taxidermy and Tanning,* Stackpole Books, Harrisburg, PA 17105, U.S.A., 1969.

Harris, R.H., 'Vacuum Dehydration and Freeze-Drying of Entire Biological Specimens', *Natural History Series 13,* vol. 7, pp 65–74, 1964.

Harrison, J.M., *Bird Taxidermy,* David and Charles, Newton Abbot & London, 1976.

Hasluck, Paul N., *Taxidermy,* Cassell & Co. London and New York, 1901, 7th reprint, 1917.

Hornaday, William T., *Taxidermy and Zoological Collecting,* New York, 1891, 7th reprint, Scribner's Sons, Charles, 1900.

Hower, Rolland O., *Freeze-drying Biological Specimens* (laboratory manual), Washington D.C., 1980.

Irvin, A.D., Cooper, J.E., and Hedges, S.R., 'Possible Health Hazards Associated with the Collection and Handling of Post-mortem Zoological Material', *Mammal Review,* vol. 2, No. 2, London, 1972.

Irvin, A.D., *The Epidemiology of Wildlife Rabies,* Surrey, 1970.

Knudsen, Jens W., *Collecting and Preserving Plants and Animals,* Harper & Row, New York, 1966.

Labrie, J., *The Amateur Taxidermist,* obtainable from Watkins and Doncaster.

Lee, Mrs. R., *Taxidermy* or *The Art of Collecting, Preparing, and Mounting Objects of Natural History,* W.R. McPhun, Glasgow, 1834.

Manesse, Abbé, *Treatise on the Manner of Stuffing and Preserving Animals and Skins,* Paris, 1786.

Maynard, C.J., *Manual of Taxidermy,* Boston, 1884.

McFall, Waddy F., *Taxidermy Step by Step,* Winchester Press, South Sheridan, Tulsa, Oklahama, U.S.A., 1975.

Metcalf, John C., *Taxidermy, a complete manual,* Gerald Duckworth and Co., London, 1980.

Moyer, John W., *Practical Taxidermy, a Working Guide,* John Wiley and Sons, New York, 1979.

O'Connor, Peter A., *Fish Taxidermy,* Watkins and Doncaster, Hawkhurst, Kent.
Phillips, Archie, *Fibreglass vs Skinmounts,* 200 52nd Street, Fairfield, AL 35064, U.S.A.
Phillips, Archie, *Fibreglass Fish,* 200 52nd Street, Fairfield, AL 35064, U.S.A.
Pray, Leon L., *Taxidermy,* MacMillan Pub. Co., New York, 1932, 31st reprint, 1979.
Roche, Jean, 'The Preparation of Osteological Specimens', original paper on the Perborate Method, *Extrait de Mammalia,* tome XVIII No. 4.
Rowley, John, *Taxidermy and Museum Exhibition,* D. Appleton & Co., London and New York, 1925.
Rowley, John, *The Art of Taxidermy* D. Appleton & Co., London and New York, 1919.
Scott, Clint, *Fibreglass Fish Reproductions,* American Taxidermist Magazine, P.O. 11186, Albuquerque, N.M. 87112, U.S.A.
Shilling, Dr. W., *The Manner of Collecting and Preparing Fishes and Reptiles,* Weimar, 1860-1.
Shufeldt, R.W., *Scientific Taxidermy for Museums,* Smithsonian Institution, Washington, U.S.A., 1894.
Simpkins, John, *Techniques of Biological Preparation,* Blackie, Glasgow and London, 1974.
Stollas, M.B., *Instructions on the Manner of Preparing Objects of Natural History,* Paris, 1752.
Wagstaffe, R. and Fidler, H.J., *The Preservation of Natural History Specimens,* vol. No. 2. Welwyn Garden City, 1968, and by H.F. & G. Witherby Ltd., London, 1955, 3rd reprint 1970.
Ward, Rowland, *A Naturalist's Life Study in the Art of Taxidermy,* London, 1913.
Ward, Rowland, *The Sportsman's Handbook to Practical Collecting and Preserving Trophies,* Simpkin, Marshall and Co., New York and London, 1919.
Wood, Neil R., *Taxidermy For You,* Tideline Books, Rhyl, N. Wales, 1980.

Many taxidermists' suppliers also carry a range of taxidermy books, especially the American firms. I would suggest that one examines the catalogue pictures of their advertised wares, on the dust covers. If the work looks poor to the untrained eye, then it is extremely poor. The likelihood is the book may well teach you to be just as useless. Many of these 'craftsmen' are no more than semi-trained opportunists, attempting to cash in on what knowledge they have. Many are in need of training themselves.

The books mentioned in this bibliography are a cross section of the books available, and range from excellent to reasonable. All are well worth reading. Look for the author's strongest subject. Normally what he has to write is well worth reading, even to the professional. If you do not like photographs of his finished work in certain fields, read how he achieved this but do not let him influence your actions. Find someone's work you do appreciate, and let him do the influencing. Remember, too, that no one person knows it all; it is a continent of a subject, and we can only truly work in a limited area, at any one time. Background knowledge of the subject or specimen being set up is as important as the skill to mount it, and should be incorporated to some degree into the finished specimen.

APPENDIX V

TAXIDERMISTS' SUPPLIERS

Watkins & Doncaster, Naturalists
Four Throws
Hawkhurst
Kent
ENGLAND

Jac Bouten &
S Veegstrasser
13 Venlo
HOLLAND

Jonas Bros.
Taxidermist Supplies
1037 Broadway
Denver
Colorado 80203
USA

Taxidermy Supply Co.
R.T.I.
Bossier City
Louisiana 71010
USA

Karl Lange
Tierglasaugen
D-8522 Herzogenaurach
Postfach 1246
WEST GERMANY

British Agent for Karl Lange:
Mr. N. P. Peters
165A Priory Road
Crouch End
London N8 8NB
ENGLAND

Nets and Sporting Supplies
P.O. Box 21
Dorchester
DT2 9TE
ENGLAND

Taxidermy Supplies
Ken Hawkins Ltd
1793 Main Street
Winnipeg 17
Manitoba
CANADA

V. E. Aussenhandels Betriel
Glas Ceromic 108 Berlin
Kronen-Str 19 & 19A
Kontor G.K.50
WEST GERMANY

Otto Linderman
Hamburg 1
Ansinch Strasse 24
Markt-Hoff
WEST GERMANY

Carola Bolz
Glasaugen
52 Sieg-Burz
Hohenzollernstrasse 21
WEST GERMANY

Rein-Lesch
Glas- und Plastikaugen Fabric
Oeslau vei Coburg
WEST GERMANY

J. W. Elwoods
Box 3507
Omaha
Nebraska
68103
USA

G. Schopfer
120 West 31 Street
New York
New York 10001
USA

Moorland Taxidermy
The Lodge
Skillington
Grantham
Lincs
ENGLAND

Snowdonia Taxidermy Studios
Llanrwst
Denbighshire
NORTH WALES

Trophy Caps & Rings, etc.
Chantry Silversmiths
55 Grays Inn Road
London WC1
ENGLAND

Glass case makers

Midland Taxidermy Services
Frankwell Quay
Shrewsbury
SY3 8LJ
ENGLAND

Glass dome suppliers

Southern Watch & Clock Suppliers Ltd.
Orpington
Kent
ENGLAND

Beech & Son Ltd.
Meridian House
Swanley
Kent
ENGLAND

Substitute beeswax suppliers (Coata AX 1230)

Kerax Ltd.
Cowling Road
Chorley
Lancashire
PR6 0DR
ENGLAND

Chrome tanning packs

Snowdonia Taxidermy Studios
Llanrwst
Denbighshire
NORTH WALES

Chemicals and old fashioned pharmaceutical materials
Pharmacos
136 Little Wakering Road
Little Wakering
Essex
SS3 0JH
ENGLAND

Index